William E.

MW00619548

Also by William E. Plunkett

The G-Man and the Diamond King
The G-Men and the Nurse

The G-men and
the Heiress

The G-men and the Heiress

The 1934 Alice Speed Stoll FBI Kidnapping Case

William E. Plunkett

ORANGE *frazer* PRESS
Wilmington, Ohio

ISBN 978-1949248-333
Copyright©2021 William E. Plunkett

No part of this publication may be reproduced in any material form
(including photocopying or storing in any medium by electronic
means and whether or not transiently or incidentally to some
other use of this publication) without the written permission of the
copyright holder except in accordance with the provisions of Title 17
of the United States Code.

Published for The G-man and the Diamond King Productions, LLC
by Orange Frazer Press

Published for the copyright holder by:
Orange Frazer Press
37½ West Main St.
P.O. Box 214
Wilmington, OH 45177

Book and cover design: Kelly Schutte and Orange Frazer Press

Library of Congress Control Number: 2020921642

First Printing

For Michael Harold, Mary Patricia, Brigette Ann, and Timothy Patrick

Acknowledgments

A very special thank you to the following:

Helen Condon Powell, Mrs. Stoll's niece, for photographs and insight.

Ruth Ann Distefano, niece of Jean Breese, for providing insight about her family.

For the assistance of the Geneology, Makers Space, and Reference sections of the Public Library of Cincinnati and Hamilton County in answering many questions.

Dr. Tom Owen, Archivist for the University of Louisville, Ekstrom Library; and Carissa Miller and Kelly Dunnagan, Louisville Free Public Library. As well as dedicated pathfinder, Jerry Spradlin, for help with logistics in Louisville.

Former FBI Special Agents who assisted with their insight: Larry E. Wack (deceased) for his excellent website, William R. Hargreaves, Edward P. Woods, J. Gregory Ellison, all of the Cincinnati office; Timothy P. Tracy, Louisville, Covington Resident Agency; and Brian E. Fazenbaker of Nashville.

In Springfield, Ohio, Natalie Fritz, Curator of Library & Archives, Clark County Historical Society at the Heritage Center, and Detective Daniel E. Dewine, Springfield Police Department.

And my editor, John Baskin, who challenged me "to be more in the story," corrected countless errors, and added value to the final text.

Ode To An FBI Agent

A man knocked at the heavenly gates,
his face was scarred and old.
He stood before the man of fate,
for admission to the fold.
"What have you done," St. Peter asked,
"to gain admission here?"
"I've been an FBI Agent, sir,
for many and many a year."
The pearly gates opened wide when
St. Peter touched the bell.
"Come in and choose your harp," he
Said, "You've had your share of hell."

—*FBI Special Agent Gale Frank Lindsey (served 1934-1966)*
(Reprinted by permission of the family)

Contents

The players

Thomas Henry Robinson Jr.—kidnapper

Frances Natalie Hauser Robinson—kidnapper's wife

Alice Speed Stoll—victim

Berry Vincent Stoll—husband of victim

Virginia and William Speed—victim's parents

Ann Woolet—maid

Thomas Henry Robinson Sr.—kidnapper's father

Jessie Lois Preston Robinson—kidnapper's mother

Jean Breese—kidnapper's girlfriend

Stephen Breese—Jean's brother

FBI

Director J. Edgar Hoover

Assistant Director (AD) Harold "Pop" Nathan

Inspector Hugh H. Clegg

Assistant to AD Edward A. Tamm

Special Agent in Charge (SAC) Earl J. Connelley, Cincinnati

SAC Herold J. Reinecke, Indianapolis

SAC Melvin Purvis, Chicago

SAC William Rorer, Nashville

SAC Orville Dewey, Louisville

Special Agent Earl Wynn, Indianapolis

Special Agent John Lawren Madala, Kansas City

Special Agent John S. Bugas, Los Angeles

Timeline

○ October 10, 1934—Kidnapping of Alice Speed Stoll takes place at her residence outside Louisville, Kentucky.

○ October 16, 1934—Mrs. Robinson Jr. delivers $50,000 ransom to Thomas Henry Robinson Jr. at apartment hideout in Indianapolis.

○ October 16, 1934—Robinson Jr. drives to Springfield, Ohio, and abandons his stolen black 1934 Ford V-8.

○ October 16, 1934—Mrs. Stoll is released, and she and Mrs. Robinson Jr. go to a Stoll family relative for assistance.

○ Late October, 1934—Mrs. Robinson Jr. and Thomas Robinson Sr. are arrested by the Division of Investigation on kidnapping charges and indicted.

○ October 7, 1935—Kidnapping trial of Robinson Sr. and Mrs. Robinson Jr. begins.

○ October 13, 1935—Robinson Sr. and Mrs. Robinson Jr. acquitted.

○ May 11, 1936—The FBI arrests Robinson Jr. in Glendale, California, on a tip from his girlfriend, Jean Breese.

○ May 13, 1936—Robinson arraigned before Federal District Court Judge Elwood Hamilton, pleads guilty, and sentenced to life in prison.

○ May 14, 1936—Robinson arrives at the United States Penitentiary (USP) at Atlanta.

○ May 27, 1936—Robinson transferred to the USP at Leavenworth, Kansas.

○ March 16, 1937—Robinson transferred to USP at Alcatraz.

○ December 19, 1937—Robinson Sr. dies in Nashville, age 66.

○ June 25, 1943—Frances Natalie Hauser Robinson's divorce from Robinson Jr. finalized.

○ August 9, 1943—Robinson's life sentence voided by Judge Michael J. Roche, U.S. District Court, Northern District of California, and Robinson ordered back to Louisville to stand trial.

November 29, 1943—Robinson's kidnapping trial begins in Louisville.

December 13, 1943—Robinson convicted and receives a death sentence.

February 13, 1944—Robinson escapes from his cell with other inmates but fails to get out of jail building.

February 15, 1944—Robinson arrives at the Federal Correctional Institution at Milan, Michigan, a more secure facility while awaiting appeals.

July 31, 1944—The U.S. Sixth Circuit Court of Appeals at Cincinnati upholds conviction and death sentence.

March 5, 1945—The U.S. Supreme Court affirms death sentence by a vote of 7-2.

March 8, 1945—Robinson is moved to Kentucky State Penitentiary at Eddyville, Kentucky, for execution.

June 6, 1945—President Harry Truman commutes Robinson's sentence to life in prison with no parole.

June 8, 1945—Robinson arrives at the USP at Leavenworth, Kansas.

July 6, 1945—Robinson transferred to the USP at Alcatraz.

April 31, 1954—Robinson transferred from USP at Alcatraz to USP at Leavenworth.

May 12, 1954—Robinson transferred to USP at Atlanta, Georgia.

May 31, 1955—Robinson brought to Louisville by order of U. S. District Court Judge Roy L. Shelbourne for a hearing on filed motion relevant to set aside his conviction.

July 18, 1956—After many defense extensions, U. S. District Court Judge Roy L. Shelbourne, Louisville, denies Robinson's request to set aside the verdict and conviction.

1959—Robinson transferred to the Federal Correctional Institution, Tallahassee, Florida.

January 3, 1961—Robinson denied parole by the U. S. Parole Board in Washington, DC.

The G-men and the Heiress

December 22, 1961—The U.S. Parole Board Chairman Richard A. Chappell at Tallahassee meets with Robinson, recommends his release on March 1, 1962.

July 21, 1962—Robinson escapes from the Federal Correctional Facility at Tallahassee, walking away from a work detail outside the facility.

July 28, 1962—Robinson arrested for armed robbery of a Chicago pharmacy netting $14 and is sent to the USP in Atlanta where he spends the next two years.

September 1, 1964—Robinson arrives at the Federal Correctional Institution at Seagoville, Texas.

June 6, 1965—Robinson escapes from the Federal Correctional Institution at Seagoville, walking away from the minimum security facility.

June 14, 1965—Robinson attempts to rob the Third National Bank of Nashville but is apprehended when recognized by a former classmate.

November 3, 1965—Robinson sentenced to fourteen years for attempted bank robbery charge and five years for an escape to run, concurrently with his life sentence, and ends up back at USP at Atlanta.

June 15, 1966—Robinson's mother, Jessie Lois Preston, dies at age 90 in Nashville.

October 15, 1970—Robinson is released from the USP at Atlanta and goes home to Pegram, Tennessee.

The G-men and the Heiress

Introduction

"Crime does not pay, but it can be a shortcut to immortality."
—William Helmer and Rick Mattix

The 1920s was a time of good fortune for the United States and its people, the end of WWI and the advent of the Jazz Age (and the fun-loving flapper) having brought about an emphasis on personal fulfillment and pleasure. Excessive drinking of alcohol, linked in the popular mind with the working-class, moved democratically upstream to the classes above—the saloon culture blossomed into the speakeasy. Indeed, the heaviest use of alcohol on campuses was taking place among the most privileged students, notably eastern men's colleges, while at other schools, among both men and women, drinking symbolized freedom from adult supervision.

The advancement of radio, talking Hollywood pictures, and the automobile brought to the general public new venues for escape from the stifling facets of a lingering Victorian Age. It would need this—and more—to circumvent the effects of the market crash in October, 1929, which ushered in the 1930s with a rare despair and economic hard times. A quarter of all Americans went jobless, and hundreds of thousands lost their homes. Soup kitchens and bread lines were standard, and massive parts of every big city saw suffering residents living in shacks. Five thousand banks closed and nine million savings accounts evaporated. No part of the country escaped unaffected.

What was called "the Golden Age of Radio" brought about a measure of relief, offering news and entertainment and serving as a secular pulpit that tied Americans together. The radio was often a family's most prized possession, and by the end of the decade upwards of thirty million households had at least one. There was another escape as well; for those who could afford a ticket, Hollywood would provide entertainment—a double feature cost merely a dime. Eighty million film tickets were sold a week as a panoply of diversion poured forth from screenland gangsters, monsters, cowboys, mustachioed leading men, and glam hoofers, which allowed a downcast America to flee its predicament, even if only for a time.

The Great Depression had blanketed the nation, and with it, the public attitude changed; it was more receptive to the federal government stepping in to assist its citizens. The New Deal was a series of laws and presidential executive orders signed

$ The Roosevelt Special (and then some).

by Democratic president Franklin Delano Roosevelt, which helped farmers, produced jobs, offered low-cost housing, and safeguarded the financial interests of taxpayers. The nation was beginning to form an identity, and the public would accept a helping hand, indeed, *needed* a helping hand. A side benefit of the New Deal, at least as far as the Democratic Party was concerned, was to increase and consolidate its base, allowing them a foothold with the public for the next twenty years.

When Prohibition ended in 1933, most Americans said "Good riddance." It had been an abysmal failure, except for the illegal sales that enriched the various gangsters and racketeers whose largest detriment wasn't underfunded law enforcement but rival racketeers and various turf wars. The hoodlums, of course, were diversified—witness the complementary rackets: gambling, prostitution, extortion, bank robbery, and other nefarious activities—but none so lucrative as kidnapping.

When the famous bank robber William Francis Sutton Jr., nicknamed "Slick Willie," was asked why he robbed banks, he supposedly said, "Because that's where the money is." And while he may never have *actually* said it (a newspaper reporter probably made it up), it became known as Sutton's Law, often used in medical school as a metaphor for the most likely diagnosis. Willie's apocryphal diagnosis thus led to the 1930s being a productive decade for bank robbers.

The downside for bank robbers was the possibility of a physical confrontation, which didn't usually end well—for bystanders, police, and especially the robber. Sutton carried either a pistol or a Thompson submachine gun during his robberies but they were never loaded because, he said, "someone might get hurt." He was a gentleman in a rough trade, known for never robbing a bank "when a woman screamed or a baby cried," and he loved his work. "I was more alive when I was inside a bank, robbing it, than at any other time in my life," he said. The money seemed to be secondary.

During Prohibition, an emerging affinity for kidnapping left it at the top of lawbreakers' preferred crimes. The reason was economics, the payoff for what was colloquially

The G-men and the Heiress

known as "the snatch racket" was sometimes more lucrative than bank robbery. An additional inducement was that a Thompson submachine gun was seldom needed.

And so the criminals, spotting a vacuum, moved in. Although those who operated in this arena would have only a brief moment before news reporting, an angry public, and the relatively young federal agency, the Division of Investigation and its boss, J. Edgar Hoover—both looking to make a name—would make kidnapping as difficult as a bank job.

In the 1930s, kidnapping appeared to be an epidemic in the United States, or maybe it just seemed so as every week in the newspapers one read of yet another one. *Barron's Law Dictionary* defines kidnapping as "the unlawful taking and carrying away of a person against that person's will," and all states prohibited it. Still, with many states, it was just a misdemeanor that carried a reasonably light sentence. Criminals knew the laws and used the various state jurisdictions to their advantage, playing one against the other. On March 1, 1932, everything changed when Charles August Lindbergh Jr.—the golden-haired son

of the aviator whose nonstop flight from New York to Paris in his monoplane, *The Spirit of St. Louis*, made him world-famous—was kidnapped. As a result, the federal government passed the Federal Kidnapping Act, which made the transportation of the victim across state lines a federal crime.

When the Bureau was formed at the behest of President Theodore Roosevelt in 1908, his attorney general, Charles Joseph Bonaparte, established it with only thirty-four investigators, and it didn't even have a name; the AG merely referred to it as "special agent force." In March of 1909, with a new AG, George Woodward Wickersham, and twice as many employees, it was formally named the Bureau of Investigation.

Its next change on its inexorable march to becoming what is known today as the Federal Bureau of Investigation

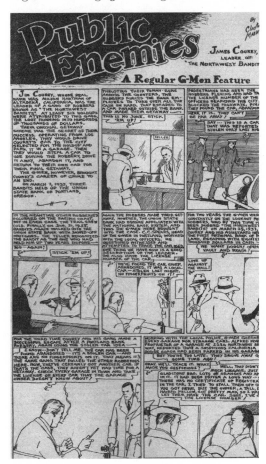

$ "They thrust their tommy-guns across the counters...."

Deer mom,
i will not
bee home to
super becaus i
am on the trale
ov a desprit
criminil but do
not wurre becaus
i have my
fatheful bludhownd
and my trusty
Eveready.
Yours Sinseerly
Sekrit Operative
9·77

$ By the late 1930s, Junior G-Men had their own boys club.

occurred in July of 1932 when it became the United States Bureau of Investigation. The next year President Franklin D. Roosevelt's executive order created the Division of Investigation (DOI), which was a combination of the Bureau of Investigation and the Bureau of Prohibition of the U.S. Department of the Treasury. The merger was to strengthen the federal effort in fighting the rise of gangsterism.

A turning point for the DOI came on June 17, 1933; the Kansas City Massacre began an eighteen-month scourge of gangsterism in the United States. It was a defining moment for the DOI when law enforcement agents and their prisoner, Frank "Jelly" Nash, a convicted bank robber and federal escapee, got off a train in Union Station. They were transporting Nash to Leavenworth Federal Penitentiary north of the city. Gunmen ambushed them and four lawmen died, along with Nash.

The DOI identified the gunmen as Pretty Boy Floyd, Adam "Eddie" Richetti, and Verne C. Miller, a former WWI Army hero. Some thought the deaths were by friendly fire. But no matter the cause of the Kansas City shootout, the result was new federal legislation, which gave the G-Men more federal crimes to pursue, powers of arrest, and the legal authority to carry firearms (previously they had carried them strictly for what was called "defensive purposes").

In 1934, the organization formed special squads or "Flying Squads" to capture the more infamous gangsters. The most celebrated were John Dillinger and Lester Gillis, known as "Baby Face Nelson," who was also one of the most vicious. Charles Arthur "Pretty Boy" Floyd, as the name suggested, was handsome but wasn't fond of his nickname. The most gentlemanly of them was southerner George "Machine Gun" Kelly Barnes, who may have never fired, let alone killed, anyone with a Thompson submachine gun, his trademark, supposedly purchased as a gift by his beautiful wife. Then there was Bonnie and Clyde, the Romeo and Juliet of the southwest criminal circuit. Ma Barker of the Barker-Karpis gang supposedly had her four sons and Alvin "Old Creepy" Karpis

The G-men and the Heiress

under her spell, and there were plenty of lesser-known and ruthless troublemakers. These and other criminals would be known and/or designated a "Public Enemy" or "Public Enemy No. 1" with much fanfare by the newspapers and, to a lesser extent, J. Edgar Hoover himself.

It would be a banner time for Hoover and his agents, and they killed all the above except Kelly and Karpis, who ended up at the United States Penitentiary at Alcatraz, and Bonnie and Clyde, exterminated by Texas Rangers and local law enforcement. Notable criminals of the era taught the nation that while crime might not always pay, it *could* be a shortcut to immortality.

Some of the more notorious and lesser-known criminals had made their living by various forms of mayhem, including murder, bootlegging, gun-running, and bank robbery until alternating or making the switch to kidnapping. Even organized crime got in on the act, converting from bootlegging.

In October of 1934, the Division was searching for a rogue of a fellow, Thomas Henry Robinson Jr., the subject of a Kentucky kidnapping case. The victim was Alice Speed Stoll, the beautiful socialite daughter of one of Louisville's wealthiest and best-known families, and Robinson would soon be designated Public Enemy Number One.

The Division in 1934 only had twenty-four offices and fewer than four hundred special agents. The case initially involved agents from half a dozen offices, which was a lot of working hours in pursuit of one man. The Division usually handled kidnapping cases by letting the payoff money walk, then tracking down the subjects through the serial numbers on the ransom money. In this case, the recording of the serial numbers was botched, and Robinson led agents—including the well-known Chicago Special Agent In Charge (SAC) Melvin Purvis and Cincinnati SAC Earl J. Connelley—on a cross-country chase.

Robinson was from a middle-class Nashville, Tennessee, family and had attended Vanderbilt University and YMCA Law School. (There actually *was* such a school—the Nashville YMCA Night Law School—in which students attended classes on a part-time basis. It was founded in 1911, still exists today, although no longer rents space from the YMCA, and counts among its notable alumni Al Gore Sr., one-time U.S. senator and father of former vice president Al Gore.) Robinson was no dummy, a small-time grifter whose kidnapping of the Louisville heiress sent him on the lam for eighteen months. Doctors, lawyers, law enforcement—even his wife—would describe Robinson as mad or psychotic.

Perhaps it all started at age 11 at his uncle's farm in Ohio when he was kicked in the head by a horse, leaving a small scar below his right eye. Whatever personal demons

Introduction

informed him, Robinson would become the first person prosecuted under the amended federal kidnapping law passed on May 18, 1934, which made it a capital offense. The case was intensely followed all across the United States, even more so by New Yorkers where the Lindbergh kidnapping had recently taken place.

Alice Stoll's kidnapping wasn't as famous as that of the Lindbergh baby, but in its own peculiar way, it was just as riveting. It featured a beautiful socialite, a troubled perpetrator tormented by his own inadequacies, a cross-country chase that went on forever, prison escapes (including one from death row), an interminable (and plucky) jailhouse defense, and the efforts by America's fledgling crime-fighting organization seeking to establish itself. Like the Lindbergh case, it, too, made *The New York Times*. (*The Times* labeled Robinson "insane," which ultimately proved too easy a designation for someone so torturously complex.) *Louisville Magazine*, as recently as 2016, called the case Louisville's "crime of the century."

What follows is the strange story of the kidnapper, the kidnapped—and the tireless G-men who worked diligently to create the country's foremost investigative agency.

The G-men and the Heiress

WEATHER
Fair Thursday night and Friday; little change in temperature.

The Herald-Post

FINAL HOME EDITION
WALL STREET TABLES

ESTABLISHED 1852—83D YEAR. NO. 140   LOUISVILLE, KY., THURSDAY EVENING, OCTOBER 11, 1934   16 PAGES   PRICE THREE CENTS

STOLL KIDNAP CAR TRACED TO LAKE LOUISVILLA ROAD; $50,000 RANSOM PREPARED

DIAGRAM OF BERRY V. STOLL HOME AND KIDNAPING

MRS. BERRY V. STOLL

ROAD WORKER TELLS OF SPOTTING AUTO

Car Maneuvers Near Lake's Edge, Drives Off Toward City; Early Report Confirmed.

Highlights of Crime

Mrs. Berry V. Stoll forced from home by lone kidnaper at about 5 o'clock Wednesday afternoon.

Fresh trail of kidnaper, unearthed by Herald-Post reporter, leads to roads about Lake Louisvilla.

Ransom note demands $50,000 and threatens further kidnaping, according to police, who refuse to divulge full contents.

Victim, in ill health, believed struck twice on head with lead pipe before being placed in kidnaper's car, but police unable to find weapon.

Maid at Stoll home and her butler-husband questioned for more than three hours. Maid tells contradictory stories; husband refuses to talk.

More than 500 peace officers engage in greatest man hunt in history of Jefferson County.

Kidnapers reported to have attempted telephone contact, but of woman ready to pay.

Search for Mrs. Alice Speed Stoll, 28, was intensified in the neighborhood of Lake Louisvilla early Thursday afternoon after a road worker reported having seen an automobile answering the description of that used in her kidnaping, near the resort late Wednesday afternoon.

The worker, Russell Williams, 48, Lagrange, said the car, a dark blue Ford V-8, passed the lake between 4:30 and 5 o'clock, stopped on a hill on the east side of the lake and turned around.

The car descended to the edge of the lake, turned down a side road and then returned to the main road and headed for Louisville. In it were a "nice looking, smooth-faced" man and a woman who wore no hat or coat and who wore a garment answering the description of the negligee in which Mrs. Stoll was attired when she was taken.

Relatives of Mrs. Stoll waited anxiously Thursday afternoon for negotiations for the payment of $50,000 ransom.

As hundreds of officers and volunteers scoured the country, detectives throughout the nation were on the alert for a sign of the kidnaper and his victim.

The local search centered about Lake Louisvilla, sixteen miles northeast of Louisville, where a trail which appeared to be that of the abductor's car had been found. Definite clues as to the identity of the kidnaper or his plans were lacking, however.

Berry V. Stoll, husband of the victim and Stoll Oil Refining Company executive, waited at the home on the "Lime Kiln Road near the Upper River Road with other relatives for word from the kidnaper.

Ransom Money

The ransom money had been drawn from the bank.

Ready to promise immunity for the kidnaper, the Stoll and Speed families were prepared to make any arrangements suggested which would insure the safe return of Mrs. Stoll.

Two private telephone lines were strung to the Stoll home early Thursday afternoon to insure the reception of a call in case the kidnaper chose that means of communication.

Early in the morning a call which was thought to come from the abductor was received by Mr. Stoll, but the connection was broken before a conversation could be opened.

George Stoll, brother-in-law of the kidnaped woman, announced shortly after 11 o'clock Thursday morning that the estate had been cleared in preparation for the safe reception of any emissary of the kidnaper.

Channels Cleared For Contacting.

Only a small squad of police remained at the entrance to the wooded estate to bar curious visitors and the patrol was ready to retreat at the request of the kidnaper.

"All channels have been cleared for negotiations with the man," Mr. Stoll said. "There will be no tricks. Our only hope is to make possible the safe return of Mrs. Stoll."

The search in the Lake Louisvilla section resulted from the first "hot lead" of the hunt. Testing a hunch of Robert L. Price, Herald-Post reporter, forty police and other officers combed the lake area.

Mary Collett, 24, who lives not far from the lake, told the investigators an automobile answering the description of the kidnap car and containing a man and woman passed her at

ugoslavs Attack Italian Emissary

by Dragged From Consulate as Mob Blames Fascists for Murder of King Alexander.

Ljubljana, Jugoslavia, Oct. 11 (INS)—The Italian consul here was dragged from his office today and beaten by a mob staging a violent Italian demonstration. Police intervened and tore out the consul, who he suffered serious injuries. Anti-Italian riots are now raging at Lessi.

The imperiled Croatian city of Ljubljana lies less than fifty miles in the northeastern frontier of Italy. It was this frontier to which the Marquis, ruling attaching an international line, was attack on the royal blood...

HOOVER SLEEPS DURING SEARCH

"Foolproof" System Bars Justice Chief From News of Kidnap.

By DAVID R. SCOTT
Herald-Post Bureau.

Washington, Oct. 11—A victim of his own "foolproof" system of protection the official slumbers being disturbed the arousal of the Stoll home and said he had come to check up on the telephone, was in the upstairs bedroom occupied by Mr. and Mrs. Stoll, in the southwest corner of the house. Mrs. Stoll was lying on one of the two beds.

Stoll Maid Tells Kidnaping Details

Servant Sees Mistress Slugged by Abductor; Forced to Bind Her Wrists.

Details of the kidnaping of Mrs. Alice Speed Stoll were related by Mrs. Ada Wooler, maid, after she had been questioned at length by police. At the Stoll home the following story was told by Mrs. Wooler:

At 5 o'clock Wednesday afternoon the maid said a man using the door-bell of the Stoll home and said he had come to check up on the telephone. The telephone was in the upstairs bedroom occupied by Mr. and Mrs. Stoll, in the southwest corner of the house. Mrs. Stoll was lying on one of the two beds.

When the maid returned, Mrs. Stoll and a man was there to see her. The telephone repairman she alone and sent into the guest bedroom in the northeast corner of the house.

The man followed with the telephone as she was doing some work on the telephone when she had the maid going before she could...

LOG OF EVENTS OF ABDUCTION

Chronological Outline of Kidnaping According to Witnesses.

Briefly stating events in the Stoll kidnaping case were chronicled as follows on the basis of information given by various witnesses and participants in the tragic drama:

WEDNESDAY

5 p. m.—Kidnaper entered Stoll home.

5:20 p. m.—Kidnaper departed with bound maid.

5:35 p. m.—Berry V. Stoll arrived home.

6:35 p. m.—Stoll phoned, mayor from home of James Clarke Jr.

7:52 p. m.—Mrs. phoned police.

8 p. m.—First report of kidnaping and description of kidnaper and Mrs. Stoll deployed by police.

9:05 p. m.—Super-radio broadcast put on wire.

9:10 p. m.—HERE and WHAS broadcast information.

4:30 p. m.—Ransom note found on front door.

9:30 p. m.—First two county patrolmen arrived at scene.

7 p. m.—Total of 300 officers at work on case. All roads from Louisville blocked; bridges guarded and thirty-five county police started search of various houses in vicinity of the crime.

7:30 p. m.—Department of Justice agents took charge of case, laying chief censorship on news.

THURSDAY

1:15 a. m.—Man believed to be kidnaper telephoned Stoll home, but connection resulted in failure of communication.

4:15 a. m.—dozens of officers start scouring countryside.

1:30 a. m.—First "hot" lead uncovered by Herald-Post reporter. He reported seeing kidnap car near Lake Louisvilla, search of roads begun.

11:05 a. m.—Police provide reveals fresh tips corresponding to those of kidnaping car. Roy returned to organize police from Jewishnative search of lake region.

11:30—Relative of Mrs. Stoll windows admit from a Louisville in preparation for negotiations.

12 a. m.—All arrangements made; drive from Stoll estate to make possible contact with kidnaper.

CITY MAN HURT IN STATE CRASH

Collision Fatal to Boy; Seven Others Injured.

Collision was fatal to one boy and seriously injured seven others...

FIRST LADY GETS CAKE

Mrs. Roosevelt Observes 50th Birthday Anniversary.

Washington, Oct. 11 (INS)—Mrs. Franklin D. Roosevelt today observed her fiftieth birthday anniversary—just because the children wanted it.

She doesn't care much for birthday cakes and parties because, she said, she personally believes "the more you forget your birthdays as you grow older the younger you stay."

Nevertheless, the five children had their way and so the time today the bakers with a large birthday party.

FOUR KILLED IN CRASH

Gaffenburg, O., Oct. 11 (INS)—Six airplanes Herman and two passengers were killed today when a Chicago Milwaukee-St. Paul & Pacific passenger train hit the automobile south of here and plunged into a ditch.

HAUPTMANN WRIT PLEA SET MONDAY

Hearing to Determine Suspect's Status.

New York, Oct. 11 (INS)—Bruno Richard Hauptmann will be given a hearing Monday on a writ of habeas corpus to determine whether he should be held for the murder of Charles A. Lindbergh Jr. when he is kidnaped in the case of March 1.

In the Bronx County Court today the extradition case against Hauptmann ruled dropping and Attorney General Harry S Buchanan today was technically new the latter of the United States. Department of Justice to investigate the said of Justice to investigate the said of Dr. Isidor Fisch...

LATE NEWS AND SPORTS

REINSTATEMENT DENIED BISHOP

Atlantic City, N. J., Oct. 11 (INS)—Appeal of William Montgomery Brown of Galion, O., deposed Protestant Episcopal bishop, for reinstatement was denied today by the committee on canons of the fifty-first triennial general convention of the church. Brown was deposed by a general convention of the church in 1925 on charges of heresy.

MOTHER OF TEN KILLS SELF

Philadelphia, Oct. 11 (INS)—Believed to have been driven to her act by prolonged illness, Mrs. Esther Gross, mother of ten children, today strangled herself to death.

Hartford, Conn., Oct. 11 (INS)—Charged with embezzling $300,000 funds of the Underwriters' Finance Corporation, Frank A. Tillman, president of this city, and Beatrice Kauffman of New York, his private secretary, were sought by police today.

SEVEN DIE IN BLAST AT APARTMENT HOUSE

Halifax, N. S., Oct. 11 (INS)—Seven persons were killed in a mysterious explosion which wrecked a three-story apartment building today.

Race Results

CONEY ISLAND (1)—Register, $3.60, $3.00, $2.60 ... Miscelanea, $6.20, $4.00 ... Clementine, $2.60 ...

NARRAGANSETT (1)—Flutterby, $9.90, $6.70, $4.90 ... Cutting, $3.20, $2.90 ... Polly Cox, $3.40 ...

NARRAGANSETT (2)—Brant ... $4.10, $7.90, $3.10 ... Comin Out, $3.60, $3.10 ... Welboy, $3.00 ...

NARRAGANSETT (3)—Peticedote, $4.10, $4.10, $3.80 ... Sport to Win, $4.00, $3.80 ... Doorkeeper, $3.70 ...

LAUREL (1)—Last Romaine, $18.40, $8.50, $4.50 ... Fair Mater, $5.70 ... Advocate Justice, $4.40 ...

LAUREL (2)—Plantime, $14.40, $7.00, $4.50 ... French Knight, $12.60, $5.40 ... Tomer, $3.90 ...

Today...

BY ARTHUR BRISBANE

Will Be Found on Page 4.

1 Caught (kid) napping!

"You're killing me."—Alice Stoll.

Alice Speed Stoll came of age after WWI, and through her travels learned to like jazz music, bobbed hairstyles, and the radical fashion of the 1920s. She drank beer, drove an automobile, and was photographed wearing a cloche hat—all images of the flapper. Her wealthy but somewhat sheltered upbringing made her ripe to wear the flapper's mantle, but she was not brash in her behavior nor did she disdain proper demeanor. The only thing she had in common with Hollywood actress Louise Brooks—the quintessential liberated flapper—was that both were born in 1906. Alice Stoll was, finally, a child of her privileged class and its manners.

Her mother, Virginia Speed, was overbearing and demanding, always fearful for the safety of her eldest daughter, and at an early age taught Alice that wealth brought predators around. One newspaper printed that she was not allowed to walk to the local corner store, attend movies, or visit the local park. When she did visit girlfriends' homes, she was accompanied by a maid. Once she became of driving age, her father, William Speed, didn't allow her out after dark. As a result of all the precautions, she never had a large cadre of friends and developed "a cool, cautious, observing nature." In adulthood, she owned a handgun and practiced shooting.

Then on October 10, 1934, what the twenty-eight-year-old had been warned about all her life finally happened. Alice Stoll was kidnapped, and the story gripped the nation's attention.

It was a typical mid-week afternoon at her residence just off of Lime Kiln Lane, a relatively modest house known as "The Cottage." It was situated on a sixteen-acre estate in the Harrods Creek area, an isolated, hilly, wooded area overlooking the Ohio River six miles east out River Road from downtown Louisville. The two-story cottage was 1,900 square feet with a brick façade and a center chimney, containing a living room, dining room, kitchen, and spare room on the first floor, with two bedrooms and a bath upstairs.

Alice's husband, Berry Vincent Stoll, an executive of the Stoll Oil Refining Company, left for work around 8:30 a.m. It was Wednesday and the caretaker, Fowler Woolet, had the day off. Frank Hardin, a part-time man who worked on the farm on Tuesdays and Wednesdays, had seen an unfamiliar vehicle in the driveway, but it turned out to be a deliveryman. Belle Stokes, the laundress, was there at 7 a.m., but as usual, she was gone by around 11:30 when she'd finished her duties and Mrs. Stoll drove her to her interurban stop.

Because there had been problems in the area with telephone service, no one thought anything odd about a serviceman showing up. In fact, one showed up at The Cottage just as Berry Stoll was leaving for work. He was Charles Henry Haunez, a repairman with Southern Bell Telephone Company. He was let in the house by the maid, changed out the old telephones for new—one at the entrance to the house and an extension in the master bedroom—and Mrs. Stoll tested the downstairs phone and found that it worked fine. The repairman left by 9:30 a.m.

$ The Stoll residence: home, sweet home.

The G-men and the Heiress

This coincidence in the intangible workings of the universe worked in favor of the kidnapper, whose impersonation of yet another telephone repairman raised no suspicion on Lime Kiln Lane. First, though, the kidnapper had to find the Stoll cottage, a small detail that surely demonstrated the impulsiveness of his character. Stopping twice to ask for directions, Hugo Kottke, an affable Bardstown Road garage owner, finally helped locate the Stoll cottage.

Once there, the kidnapper parked in the driveway and rang the doorbell. When the maid answered, he said—more statement than question—"Your number is East 2491."

"Yes," she said, noticing that he spoke in a southern drawl.

"I want to check your phone," he said.

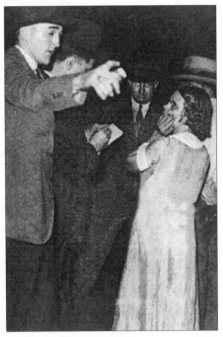

$ Ann Woolet: beyond the call of household duties.

The maid later described him as handsome, 5'8" or 5'9" (actually he was 6'0") thin at 130 pounds, with a pale white face, thick red lips, and black slicked-down hair. He seemed to be well-educated and was wearing a pinstriped gray suit, white shirt, and blue tie with a gold tie pin. She remembered him as wearing a gray hat. All in all, it was not the dress of a working man, but no one seemed to make such an observation.

The maid, 24-year-old Ann Woolet, had been with the Stolls for two years, along with her husband, Fowler, and they lived in the basement of the Stoll residence. Subsequently, the Division of Investigation conducted a thorough investigation, as well as not-too-subtle interviews of the Woolets, before finding no data to tie them to the abduction. (For whatever reason, Berry Stoll would fire the Woolets a few days after the kidnapping, and a year later—perhaps due to his impulsive dismissal—he helped Fowler Woolet find another job.)

Once in the house, the kidnapper checked the telephone on the first floor. The maid then escorted him to the basement to check the telephone box. He asked her if the Stolls would be interested in dial service at a 10 percent discount. She went upstairs to the master bedroom and asked Mrs. Stoll, who said yes. The maid went back to the basement to finish ironing, and he followed her there, wondering if there might be another phone extension. He asked if the Stolls had a chauffeur, and the maid told him no, only a gardener, who was out.

He checked the telephone line from the house to the garage, and after he had been there an hour, he asked the maid to go upstairs to the master bedroom and hold the telephone while he checked it. Mrs. Stoll, meanwhile, had moved to the spare bedroom. The masquerading repairman and the maid entered the master bedroom, and when the maid turned around, he was pointing a gun at her. He ordered her into the other bedroom where a startled Mrs. Stoll demanded to know what he was doing.

"You know I have got a forty-five," he said, and told her she was being kidnapped.

$

OUR LADY FAIR

Mrs. Stoll had been caught off-guard; suffering a bad cold, a headache, and a temperature of 103, she was wearing a kimono and had been trying to nap. At first, she tried to reason with her kidnapper.

She offered to pay him but she had only $10 in cash. Then, to no avail, she tried to write him a personal check. She said that her family "was in bad financial circumstances and could not pay a ransom."

The kidnapper told the maid to tie Mrs. Stoll's wrists, using two-inch adhesive tape and wire he brought with him, but the maid was too nervous. The kidnapper laid his handgun on the bed and went to do it himself when Mrs. Stoll tried to grab the handgun. The kidnapper pulled from his pocket an improvised blackjack made from a piece of iron pipe wrapped in brown paper and hit her twice, the first time on the forehead over her right eye, which formed a welt, and because she was still struggling, he hit her a second time, this time above the right ear. She fell onto the bed, blood oozing through her hair and onto the bedspread, making two large stains.

"You're killing me," she said, matter of factly.

As he finished taping her mouth, she said, "Take me with you before Berry comes," worried that the kidnapper might harm him.

"Go on," the maid said bravely to the kidnapper. "We don't want anyone else hurt."

Then she asked what he was going to do with her.

"I haven't got any money," she said.

The kidnapper made the maid sit on the floor and tied her hands and ankles with wire and adhesive tape. He left his ransom note, sealed in an envelope, on the bed. The note had black typing on the envelope: "To members of the Stoll family" and printed in pencil: "And Mr. Speed." In red-colored typing was written, "Do not call the police, but read this letter, or you will never see Stoll again, either dead or alive."

The G-men and the Heiress

It seemed the kidnapper was at first uncertain as to exactly who he was kidnapping. Almost as an afterthought, he had printed, "$50,000 for Mrs. Stoll."

Next, he went into the master bedroom where he retrieved a coat from the closet and draped it over Mrs. Stoll's shoulders. It was an almost solicitous gesture from a man who, moments before, had slugged her with a crude blackjack. The weather was in the high 70s that afternoon, so Mrs. Stoll didn't need the coat, but she was still wearing only a light kimono.

Carrying his .45, he left the house with Mrs. Stoll, telling her to lie on the floor in the back

💲 Alice Stoll: her wayward adventure begins.

of his car. He tied her legs and covered her with newspaper and a blanket. The maid heard the engine start, and the kidnapper and Mrs. Stoll drove off in a stolen black 1934 Ford V-8, Model 40 Tudor sedan. He drove towards Louisville, and on the way, the kidnapper thought he saw Berry Stoll pass him, heading in the direction of the cottage.

Stoll arrived home around 5:30 p.m. and heard the maid yell from the upstairs. He found her with her hands tied. She had gotten her ankles free, then stood by the window in the master bathroom waiting for him. When he saw the blood on the bedspread, he thought his wife was dead. They ran nearby to the house of the James Clark family, located across Lime Kiln Lane, because the kidnapper had disconnected their telephone line. Stoll called the city and county police, Louisville Mayor Neville Miller, and family members, then waited for their arrival.

Stoll found the ransom demand on the bed upstairs, which he had initially overlooked. Most kidnappers prefer a terse brevity in their demand notes: "We have your relative. We will be in touch about the ransom. No police." Mrs. Stoll's kidnapper, however, left a circuitous and revised note that provided some insight into his mindset, which appeared to be impetuous and careless.

💲

RANSOM MANIFESTO

The ransom note contained two pages typed on legal paper, with handwritten corrections and additions made by the kidnapper. He initially wanted $30,000, which was

$ The Stoll estate, a bird's-eye view of where it happened.

crossed out and changed to $50,000 (almost a million in today's dollars). He asked that half be in $10 bills and the other in $20 currency; he was not specific about the denominations of the additional $20,000. Mrs. Stoll's father-in-law, C. C. Stoll, was listed as the original target but then his name was scratched out. Even choosing the Stoll family as his target seemed whimsical, for the net worth of Alice's family, the Speeds—whose name and address was pencilled on the note, too—was significantly larger.

The kidnapper typed the letter as if he had accomplices. He complained about capitalists and specifically about C. C. Stoll being miserly. Stoll would not spend money to have his filling stations repainted, the kidnapper said, and now that money would go to *him*, a kind of punishment for his greed.

The kidnapper cautioned the Stolls not to copy the serial numbers of the currency, nor contact the police, nor publicize the event. The authorities duplicated the serial numbers but the record was somehow botched and the family *did* contact the media, all to the dismay of the Division of Investigation boss, J. Edgar Hoover, a man made happy only by perfection. The kidnapper warned that disobedient family members could be shot from a distance, with a .30-30 rifle, and his note asserted that if double-crossed, he would kill Mrs. Stoll, "burn the body, and dump the ashes in a stream."

Former agent J. Gregory Ellison, a statement analysis expert who was provided a copy of the note for insight, noted the author's use of "corpus delicti" and "aggravate our offense," which denoted a familiarity with legal/law enforcement terms, and was above the usage of a regular citizen of the 1930s. The author's use of the term "we" suggested co-conspirators were involved. Threats that seemed to have an omniscient level of awareness about the Stoll or Speed families' subsequent activities also indicated the involvement of

The G-men and the Heiress

confederates although, historically, ransom notes tended to reveal such claims were often a ploy.

The language of the note denoted a person of white-collar attributes, with an equivalent level of education and experience, and having some knowledge of insurance and banking. A kidnapping/extortion might be characterized as potentially "high-risk and high-reward," said Ellison, because so many things can go wrong. Such an undertaking, he said, required a high level of audaciousness—or foolishness.

Berry Stoll was careful with the ransom letter, making sure he left no fingerprints. It was given to Officer Robert Krieger of the Louisville Police Department, who passed it along to

$ The young Alice Speed, when the headlines were on the society pages.

its fingerprint examiner, Lieutenant John Messmer. Messmer was the expert who would also dust the cottage for latent prints.

Copies of the ransom note were made, and the original turned over to Agent Stuart R. Kerr of the Divison of Investigation. On October 13, Messmer turned over to Agent Francis E. Hurley items obtained from the Stoll home on the day of the kidnapping. They were: a screwdriver, one small table knife, one gas pipe two feet long wrapped in manila paper, one black enamel telephone box, one telephone transmitter. Also included was one silk laundry bag the kidnapper used to wipe his hands, a roll of adhesive tape, and three small cotton-covered copper wires. The Divison's laboratory was unable to find fingerprints on any of the items; the Louisville Police Department had previously found prints on the telephone box, which were later determined to be from Robinson's right middle finger.

The Divison Laboratory conducted hand-printing analysis and looked for fingerprints on the ransom note, and it wasn't hard to ferret out the kidnapper's identity. The intermediary, T. H. Robinson, was a well-known Nashville engineer and bridge builder. His son, Thomas Robinson Jr., however, had few of his father's credentials. He was a law school dropout and layabout whose eccentric behavior would prove to befuddle federal investigators, at least two wives, and a host of psychiatrists for years to come. Thus the investigators knew immediately where to look. And from the start, young Robinson's cockeyed schemes and strategies seemed to indicate a deathwish, which in the not-so-distant future, occurred as a very real possibility.

DAILY **NEWS**

BROOKLYN

NEW YORK'S PICTURE NEWSPAPER

Copyright, 1934, by News Syndicate Co. Inc. Reg. U. S. Pat. Off.

Entered as 2nd class matter Post Office, New York, N.Y.

2 CENTS IN CITY LIMITS

Vol. 16. No. 98 100 Pages

New York, Thursday, October 18, 1934*

2 Cents

ASK DEATH FOR STOLL KIDNAPER

Story on Page 3

HAUPTMANN ALIBI WITNESS.—Joseph M. Furcht (above) construction superintendent, told The News yesterday that Bruno Hauptmann worked all day in New York March 1, the day the Lindbergh baby was kidnaped, in the Majestic apartments, in W. 72d St.—*Story on page 3.*

Thomas H. Robinson Jr. (above), charged with the kidnaping of Mrs. Berry V. Stoll of Louisville, Ky., was being hunted by Federal agents and local police in Chicago yesterday.

The wages of sin made plaintive in headlines.

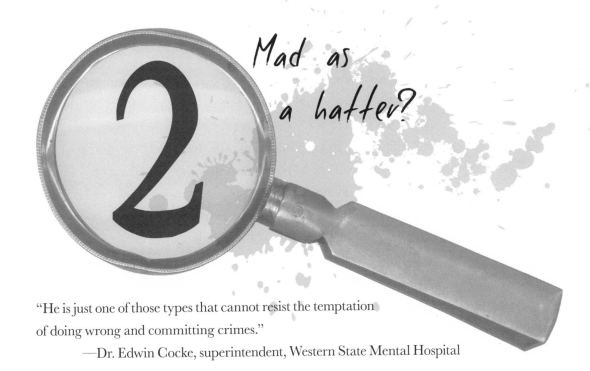

Mad as a hatter?

"He is just one of those types that cannot resist the temptation of doing wrong and committing crimes."

— Dr. Edwin Cocke, superintendent, Western State Mental Hospital

Thomas Henry Robinson Jr. was born in Nashville, Tennessee, on May 5, 1907, which he would describe as "in the year of the panic, and it has been a panic ever since." He was referring, of course, to the Panic of 1907, the first great financial crisis of the new century, as though he planned on adding his own personal turbulence to the nation's zeitgeist.

He was the only child of Jessie Lois Preston Robinson, originally from Zanesville, Ohio, and Thomas Henry Robinson Sr., a general contractor from Tennessee. They were from Scottish and Irish stock, and he would describe his mother as religious, a good housewife and nurturer. She was an accomplished piano player and organist, and passed her musical ability to her son.

Robinson Sr. was a self-made man (which, H.L. Mencken said, absolves the almighty of an awesome responsibility). He was orphaned at five, and sold newspapers to pay his way through grammar and high school. He was a professional baseball player, a boxer, and an accomplished gymnast. He obtained his civil engineering degree through correspondence and night classes and became a well-known bridge builder. At 45, he studied law through correspondence courses and the Y.M.C.A. Law School, which is most likely why his son would show a similar interest in studying law.

Robinson Jr., by his own admission, implied that initially his home life was ideal, although that changed during his grammar school days when his father started to drink heavily and became involved with prostitutes. His mother covered up most of his father's drinking and his indiscretions, in an attempt to spare them all embarrassment.

Robinson Jr. had above-average grades in elementary school, took piano lessons, and at age 12 joined the Boy Scouts, although a weakened constitution kept him from the Scouts' more physical activities. His fellow scouts considered him to be eccentric and at some point, for some unknown offense—perhaps nothing more than his egotistical personality—he was punished by a jury of Scouts, which he considered a kangaroo court.

Early on, it seemed that Robinson was developing a two-sided personality, complicated by his health: he contracted measles, mumps, and chicken-pox, a touch of rheumatic fever, and at age 13, malaria. Two years later, he had pneumonia and pleurisy that developed into tuberculosis and spent almost a year at the Davidson County Tuberculosis Sanitarium. Employees there described him as aloof and condescending. The tuberculosis would come back in varying degrees during adulthood. Adding insult to such medical injury, he had already begun to wear glasses.

On his sixteenth birthday, his parents purchased an expensive Buick coupe with his initials monogrammed on its doors. Having a car increased his popularity at school, which may or may not have been why he had many friends and was constantly invited to social gatherings while escorting prominent young ladies of the city. One of them, a young lady named Cora Thomas, dated Robinson perhaps a dozen times, yet what she remembered most about him was that he had a car. As for Robinson, he justified its purchase by saying how far he lived from school (and when speaking of it, he inflated its $800 purchase price).

DRESSING UP

He was seen as being a typical male, although a bit effeminate, perhaps because he was so meticulous about his appearance. (Recall that he had committed a kidnapping while masquerading as a telephone repairman who was wearing a pinstriped suit.) Probably atypical, he was expelled from more than one school before, at age 16, enrolling in the Wallace Preparatory School for Boys, a feat that seemed to be accomplished by his mother's friendship with the founder.

During his senior year, he was the business manager of the school newspaper, *The Wallace World*, where he embezzled subscription receipts. Somehow, he managed to survive (a testament, perhaps once again, to his mother's relationship with the founder), and despite his depredations, he did well academically while taking college prep classes,

The G-men and the Heiress

received a prize for the highest grade in Latin studies, and graduated with a high school equivalency diploma.

From 1926 to 1928, he attended Vanderbilt University where, again, he was considered an intelligent student (later, in various tests, his I.Q. was said to range from 104 to 118). He was a member of Pi Kappa Alpha and Gamma Eta Gamma, a legal fraternity, and active socially. He occasionally drank and enjoyed gambling, mostly dice, which he later pursued with abandon. He was also described as a "playboy," dating the nice girls such as Sammy Meeks, a fashion model, as well as being a frequent escort of Ethel Reed, a known prostitute. His extracurricular activities left him with a souvenir of his campus years: he was treated for gonorrhea (later, in 1932 and 1933, it was syphilis; his campus lifestyle seemed to be the gift that kept on giving). His extracurricular pursuits apparently took a toll on his education, though; he became bored with his studies, cut classes, and dropped out.

But there was more to the story, which began with the most universal love-story line in existence: He met a girl. This happened, he said, at the end of his freshman year at Vanderbilt. Her name was Sue Ann Tubbs, whom he discovered as she was waiting for a streetcar. He stopped and offered her a lift home. (While we don't know what he said, it had to be one of the original pick-up lines.) They had a few dates, went to some parties, then drifted apart. When she came back into his life, she brought along a surprise—his baby, she said. He said the child she was carrying wasn't his.

When interviewed by the Division in October of 1934, Sue Ann Tubbs was still using the last name of Robinson, even though she confirmed they had divorced in 1929. Her interview resulted in a twenty-nine-page transcript, beginning with their meeting, which, according to her, happened *not* while Robinson was at Vanderbilt (which is what he told her) but while he was in prep school. (This also raised issues of her being underaged.)

She said that, although she had no evidence she thought she'd been drugged the first time they had sex. After being together for more than a year, she got pregnant, and they talked about marriage. He brought up the possibility of an abortion. Tubbs's aunt entered the picture where her persistences—*and* the possibility of Sue Ann being underaged—ended at the courthouse with a shotgun wedding. Robinson appeared to take it all in stride, and he contacted neither his father nor an attorney.

$

CLASS ACTION

They were married on January 18, 1927, and she gave birth at home six days later. During the marriage, they never lived together, and Robinson provided no support of

Mad as a hatter?

any kind. (She paid for the license and later purchased a ring herself.) She did receive anonymous gifts through the mail for the child, which she believed was from Robinson.

She heard Robinson had wanted to come and visit her, but that his parents kept him locked in his room. Which seemed difficult to believe but something—perhaps his own inertia—kept him away. She never discussed the matter with Robinson Sr., nor did he try to buy her off (another rumor). She did feel, though, that his parents didn't think she was good enough for their son, and they hadn't condoned the marriage because, Tubbs said, "they looked down on me as being very low class."

Robinson began annulment proceedings in March of 1927, and the only time he saw his daughter was in court. His request for an annulment was denied; he had better luck with the divorce, which was granted. In the proceedings, her reputation was repeatedly attacked. She said he was the only man she had been with. He said she had tried to shake down another man as the father, and later *his* father, Robinson Sr. Finally, she just wanted the proceedings to be over, and the divorce was granted in March of 1928. Grounds: cruel and inhuman treatment.

Through it all, she had nothing derogatory to say about Robinson and retained fond memories of him. After all, their relationship had produced a daughter, Nancy Jane, who was then eight. It was a testimony to either her immeasurable charity or poor judgment, but she thought of him as "a regular guy" and recalled him visiting her and playing the piano (obviously something *diminuendo*).

Her acrimony was reserved for Robinson's parents, and she always felt she and Robinson would have stayed together if it had not been for them. After the divorce, though, when he telephoned her and wanted to meet, she had the good sense to say "No."

Undaunted by his experiences, Robinson married again the next year. The bride was Frances Natalie Althauser, tall and thin with gray eyes and dark brown bobbed hair. They were married in Nashville at the Episcopalian Church of the Advent and began married life on Harding Street. At first, their union went well. Robinson was working at the Wayne Lumber Company and going to school nights, studying law at the Y.M.C.A. Law School. His work was highly satisfactory, and while with the company, Robinson made compelling and innovative suggestions about company timekeeping.

His wife was taking a secretarial course at Watkins Day School. Then one day, Robinson, on his way to the bank, saw his wife and her girlfriend on a streetcar when she should have been in class. Robinson talked to the head of the school and learned Frances had been in class only one day in the previous month. He confronted her, they argued, and Robinson, in a fit of anger, pulled a handgun from a drawer. In his recollection, he

The G-men and the Heiress

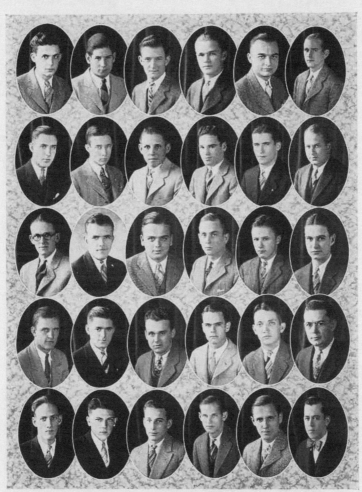

Top Row—Settle, Tanksley, J. Manley, Babington, Klilman, Miller
Second Row—Stockman, Hargroves, Crane, Noel, Beasley, Crum
Third Row—Radford, Daugherty, Pierce, Holt, Vaugha, Robinson
Fourth Row—C. Lackey, Bramwell, Hollabaugh, G. Patton, Cox, Regen
Fifth Row—W. Patton, Gore, Gordon, B. Manley, H. Lackey, Hill

156

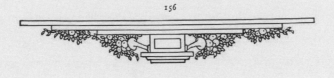

$ School Daze: Robinson at Vanderbilt, third row down, far right.

Mad as a hatter?

15

dropped the weapon on the floor and it accidentally went off, the bullet striking her in the leg. She would describe the incident as something less of an accident.

By his own admission, he couldn't concentrate on anything, whether it was work or his new domestic life, and he dropped out of school. He began drinking, lost his job, and the couple moved in with his parents. It wasn't an ideal situation. The house was new, and his mother complained about his wife wearing high heels and marking the floors. She also objected to smoking indoors, dancing, and, in general, whatever activity Frances might be involved in.

Robinson Sr. was drinking again and had to be retrieved from various Nashville dives known as "blind pigs," those low-end, usually illegal bars that sold booze during Prohibition. Robinson Jr. was at his wit's end, and he was about to do something that would make his life go from bad to worse.

$

LAUNCHING A NEW CAREER

In June of 1929, Robinson, wearing a badge he had purchased for a dime, was arrested in Nashville by Detective Sandford Egan for impersonating a deputy sheriff. In March, he had entered the homes of two separate wealthy women. He flashed the badge, pretending to be looking for alcohol and showing what he said was a warrant.

At the home of Mrs. Mary Gee Lamb on Jones Avenue in Nashville's Hillsboro section, he herded three women into a room and stole diamonds, watches, pins, and rings worth over $4,000. Then, before abandoning it, he drove Mrs. Lamb's new car to his next caper. There, at Clarence Waggoner's home on Harding Road, he locked Nellie White Waggoner and the maid in a closet, taking some $3,000 worth of valuables.

Interviewed by detectives, Robinson admitted the crimes, was charged with grand theft, and indicted on June 10 for assault and robbery. Robinson didn't deny committing the crimes but said he was victimized by his own personality (which was the perfect rationale, after all, for the vast amount of perfidy in the human condition). With some awareness of his own, he was already demonstrating the contradictory elements of his nature that would continually override his better self.

Lamb and Waggoner agreed not to cooperate with the prosecution after assurances they would get restitution. Robinson Sr. returned the stolen items to the victims and paid for additional expenditures incurred. Then their attorney arranged for Robinson to plead insanity to one of the robberies, and the criminal court placed him in a facility for a mental evaluation.

$

PIXELATED AT THE CUCKOO'S NEST

The Davidson County Circuit Court ordered a two-week assessment at the Central State Hospital for the Insane in Nashville, which Robinson began in early June. Previously called the Tennessee Lunatics Asylum, it was, as were many institutions of the period, overcrowded and underfunded, with a limited staff. It was a place where authorities and families placed those with various maladies: depression, substance abuse, mania, and psychosis.

Upon Robinson's arrival, four different doctors conducted Robinson's examination. He would later have three more assessments by the same doctors. In their opinion, he displayed delusions of grandeur, having made comments that he was so intelligent he could commit any crime without getting caught. (As Robinson was in CSH for committing grand larceny, this suggested Robinson suffered from other pathologies, as well.)

He said he opposed preachers and churches. He told one of the doctors that he'd threatened his father with a pistol. He told Dr. W.L. Farmer that he had sex with his wife at least three times a day while performing acts of self-gratification one to two times a day as well. (If true, Robinson likely would have had little time for larceny.) Dr. Farmer also learned that upon occasion, Robinson would leave work during the day, break into his own home, and sexually assault his wife. Farmer believed the stories and felt Robinson was a danger to society.

The attorney general of the Tenth Judicial District of Tennessee, Richard Atkinson, worked out a deal with the Robinsons and their attorney. The indictments would be dropped, with the understanding that Robinson would remain at the CSH for treatment. He was assigned the ward for the criminally insane, which would forever be "indelibly imprinted" on his psyche. He was rooming, he said, with a murderer adjudged insane, and he couldn't believe the cruel practices to which the patients were subjected.

After a stay of almost a year at CSH—and unknown to the prosecutor, Atkinson— Robinson was released into the care of his father. The hospital permitted him to leave, saying he was "improved but still insane." (There was apparently a sliding scale on insanity, and the expert opinion was that Robinson was on it somewhere.) His discharge was on May 20, 1930, and five days later, he was committed again, this time to the Western State Mental Hospital at Bolivar, Tennessee. There, he was a private pay patient, the expenses covered by his family. The record is unclear as to exactly how and why this occurred, but apparently it, too, was due to the influence of Robinson Sr.

WSMH was the antithesis of Robinson's former hospital; he participated in tennis, swimming, and attended socials where he hit the dance floor with some of the doctors'

Mad as a hatter?

Being mental in the 1930s

Thomas Robinson's brush with fame may have actually begun with meeting Dr. Edwin Cocke at Tennessee's Western State Mental Hospital. WSMH was a Gothic Revival pile built in 1885 and Cocke, its administrator, not only wrote the 1919 state law that dealt with the legal aspects of patients' treatment, but he was a pioneer in that treatment. He worked on the first therapeutic fever in the treatment of syphilis of the brain (which surely piqued Robinson's interest), and he was also a pioneer in insulin shock therapy.

By and large, though, the Depression was no time to need psychiatric treatment because there wasn't much of it, and what there was resembled plot devices from horror movies yet-to-come, in which lobotomies were performed with ice picks and children were chained to radiators.

There was no suitable treatment for schizophrenia, which was treated with sedatives that suppressed the patient's nervous system. Prescribed therapies included electroshock, induced comas and fever, and hot and cold baths. One asylum superintendent was renowned for his theory that infection led to mental illness. (His treatment was to surgically remove any place he suspected might harbor infection, from teeth and gallbladders to thyroid glands and parts of the colon. Ultimately, it was his theory that proved to be infected.)

$ Robinson early on: always a patient.

The essential improvement of the day was that the mentally ill were no longer treated by having their illness beaten out of them (although shocking was a close second).

The treatment centers like Western State were overcrowded, and Robinson with his tennis court times was given an unheard-of accommodation. By the beginning of the next decade, the country had a million psychiatric patients and the inmate population was growing by eighty percent annually. This meant that more and more patients were simply warehoused.

Robinson's jaunt through the psychiatric institutions was both brief and merciful, and in this, fortune had once again favored him.

The G-men and the Heiress

daughters. On occasion, he had lunch in the supervisor's apartment and was even allowed to drive an automobile for errands. At least that's what Robinson told the FBI in 1937. Again, the record is unclear as to why a patient with such a diagnosis was released. And, again, staffers were unhappy about it. Dr. Edwin Cocke, the superintendent, reluctantly agreed to the release but not before obtaining a signed statement from Robinson Sr. that covered himself and his institution.

The entire staff signed a statement asserting Robinson suffered from a psychopathic personality, that he was *not* insane, that he had never suffered from dementia praecox, but persistently demonstrated "an air of superiority," as well as a disregard for every regulation. Because of the latter, his privileges were taken away and he was locked up, which is when Robinson's father intervened.

Dr. Cocke was explicit in his appraisal. He said Robinson was an institutional patient and that with his experience with such cases, he felt the probability was that Robinson was "a menace to society." He, too, emphasized the term "psychopathic," which is the personality disorder characterized by a persistent antisocial behavior, impulsivity, and ego-centricity. (The modern day Hare Psychopathy checklist is made up of twenty items—i.e., manipulation, grandiose sense of self-worth, lack of realistic goals, parasitic lifestyle, short-term marital relationships—every one of which would be checked on Robinson's profile.)

Said the perspicacious Dr. Cocke, "He knows right from wrong as any normal person would, but he is just one of those types that cannot resist the temptation of doing wrong and committing crimes." And, in a final note, "He will continue to cause me a great deal of trouble." Or if not Dr. Cocke, *somebody*.

Robinson was out, but he was back home with his parents and all its familiar but menial routine. Looking for work, he found that having been in a mental hospital was a considerable handicap to his résumé. The Electrolux Corporation at Evansville, Indiana, was hiring, and he ended up on the factory floor tightening bolts, a job that lasted one fourteen-hour shift. (He said the work "disabled him," and he was unable to report back the next day.)

Robinson was also unable to stay out of trouble. In the spring of 1931, Nashville fireman, W. P. Ackerman, was proceeding down Murphy Road in Nashville around midnight when he saw a person peeping in a house window. Observing more closely, the person appeared to be a man dressed in women's clothing. Ackerman grabbed the person and took him to Firehouse 17 where he telephoned the police.

Policeman Lem Barker showed up, took the wig off the person's head, and took him to the police station where the arrestee identified himself as Thomas Robinson Jr. The lieutenant on duty was J. L. Redman, a good friend of Robinson Sr., so Junior got

Mad as a hatter?

another break and was released without process. He told the officer he was pulling a prank on a friend and his wife had helped him with the outfit. When Barker contacted Mrs. Robinson, she denied any knowledge of her husband's sexploits.

$

PERPETUALLY SQUARE ONE

In June of 1931, Robinson found a position with the Stoll Oil Refining Company of Louisville, making $65 a month. His father was friends with the owner/president Charles Christian "C. C." Stoll, so he was hired. (Nepotism seemed to be firmly entrenched in the Robinson family dynamic.) Robinson was to work sixteen hours every other day as a gas station attendant. On the days between, he was to sell gasoline, fuel oil, and coupons for commercial accounts.

One of his successes was opening a new account for the Ohio Valley Rock Asphalt Company of Summit, Kentucky, for fuel oil along with an installation of a new gas station. He brought his wife with him to Louisville but soon left the oil company for a job with Mutual Life Insurance Company of Baltimore. There, he was a salesman and collector in its Louisville branch, but the work was high-pressure sales, and many of the policies he sold were to workers in manufacturing. When their factories closed, they were unable to pay the premiums, his earnings stopped, and he lasted only a few months.

In the summer of 1932, he moved to Winnetka, Illinois, for a position with the ABC Oil Burner Corporation headquartered in Chicago but found selling oil burners difficult. It was on commission; he earned no money during August and September. One of the employees would later describe him as "egotistical, conceited, sleek and silky." While there, he was sometimes seen in the company of Blanche LeFleur, part owner of the Chambers Café in Winnetka who described him as "quite the braggart."

Moving back to Nashville, he was again at square one—living with family. (His in-laws were not happy that he had moved the family "up north where all of those foreigners were.") He asked his father-in-law for financial help in getting established in another city and received no help. He got involved in another sales venture, but it was like all the rest, a bust, involving a great deal of travel while he needed a better wardrobe and his vehicle was in poor condition. He needed money to make money.

In the fall of 1932, Robinson went to work at Andrew Jackson University of Nashville as a student recruiter. He lasted four months, having recruited only twenty students. In early 1933, he bluffed his way into a job at the Mar-Main Arms Apartment in South Bend, Indiana, as a maintenance worker with knowledge of steam-fitting, plumbing, boil-

The G-men and the Heiress

ers, heating equipment, painting, electrical work, and as all-around handyman. He had no experience with any of this work, so it wasn't surprising he was let go after his three-month contract.

In October of 1933, he was a timekeeper on a construction job for a few months, considered by his supervisor to be a good employee and even received an increase in pay. When describing Robinson, the descriptions were what one might expect—attractive, well-educated, having common sense. The company let him go when it learned he had a record, which meant the company would have to notify its bonding company.

By this time, Robinson's old criminal impulses resurfaced and he began targeting unsuspecting young women. Nashville agent Hugh Small interviewed one victim, Irene Johnston, who said that in early April of 1934, she was standing on a street corner in downtown Nashville around 8 p.m. when Robinson Jr. drove up

💲 A dapper young Robinson before the fall.

in a new Pontiac. He offered her a ride home, and when she objected, he forced her into the vehicle and started driving towards Nashville's Bellemeade area. During the ride he made physical overtures, then threatened and choked her, saying he was going to rape her.

To keep her from screaming, he hit her once on the head, which dazed her. He grabbed her purse, which contained $3, and her fifteen-jewel watch, stopped the car, and let her out. She was in some pain from the choking and visited a doctor the next day, but she didn't report the incident to the police because, she said, she didn't want to upset her mother, who suffered from nervousness.

On April 22, 1934, he was arrested on a complaint about a different robbery. Sometime in March, it seemed, he was driving near downtown Nashville and picked up Katherine Smith, age 20. She was walking alone towards town, it was snowing, and Robinson offered to take her to the center of the city.

They started talking, and she didn't notice he had detoured from town. They ended up on the outskirts of the city where he parked on the side of the road. He took her two diamond rings and her watch. He also tried to hug her (which was contrary to the usual practice of *giving* diamonds for affection). When she pushed him away, he slapped her and cursed at her. Then he ordered her out of the vehicle and threatened to shoot her.

In early May, Robinson pawned Smith's seventeen-jeweled Hamilton watch at a shop on West Market Street, using the name John Ward. Smith did not press charges—she said she didn't want the publicity—but the grand jury indicted him for the robbery. Robinson, disillusioned by his troubles—and his apparent inability to become a first-rate stickup artist—had skipped town earlier in the month.

Arriving in Chicago by train, he made contact with a childhood friend, Orville Carter. He told Carter he'd left Nashville as two detectives had come to his home to arrest him. He managed to grab $90 from a dresser drawer in the bedroom and jump out of a window. He left behind a recently purchased Plymouth automobile and his wife, who inherited the payment-in-arrears on the Plymouth.

Carter helped him obtain a position as a janitor at the Forsythe Building where Carter had previously been employed. Robinson's shift was from 1 a.m. to 8 a.m., although sometimes he worked until two or three in the afternoon. Robinson was on the run both mentally and physically, but not going very fast or very far. The night job in the summer heat was wearing him out physically, aside from having contacted a venereal disease. Treatment began at the Chicago Public Health Institute and if Robinson followed the prescribed regimen, treatment would be complete after some twenty visits and eight months.

Because of the difficulty of the job and his perpetual lack of funds, he didn't see how he could go on. He was also freighted by recollections of patients at the hospital who'd had the same disease—and what its latter stages did to the brain, causing paranoia and dementia, perhaps meningitis.

Then Robinson was fired from his position at the Forsythe Building for neglecting his duties. The fact is that he couldn't—or wouldn't—do any job for very long, and he'd be on to the next thing, an endless merry-go-round of lost opportunity and deadends. Robinson had tried everything; numerous occupations, family connections, a new start in different cities, with always the same result—failure. But a small seed had been planted and was growing in his mind. A notion to set him up financially, if not for life then for quite some time, but did he have the nerve to execute it?

$

KIDNAPPING ON A GRAND SCALE

The idea of kidnapping came to him from reading various crime magazines with stories about the high profile ransom kidnapping cases of the day. He was with his wife on October 8, 1934, when they drove to Louisville. He put her on a train back to Nashville, then under a fictitious name checked into the Tyler Hotel in the northern part of downtown. His plan was to kidnap C. C. Stoll, the executive of the Stoll Oil Company, the next day.

Even the hours leading up to Robinson's new caper was fraught with his ever-present lack of concentration. Sometime in the evening, he ended up in a pool hall, which happened to be across from the offices of *The Courier-Journal* where he began shooting pool with one of the reporters. He got drunk, told the reporter his real name, that he had been in an insane asylum, and began ranting about C. C. Stoll. He was so intoxicated, the reporter helped him back to his room, apparently unaware he had just helped tuck the newspaper's future front-page headliner into bed.

Robinson selected Stoll as the kidnap victim because he had a grievance—or thought he did—for in the summer of 1934, he had returned to Louisville and asked Stoll for another job. Stoll either advised him that his son did the hiring, or it was company policy not to rehire a previous employee.

In the mid-afternoon of October 9, Robinson drove to C. C. Stoll's residence on Cherokee Parkway, an affluent part of town. There, he rang the doorbell and when the maid answered, he represented himself as a telephone repairman. Seeing that C. C. Stoll was not home, he excused himself and went next door to the home of Stoll's oldest son, George Jungerman Stoll, who was not present, either. Next, he went to the Glenmary Avenue home of another son, Charles Ernst Stoll, also absent. It did not seem to occur to Robinson that most people were at work during the day. (Check Hare's twenty-item psycopathy diagnostic for "impulsivity.")

With only $17 in his pocket, he thought of returning to Nashville but instead checked into the Henry Clay Hotel. On October 10, he drove to the residence of yet another son, Berry Vincent Stoll. Later, he would tell investigators he hadn't planned on kidnapping anyone; he simply wanted financial help. He would also say his wife should have insisted he return to Nashville with her, or that she should have gone to his father and, because of his state of mind, they should have hospitalized him.

He thus faulted his wife, his family, the medical profession, in short, almost everyone but himself. He had escalated his antisocial behavior until he was on the cusp of graduating into a capital crime. Soon, his mental acuity would be tested almost day to day, for he would be under the constant pressure of a man wanted not just by local law enforcement officers but by the new and formidable presence of the Division of Investigation's G-Men.

Mad as a hatter?

Alice Stoll, "the young society wife," and her husband, Berry.

3 Louisville debutante

"I've had difficulties." —Alice Stoll

The Ohio River cradles Louisville on its way south, making a small detour west before heading back southward, as if it were accommodating itself to the city and surprising no one that the city was an early transportation hub on the Falls of Ohio. The city itself is a cross-section of southern hospitality, Midwestern diligence, western initiative, and eastern custom all rolled into one. Named in 1780 for monarch Louis XVI of France, it was a city fit for royalty. It had the charm and graceful architecture of the old South, and was known for its hemp and tobacco crop in addition to plenty of bourbon production.

It also profited massively from its pre-Civil War slave trade, with slave labor adding significantly to the building of the town. (The opprobrious term, "Sold down the river," is thought to have originated here.) Its harmful aftereffects would be seen well into the next century, a significant backstory to bluegrass, horse farms, and the yearly run for the roses, the Kentucky Derby at Churchill Downs.

At the time of the Stoll kidnapping, the Great Depression was in full swing, and Louisville suffered along with similar-sized cities. Prohibition merely added to the woes. It eliminated jobs and caused a hike in Louisville's criminal activity with a burgeoning underground market for alcohol that floated entire city districts (one police precinct reported eighty-three raids on bootleggers in one week, to small effect).

When repeal occurred the year before Alice Stoll's kidnapping, employment rose among Louisvillians. (After repeal, Louisville's first beer license went to a city police captain.) The distillery business came roaring back, and thirty-three new ones opened in 1933, including the new Seagram & Sons, the world's largest. The fortunes of Louisville

tobacco companies were never much impacted by Prohibition, in fact, they were probably enhanced by the jangled nerves of people unable to find a good bootlegger. In 1932,
for instance, they turned out eleven billion cigarettes, tripling the previous year's totals
and unable to keep up with demand.

Into such an unsettling decade, the Speed family was about to gain unwelcome
new exposure. The Speeds were a time-honored tribe of blue-blood Kentuckians who'd
acquired early prominence when Abraham Lincoln named James Speed as his attorney general. (He loaned the president books from his own law library.) Speed's nephew,
James Breckinridge Speed—known as "J.B."—was Alice's grandfather. Missouri-born
in 1844, he came to Louisville at age 11 upon the death of his mother and was raised by
an aunt, Lucy Fry Speed Breckinridge. When the Civil War began, he enlisted in the
First Ohio Battery, was promoted to Adjutant of the 27th Kentucky Volunteer Infantry
Regiment, and saw action with Major Generals George H. Thomas and William Te-
cumseh Sherman during the Knoxville and Atlanta campaigns.

Mustering out in the spring of 1865 and back in Louisville, he became a financial
leader with a significant role in the building of the city. As president of the Louisville
Cement Company, he foresaw the uses cement would play in the forging of the country. He branched out into cotton mills, coal, and telephone communication. His most
significant contribution to Louisville may have been his involvement as president of the
Louisville Railroad Company, investing heavily in the stock of the company and serving
as president, then chairman of the board, until his death.

In March of 1911, the newspapers reported Speed on his deathbed, but the news
was at least somewhat premature. He donated some $40,000 for a fourteen-foot, twen-
ty-five-ton statue of Abraham Lincoln located under the dome of the state capital at
Frankfort. It was dedicated in November of 1911 by President William Howard Taft
and little Alice Speed, age five, who was dressed in white with a blue cape. (Her job
was to pull the string that unveiled the statue.) The Speeds arrived by private train
with two hundred and fifty friends from Louisville although J.B.'s health kept him
from participating in the official presentation.

(There was a well-intentioned sidelight: twenty former slaves owned by various
branches of the Speed family were brought for the unveiling of the statue of the man
who'd set them free. "The former slaves will have a special place in the Capitol reserved
for them, so that they will be able to see and hear all that is done and said," read *The
Courier-Journal's* account, with its attendant whiff of condescension, which was, after all,
entirely in keeping with the times.)

The G-men and the Heiress

$ Alice and her grandfather, J.B. Speed—from a time-honored tribe.

In July of 1912, while convalescing at the Hotel Samoset in Rockland, Maine, he succumbed from heart problems and Bright's disease. His reported worth was $15 million. In 1925, his children established the Speed Scientific School at the University of Louisville in his honor. His second wife, Hattie, founded the J. B. Speed Memorial Art Museum in the same year, which is now known as the Speed Art Museum, located next to the University of Louisville.

Louisville debutante

SOUTHERN BELLE

Alice Helen Speed, J.B.'s granddaughter, was born on February 2, 1906, to Virginia Herndon Perrin and William Shallcross Speed. Her mother was tough and somewhat overbearing while her father may have suffered from depression. He was the only son of J. B. Speed, although Alice had another famous relative, her uncle, Frederic Mosley Sackett, a United States senator and Herbert Hoover's ambassador to Germany. Sent to Germany to assist with economic difficulties, he wasn't in the country long enough to affect conditions and was relieved of duty when Franklin Delano Roosevelt became president.

Alice's parents founded the Louisville Collegiate School in 1915 and continued their patronage of the K-12 preparatory school, which was primarily for girls. Alice and her sister both attended the school, and Alice would leave it $10,000 upon her death in the 1990s.

Beginning early in the century, Alice made more than a dozen Atlantic Ocean crossings. In June of 1914, she and her immediate family boarded the *RMS Lusitania* in New York City and sailed to Liverpool, England. (Good timing, for almost a year later, the *Lusitania* was torpedoed by a German U-boat off the coast of Ireland. The ship sunk in half an hour, and of the almost two thousand passengers and crew, only around eight hundred survived. Congress, the press, and some citizens wanted war, but President Woodrow Wilson held fast to neutrality, and the U.S. didn't enter WWI until two years later after Germany sank more U.S. ships.) In 1924, the Speeds sailed to France on the *S.S. Majestic*, vacationing in St. de Luz, and in 1925, they sailed from New York on the *Mauretania*, and motored through England.

With all her travels, Alice was still a shy, reserved, dignified person with an independent streak, which she inherited from her mother. With such an old and honored

$ Classmates at the Louisville School, Susan Stewart and Alice, 1922.

The G-men and the Heiress

$ Alice Stoll's wedding: Alice on right, and her sister, Virginia, on the left.

Kentucky name—and money—one would have expected her to emulate the society she was from; in truth, she seemed to be uncomfortable with it.

In 1925, she entered Bryn Mawr, an all-women's college near Philadelphia run by the Quakers. She majored in French, and at some point told a relative that France would have been her preferred place to reside. If she disaffirmed the life of the socialite, it was difficult to tell for the student social calendar was filled with afternoon tea socials, dances, buffet dinners, and theater parties, and her name was at the top of a *Courier-Journal* list of students. She spent Christmas vacation with her parents in Louisville, and in the spring they visited Washington, DC, together.

Because of the intervention of Cupid, she did not graduate from Bryn Mawr, and in 1927, after a brief engagement, she married Berry Vincent Stoll at the St. Paul Episcopal Church in Louisville. It was one of Louisville's social events of the year and even made *The New York Times*. The newlyweds spent two months in Europe visiting Milan, Venice, Florence, Rome, Naples, Sorrento, and the Island of Capri, returning to the United States in late August.

Upon their return, the couple took up residence with Alice's parents until their home was ready on Grinstead Drive, not far from the Louisville Collegiate School. They moved into the house known as The Cottage—where the kidnapping would occur—off Lime Kiln Lane in the early 1930s. Visitors entering a side door are now welcomed by a plaque reflecting its history as a "1920s Honeymoon Cottage," a bit of a mystery as the house was listed as built in the 1930s.

Oilman Extraordinaire

Charles Christian Stoll started his career in oil in the late 1880s, a time of vast monopolization in the industry. The independent company—in name only—for whom he worked followed Standard Oil's lead trying to monopolize producing, refining, transporting, and marketing, and driving out anyone in opposition. C.C., a man of principles in an unprincipled era, wasn't happy with Standard Oil's ruthless methodology, so when he returned from his wedding trip to find his employer had been taken over by Standard Oil, it was all the impetus he needed.

He borrowed on his house, bought some river property in Louisville, and started his own company. It was a brash move against cold-blooded competition, but in 1911, the Standard Oil trust was broken up, new oil fields were opened near Louisville, and C.C. was on his way. By 1924, Stoll Oil operated ten gas stations in Louisville and expanded across Kentucky, southern Indiana, and Ohio. By the war years, Stoll Oil had a thousand outlets selling its gasoline and other products. (His granddaughter remembered that as children, gasoline was eleven cents a gallon, and she and her playmates bought "play" gasoline for their bicycles.)

Stoll Oil, by all accounts, was "a vibrant company," reflecting C.C.'s values as a spiritual man active in his community, and it was run, said one report, "with great personal attention to the welfare of employees and customers." The old man died in 1943, his company left to his four sons, who came up against their father's original difficulty: targeted expansion by the large companies. And this time, the big boys won; Stoll Oil was subsumed by Sinclair Oil in 1952.

Sinclair kept the Stoll brand on the Louisville products for a few years, then in 1956 the name "Stoll Oil" vanished from the city directory, its former address on River Road taken over by gentrification. Tough but righteous old C.C. was merely one more ghost lost in the past.

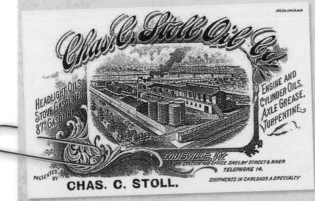

$ Stoll Oil: skirmish with the Big Boys.

The G-men and the Heiress

Alice's father-in-law, Charles Christian Stoll, known as "C. C.," founded the Stoll Oil Company in 1911, selling almost a hundred petroleum products, beginning with motor and transmission oil, gear lubricant, and transmission grease. In 1918 its name was

"A Profit in Every Sale" Should Be Slogan for Distribution in 1928

By BERRY V. STOLL
Vice President, Stoll Oil Refining Co.

I feel that the entire situation can be covered by the statement that the oil men as a whole have been too selfish. They cannot stand to lose an order. The producer cannot stand to think that someone

might be getting some of the oil he might get if he pumps his wells a little harder. The refiner, if he loses one order, cuts his price lower to get the next and all along the line this selfish policy of not letting the other fellow have his share but cutting to get all of it, has demoralized prices and demoralized general conditions.

There is going to be a tremendous increase in the consumption of oil and gasoline. Cities are spending large amounts of money to put in the right kind of airports for airplane use. Read Lindbergh's book "We" and you cannot help but realize that the future year holds a new customer for gasoline. It only takes a straw to break a camel's back and if the various oil refiners and producers and jobbers were willing to get their share and not try to increase each year and sit idle for one year—it would not take long for consumption to catch up with production and for the whole industry to go back on a healthy basis.

The oil industry has as good brains in it as any other industry—in fact too good, and what we need now is for the whole industry not to be so progressive and to be better satisfied with a normal business and a normal profit, and a slogan like "A profit in every sale" would not be a bad one, or "Volume at a profit."

$ Berry Stoll: normal business and a normal profit.

changed to the Stoll Oil Refining Company, and a 1921 newspaper article mentioned that Berry Stoll had invented an outlet valve which extinguished leakage of oil thus eliminating danger during unloading.

A 1924 article in *The Courier-Journal* said that Stoll Oil owned a twenty-mile pipeline in Lee County, Kentucky, receiving crude oil from over a hundred surrounding wells. It was then carried to storage tanks and loaded on to one of seventy-five company-owned tank cars near Beattyville, to be shipped to the Louisville oil refinery where 1,500 barrels of fuel and transmission oil was processed daily and shipped by tanker cars across the United States.

All four of C. C.'s sons worked for the company: the oldest, George Jungerman (vice-president of sales), Berry Vincent (vice president of refining), William Arthur (treasurer), and the youngest, Charles Ernst (secretary). C. C. died in 1943 and George became company president. It was sold in 1952 to Sinclair Oil. While the sale price was not mentioned, the company was believed to be worth nearly $2 million. Charles stayed on as president, and the Stoll Oil Refining Company name stayed on signage for some years before being phased out.

Berry was an officer with the Army Reserves just before, during, and after WWI, and had a law degree from the University of Louisville. He was at one time president of the Board of Park Commissioners, and in 1923 he helped facilitate the purchase of seven hundred acres for the city. (Part of the acquisition was Bowman Field, currently the oldest continuously operated commercial airport in North America, and the land also included the nearby Seneca Park.)

Upon the sale of the Stoll Oil Company, Berry became director of various entities, and he was involved in the United Refining Company, Louisville Transit Company, Louisville Cement Company, Black Star Coal Company, and the Pioneer Coal Company. Relatives described him as difficult, temperamental, possibly unstable. He had threatened one relative with a gun and gossip in the Louisville community said he was a gold-digger who'd married his wife for the money.

At the couple's island retreat in Pease Bay, Grand Cayman, Berry managed to sell sand from the beach to those willing to pay. Back in the states, it was thought he dumped oil waste on their property (possibly without Mrs. Stoll's knowledge). On the day of the kidnapping, the Division of Investigation said a Stoll Oil Company truck drove onto the Stoll estate at noon and dumped oil waste into a sinkhole. After Alice's death in the late 1990s, the estate had to spend $250,000 for an environmental site cleanup before the land could be turned over to the Speed Museum and sold.

The G-men and the Heiress

In addition to whatever private life Alice once had, she was about to inherit a vastly public one. Her life would be turned upside down by a disordered Tennessean, and the experience would reverberate throughout the rest of it. Already shy, Alice would become more cautious and ever more reclusive. She resisted any complete revelation about the kidnapping, saying only, "I've had difficulties."

In later years, Mrs. Stoll told her niece, "I had a hard time being my own person." It was surely a reference to her overbearing mother, her moody sister, her temperamental husband—even her kidnapper. Raised with every advantage and sheltered by family and wealth, her life was still an ardent demonstration of how easily happenstance might invade even the most heaven-sent existence.

$ Quick start—park your winter driving troubles at the Stoll station nearest you.

DARING DETECTIVE'S SHOW-UP

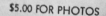

$5.00 FOR PHOTOS

Daring Detective will pay $5.00 each for photos of wanted men and women when they are accompanied by descriptive matter, details of crimes for which they are wanted and other necessary particulars. Only original photos, or copies of originals, can be used, and all photos and records used must be fully authenticated from official sources. It will be impossible to use all photos submitted, but those accepted will bring prompt checks. Address pictures to *The Show-Up, Daring Detective, 22 West Putnam, Greenwich, Conn.*

This photo of Thomas H. Robinson, Jr., was made in 1932 and is said to be an excellent likeness of the fugitive.

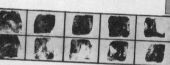

Law enforcement agencies everywhere have been supplied with fingerprints of Robinson, as reproduced above.

Another pose of the much-sought snatcher emphasizes the prominent cleft in his chin, one of the outstanding characteristics of his physical appearance.

SOMEWHERE, in hiding, is a man for whom every agent of the Federal Bureau of Investigation, and every other law enforcement officer in the country, is looking.

That fugitive, sought for the kidnaping of Mrs. Alice Speed Stoll from her home in Louisville, Ky., on October 10, 1934, is Thomas Henry Robinson, Jr., whose photographs and fingerprints are reproduced on this page.

Robinson is one of the few snatchers now at large. That is one of the reasons the G-men are closing in on him, making a determined drive to take him into custody.

Robinson, whose aliases include John Ward, Jr., John E. Ward, John W. Ward, Thomas W. Kennedy, Jerry Dobson, Henry Saunders and Mr. Knapp, is described as 28 years old; build, slender; height, six feet; weight, 149 pounds; hair, dark brown; eyes, gray; complexion, sallow; beard, heavy and dark; ears, no lobes; chin, prominent cleft; occupation, attorney's clerk. On occasion he is reported to have masqueraded as a woman to escape detection and capture.

Fingerprint classification:

$$\frac{21 \quad 27 \quad W}{15 \quad rW \quad 20}$$

Readers of DARING DETECTIVE are urged to watch for this fugitive. If apprehended, or if you have information regarding his whereabouts, communicate at once with J. Edgar Hoover, Director, Federal Bureau of Investigation, Washington, D. C., or with the nearest office of the Bureau.

It is possible, in order to avoid detection, that Robinson may be masquerading as a woman. An artist, using the photo at upper left, here shows how he may look in feminine disguise.

Daring Detective Magazine

"Watch for this fugitive!!!"

The kidnapping racket

4

"Well, Bud," he said, looking at me, "I'll be damned if you don't go to a lot of trouble to have your fun. Kidnapping, then fighting. What do you do on your holidays? Burn houses?"—William Faulkner

Most of the headline-grabbing kidnappers of the 1930s were career-hardened criminals with very little education, such as the members of the Barker-Karpis gang. And kidnappings and abduction were around long before Thomas Robinson got the idea, which came into popular view in 1874 when Charley and Walter Ross, the four- and five-year-old sons of a Philadelphia dry goods merchant, were taken from the Ross's front yard after being promised candy and fireworks. Walter was released but the kidnappers kept Charley.

Charley was a beautiful child with a cherubic face, dimpled chin, and curly hair down to his shoulders. Best liked by the family, timid, unassuming, and sensitive, quickly brought to crying. With his thorough manner, careful and old-fashioned, his relatives nicknamed him "Little William Penn." Charley's father received notes asking for $20,000, and although the Ross family lived in a mansion, they weren't wealthy, having lost considerably in the stock market crash of 1873. Unable to pay, Ross reported the matter to the police.

The police, fearful of copycat kidnappings, prodded him not to pay, even as sympathetic citizens offered to contribute. The case became a national *cause célèbre*, the famous Pinkerton detective agency got involved, and millions of posters were printed with Charley's likeness on them. (The missing-child poster was a first, which then became an initial response measure in future child-takings.) When Ross, in a newspaper ad, agreed to the ransom, it appeared that the unprecedented deluge of media

$ Charley Ross at age four—and never seen again.

coverage had made the kidnappers wary, and all communication stopped.

Five months later, two men were shot during a burglary. One of them, in a death-bed confession, admitted taking Charley Ross. Charley's brother, Walter, identified the man's body by its impaired nose (said to have been disfigured by syphilis), and for most, the case was considered closed. But Charley was still missing.

The Rosses looked for their son the rest of their lives. They interviewed nearly six hundred people who said they'd seen him and spent a small fortune chasing leads. In 1924, on the fiftieth anniversary of Charley's kidnapping, the child was still in the news. His brother, Walter, then a middle-aged stockbroker, said he and his sisters were even then receiving letters from men claiming to be Charley.

No kidnapping had ever caught the attention of the country quite like it. There was a popular song, "Bring Back Our Darling," and the warning to "never take candy from strangers" is thought to have originated with Charley's kidnapping. There was even something called "the Charley Project," a missing persons database founded early in the twenty-first century.

The more important result was that it demonstrated the inadequacy of both existing laws as well as police responses and focused public attention. Pennsylvania law was changed by a unanimous vote of the state legislature, making kidnapping a felony. Charley Ross, perpetually age four, had entered history with an unlived life, and would be forever known as one of the most famous disappearances in American history.

The next kidnapping to occupy so much public attention was that of Ion Perdicaris, a Greek-American playboy kidnapped in 1904 by a Tangier brigand known as Raisuli, who snatched wealthy Europeans for ransom. He had a colorful reputation that, depending upon the source, could be either chivalrous or cruel. He promised to defend Perdicaris from any harm, but he had also returned the head of one of his victims in a basket of melons.

The G-men and the Heiress

Raisuli had not reckoned on the temperament and resolve of the U.S. president, Theodore Roosevelt. Peeved by the kidnapping, Roosevelt dispatched seven warships and several Marine companies to Tangier, leading the American secretary of state, John Hay, to say that the American government wanted "Perdicaris alive or Raisuli dead." The international display, of course, did nothing to harm Roosevelt's profile for that year's presidential election.

The incident was also made into a film, *The Wind and the Lion*, in 1975 and Raisuli's labyrinthian personality was given over to Sean Connery, who rendered Raisuli in such a swashbuckling fashion that even Raisuli himself would have applauded. Brian Keith was a vibrant Roosevelt and poor Perdicaris became Candice Bergen because Hollywood thought the victim should be a woman. Then-president Gerald Ford had it screened in the White House and loved it.

$

THE CRIME OF THE CENTURY

Charles Lindbergh's fame helped bring about a public outcry when his twenty-month-old son, Charles Jr., was snatched outside Hopewell, New Jersey, on March 1, 1932. He was taken from his nursery window and down a homemade ladder, left broken at the rear of the house. A note requesting $50,000 ransom was on the window sill, later paid, but Little Lindy was already dead.

Local and state police investigated for two years without much success. The Bureau of Investigation had no jurisdiction until President Franklin Roosevelt ordered them to take the lead. Then, in September of 1934, police arrested a German immigrant carpenter named Bruno Richard Hauptmann for passing some of the ransom money. An alert gas station owner had written Hauptmann's license plate number on a bill. The deliverer of the ransom money identified Hauptmann, and Lindbergh Sr. said he recognized his voice (others doubted Lindbergh Sr.'s hearing recall). A significant

$ It was the nightmarish case that rewrote federal laws.

amount of ransom, $14,000, was found in Hauptmann's garage, the telephone number of the man who delivered the money was written on a panel in Hauptmann's closet, and the Divison identified Hauptmann's handwriting on the ransom note.

The most damning evidence may have been expert testimony that a piece of wood in Hauptmann's attic matched wood in the ladder. He was convicted and executed for capital murder on April 3, 1936. Some who examined the evidence questioned the investigation and believe he had only a minor role in the kidnapping. Even Hoover had a problem with some of the evidence, because the fingerprints on the ransom note and money didn't match Hauptmann's.

His widow, Anna Schoeffler Hauptmann, spent the rest of her life trying to clear his name, which was wishful thinking on her part. While he may have been innocent of taking the child, he was surely part of the conspiracy.

Congress had been debating the issue for some time; the Lindbergh kidnapping made them serious about enacting a new law. Some advocated states' rights— letting the locals handle the crime—worried that the federal government would overreact. They might have been onto something, because Congress pushed to make kidnapping a capital punishment. While the Lindbergh case was pending, though, Congress held off on a decision. Then when the baby's body was found on May 12, 1932, Congress acted, forwarding the Federal Kidnapping Act to President Herbert Hoover, who signed it into law on June 22.

$ The monoplane that made the first nonstop flight across the ocean.

The G-men and the Heiress

Known as the Lindbergh Law, it prohibited kidnapping and transportation of victims from one state to another. The Bureau of Investigation had a seven-day waiting period before it could assume the victim had been transported across state lines, which allowed agents to be involved. Any victim not released within a day was covered by the law, excluding parental kidnapping.

Before the law, a kidnapper's best bet was taking the victim to the next state—or farther. Thus the original state jurisdiction would be out of reach. Extradition procedures were seen as weak, inept, or lacking. By the time law enforcement followed the processes and obtained assistance from some counterpart in another state, the case—in most instances—would have run cold.

Congress decided it was better to have federal authorities coordinate cross-state efforts, which would be more efficient and effective in investigative efforts. It seems the act wasn't the deterrent they had hoped, for in 1933 the number of significant ransom cases doubled to twenty-seven from the year before. In Depression-era America, there were so many kidnappings that newspapers tended to use smaller type to list the less sensational ones. Ransom kidnapping seemed to have become an epidemic.

$

RUFFIANS BRANCH OUT

In the early 1930s, kidnapping and extortion were so bad in the Midwest that a Kansas City insurance agent offered businessmen policies through Lloyd's of London. Maximum coverage was $50,000, later upped to $100,000, with children's coverage costing $50,000. The company also offered an additional plan for adults if injured during the kidnapping. As companies offered this new coverage, they generally insisted upon two things: (1) the policy had to be kept secret and (2) the company only paid once the ransom was paid—it never fronted the money. (Company thinking was that paying a large ransom quickly incited future kidnappings.)

Thomas Robinson, in his ransom note, made it plain that he was aware of the famous kidnappings of the day: Nell Donnelly was taken in 1931; the Lindbergh baby in 1932; wealthy brewer William Hamm Jr., Jake Factor (the less-famous brother of Max Factor), and Charles F. Urschel, stolen away from a bridge game, all in 1933. Banker Edward Bremer and businessman Charles Boettcher II were grabbed in 1934.

Robinson must have studied each case because he knew that police and the federal men were involved. All the families except Donnelly's paid the ransom. Robinson even said in his ransom note that Mrs. Stoll's family shouldn't "deal secretly with the police

The Barker-Karpis Gang, professional kidnappers

The gang pulled off kidnappings of William Hamm Jr. and Edward Bremer in the early 1930s, netting a combined $300,000 and plenty of notoriety, which led to its eventual undoing. Involved in everything from harboring fugitives, bank burglary and robbery to violent kidnappings and murder, the gang was an equal opportunities offender. Historians differed on whether a woman called "Ma" Barker was the leader or just an associate (members got a kick out of being asked if she was the leader). Alvin Karpis portrayed her as an elderly hayseed who dumped her husband but stayed close to her four sons because they were her world, and she conveniently provided a decoy for the gang's operations.

The gang originated in 1931 when Fred Barker and Alvin Karpis met in prison, and they were basically bank robbers until the mid-1930s when they segued into kidnapping, which they thought would be less risky. After Hamm and Bremer, Doc Barker was arrested in early 1935 and agents found a map with a penciled circle around the town of Ocklawaha, Florida, which ended up being the Barker hideout. On January 16, 1935, during a raid led by SAC Earl J. Connelly, thousands of rounds were fired into the house and both Fred and his mother were killed.

Ma should have come out with her hands up. The public had been convinced by all the colorful reporting that she was the brains of the outfit, even though she had never been arrested or fingerprinted. The record isn't clear, but in all probability Ma never held a Tommy Gun, let alone used one.

💲 The fabled Machine Gun Ma, as rendered by Katie Roden.

Doc was convicted of the Hamm and Bremer kidnappings and sentenced to life in prison. In January of 1939, five prisoners tried to escape the Federal Penitentiary at Alcatraz; they made it out but ringleader Doc was shot, wounded in the head. Before he died in the prison hospital, he said, "I am crazy as hell. I should never have tried it." He really should have known better; it was Friday the 13th.

By the end of 1936, most if not all of the primary gang members were either dead or captured, ending one of the most ruthless criminal gangs in American history.

either. There is always a crooked cop who will tip off a newspaper reporter for a sum of money." Thus it appeared Robinson had been contemplating a kidnapping longer than anyone initially thought.

As in the Stoll case, Nell Donnelly was not the original target; her husband was. But he was ill and not taken because he never left the house. His young, attractive, blue-eyed wife was a fine substitute. She had started the Donnelly Garment Company in 1919 with money from her husband. By 1931, it was a $3.5 million-a-year business in which a thousand employees made affordable dresses, aprons, smocks, and pajamas. Success made her a target, and in mid-December of 1931, Nell and her chauffeur were grabbed by three men who demanded a $75,000 ransom.

A friend of the family, James A. Reed, a former U. S. senator, led the search for her. He allegedly turned to Johnny Lazia, an infamous Kansas City organized crime head, for assistance. Through their efforts and those of the Kansas City Police Department, Nell and the chauffeur were released after being held captive for thirty-four hours—and without payment of a ransom. The kidnappers initially escaped but were later captured, tried, and convicted. Nell ended up divorcing her husband, buying his interest in the company, and marrying Reed—who was over twenty-five years her senior—in 1933.

Robinson, more than likely, would have paid little attention to the ransom *not* being paid. His ego would not let him believe *his* kidnapping would not be successful.

In June of 1933, William A. Hamm Jr., 39-year-old president of the Theodore Hamm Brewing Company of St. Paul, Minnesota, had just left his office when he was snatched by four men and shoved into the back of a car. Driven to Wisconsin, he was forced to sign four ransom notes. Moved to a hideout in Bensenville, Illinois, he was held there until the $100,000 ransom was delivered. The Bureau Crime Lab cracked the case using cutting-edge engineering and a technique later known as Latent Fingerprint Identification, which allowed fingerprints to be pulled from surfaces that couldn't otherwise be dusted for prints. (Items were painted with silver nitrate and its chemical reaction with the naturally-occurring perspiration on fingers produced sodium chloride, visible under UV light.) Fingerprints of the Barker-Karpis gang were found on the ransom notes, and they were arrested and convicted. It was the first time the method had been used successfully.

On January 17, 1934, Edward George Bremer, 36, a wealthy banker and heir to the Jacob Schmidt Brewery fortune, was kidnapped from St. Paul, Minnesota, while on his way to work. His father, Adolph, was a financial supporter of President Franklin Roosevelt, and when FDR mentioned the kidnapping during one of his fireside radio chats, significant heat was put on the perpetrators. One of Bremer's attackers was Arthur

$ Thomas Robinson: following in the footsteps of the previously indicted.

"Doc" Barker, who punched and pistol-whipped him. Bremer was taken to Illinois, where the culprits received $200,000 in ransom.

Bremer was released after twenty-two days and, once at home, he quickly downed two glasses of beer and told the Division of Investigation agent at his house he never got a look at the kidnappers. He was reluctant to give details because the kidnappers had threatened the life of his wife and children. Finally, though, Bremer revealed what he knew, which was considerable. His information, along with an abandoned gas can that contained a single fingerprint of Doc Barker—as well as serial numbers of the ransom money—helped. Twenty-five people were eventually convicted in connection with Bremer's kidnapping. Among them, six received life and others received combined sentences of one hundred years and a day.

The Barker-Karpis kidnapping of both Hamm and Bremer were lucrative, but Robinson might have reconsidered following in their footsteps if he had paid attention to how things turned out for them.

AGENTS WORK OVERTIME

In May of 1934, Attorney General Homer Cummings pushed for additional legislation that re-enforced the federal kidnapping statute. It created a presumption of interstate transportation after three days, allowing the Division of Investigation to enter the case (reduced from the original seven). It also allowed the jury to recommend capital punishment, even if the victim was released unharmed. Other laws made federal crimes of bank robbery, interstate transportation of stolen property, the unlawful flight of fugitives across state lines, racketeering in interstate commerce, and assault/murder of a government agent. Most important, it enhanced the Division of Investigation, commissioning its agents to carry firearms, serve warrants, and make arrests.

That fall, the Division advised the Associated Press of seventy-four kidnapping convictions resulting in 1,500 years of jail time (including two death sentences and sixteen

The G-men and the Heiress

life terms). In January of 1935, *The New York Times* reported that kidnapping was on the downswing. Its story headline came from the number one public relations representative of the Division, the Director himself, J. Edgar Hoover. The timing wasn't perfect, however, as one of the most famous kidnappings of the decade—that of nine-year-old George Weyerhaeuser, the son of a wealthy lumberman in Tacoma, Washington—had occurred a little over a week before. Hoover and the Justice Department were pushing the line that kidnappers had a better chance of being caught than escaping.

Since the Lindbergh Law had been passed three years prior, agents were having success capturing the perpetrators, but they blamed the newspapers for publishing stories about the wealthy, making them easy marks for hard-hearted risk-takers. The payoff could reach $100,000 or more, and that, of course, was the prime mover of any criminal enterprise. Hoover's answer was to find the perpetrators, arrest them, and convict them, swiftly and harshly. He thought kidnappers were afraid of only one thing, and that was getting the electric chair (or in the slang of the day, "the hot squat").

On February 9, 1936, Walter Winchell, the syndicated gossip columnist with a sixth-grade education but some fifty million fans, said during his Sunday night radio broadcast that all ninety-five of the agents' kidnapping cases were solved. Then he received a letter from a listener, Edward Davis of Berea, Kentucky, wanting to know under what category the Stoll kidnapping case fell because Thomas Robinson was still on the loose. Winchell, one of Hoover's good friends, passed the letter along to the Director, who then explained in a letter to Davis that "although Thomas H. Robinson Jr., has not yet been apprehended, the Stoll Kidnapping Case has been solved." Hoover said the case wasn't over until all perpetrators of the crime were caught and convicted but, in practical terms, he knew Robinson was already a convicted man walking. Or running, as the case might be.

As for Robinson, he knew that in Kentucky, ransom kidnapping was a felony with punishment decided by a jury. Depending on how jurors leaned, they could hand out life in prison or death by electrocution. He also knew that the federal government's method of capital punishment was usually hanging, with the judge having the final say. In the 1930s, the federal government executed nine by hanging and one by electrocution. Forty-five states also had capital punishment, and the federal government and states conducted more executions in this decade than any other (and by a fiendish variety of methods)—two by firing squad, 114 by gas chamber, 357 by hanging, and 1,206 by electrocution.

If caught and convicted, Robinson was, at a minimum, looking at a lengthy prison stay. Paying the ultimate price—death by electrocution or hanging—was also a possibility. As usual, the impulsive Robinson did not see the bigger picture.

The kidnapping racket

Comic Strip "War on Crime" The Akron Beacon Journal
(Akron, Ohio), August 17, 1936, Pg. 13.

5

Manhunt: wanted by the Division of Investigation

"This was a brave and selfless squad of men. They were heroes, and your father was one of them, and it was a hell of a thing to be."
—Doris Rogers Lockerman, Melvin Purvis's secretary, to Purvis's son

In October of 1934, the Stoll kidnapping wasn't the only crime making the news. On October 17, Harry "Pete" Pierpont, a bank robber and mentor to John Dillinger and a member of his gang, made the front page of the newspapers when he was executed at the penitentiary at Columbus, Ohio, for the murder of Sheriff Jesse Sarber while breaking Dillinger out of the Allen County jail in Lima, Ohio. Pierpont's eyes were swollen red from weeping before his execution, but at the end he was reported as wearing a slightly cynical smile. (It was Pierpont's girlfriend, Mary, who gave the best description of John Dillinger: "Johnnie's just an ordinary fellow. Of course he goes out and holds up banks and things, but aside from that, he's really just like any other fellow.")

The capture of Charles Arthur "Pretty Boy" Floyd, a prolific bank robber, was more big news. He was designated "Public Enemy No. 1" after John Dillinger had been killed. On October 22, almost three months later to the day, Floyd occupied the front-page headlines of most newspapers, and the Stoll kidnapping was relegated to a smaller story on the lower half of the page. Floyd met his end in a cornfield behind a house in East Liverpool, Ohio, shot in a one-sided gunfight with local law enforcement and Division agents led by SAC Melvin Purvis of the Division's Chicago office. Then in January of 1935, the famous Lindbergh kidnapping took up major front-page territory when the trial of the baby's alleged kidnapper, Bruno Hauptmann, got underway.

SA Michael F. Glynn

SA William C. Ryan

SAC Melvin H. Purvis, Jr.

SA Herman E. Hollis

SA Daniel P. Sullivan

SA Allen E. Lockerman, Jr.

SA Raymond C. Suran

SA Charles G. Campbell

SA Earle L. Richmond

SA James J. Metcalfe

SA Ralph D. Brown

SA Charles B. Winstead

SA John T. McLaughlin

Clarence O. Hurt

SA Thomas J. Conner

SA Val C. Zimmer

SA Robert G. Gillespie

SA Joseph P. McCarthy

Inspector Samuel P. Cowley

SA Grier C. Woltz

$ The men who brought John Dillinger to bay.

The G-men and the Heiress

$

WEDNESDAY, OCTOBER 10, 1934

The first Indianapolis Division of Investigation agent to become aware of the Stoll kidnapping was Earl Wynn, who happened to be staying at the Tyler Hotel in Louisville. He learned about it from Lieutenant Roy Parsons of the Louisville Police Department, then telephoned his boss, Herold Reinecke, the Indianapolis office SAC.

Reinecke was famous in the agency (and out of it) because John Dillinger's girlfriend, Billie Frechette, had testified at her trial that Reinecke slapped her, whereupon Dillinger vowed to kill him. Reinecke denied hitting her, but the Dillinger name was now attached to Reinecke's reputation, and as late as 2009, he was badly fictionalized in the Michael Mann film, *Public Enemies*, in which Adam Mucci, in a breakout performance, depicted Reinecke as a frenzied, overweight agent. (Said sultry Billie in the film, "And when my Johnny finds out how you slapped around his girl, you know what happens to you, fat boy?")

The Indianapolis office territory covered Louisville, so during the investigation it was the office of origin and—immaculate timing—other Indianapolis agents were already in Louisville for federal court, handling War Risk Insurance investigations. (This WWI program, by and large, provided insurance for shipping vessels, and the Treasury Department had jurisdiction over claims.) Reinecke told Wynn to get the other agents and meet police at the Stoll residence where they were to interview the family and other witnesses and report immediately back to him. They arrived into chaos, with numerous city and county police, reporters, family, and curious spectators milling about the grounds.

Wynn conferred with Major Edward McElliott, the Louisville Police Department's chief of detectives, and they agreed the Division would take the investigation's lead. Assistant Chief of Detectives William Oeltjen, a former WWI intelligence officer, had kicked off the police department's efforts by alerting surrounding municipalities and other police agencies, telling them to be on the lookout for a dark Ford V-8 automobile. Based on the ransom note, he identified the kidnapper and laid the groundwork for the Division's efforts.

SAC Earl Connelley of the Cincinnati office, who'd investigated some of the critical Division cases of the 1930s, arrived in Louisville late in the evening. Connelley had learned about the kidnapping from the victim's uncle, the former senator Fredric M. Sackett, who was staying at the Netherland Plaza Hotel in downtown Cincinnati. Sackett told Connelley what he knew, which wasn't much, but gave the agent a brief description of his niece. (The initial descriptions of the kidnapper, meanwhile, were vague and sketchy.)

$ The chaos outside the Stoll house: no turn unstoned.

The Division would quickly acquire a much more accurate description of Mrs. Stoll, and the maid, upon reflection, gave a more reliable one of the kidnapper, with such sharp details as his having a sallow complexion and a sunken chest (which led Connelley to think the description fit someone in the advanced stages of tuberculosis, a prescient observation as Robinson had already been treated in a sanatorium).

Agent Wynn contacted the general manager of the Southern Bell Telephone Company and made arrangements to have an operator cover the Stoll's number—East 2941. The Division gave the manager telephone numbers of the Stoll and Speed families, and their friends and business associates whom the kidnapper might contact, and operators were put in place to monitor them. An agent was designated explicitly to answer any calls to the Stoll residence, with a second agent added a short time later. An exclusive line was placed in the house to trace incoming calls and a second such line was quickly added, strung from five miles away just for Division business.

The G-men and the Heiress

The agency, on tap

In 1927, a former Seattle police lieutenant and bigtime bootlegger, Roy Olmstead, was caught through telephone wiretapping, and the case went all the way to the United States Supreme Court. A year later, in a 5-4 decision in *Olmstead v. U.S.*, Chief Justice William Howard Taft presented for the majority, which said rights of the defendant weren't violated (although he had his own reservations).

Once he became attorney general in 1929, William Mitchell went so far as to prohibit the use of wiretapping by the DOJ. Hoover, caught up in the controversy, was asked by members of the House Appropriations Committee as to whether the Bureau's 1930 fiscal budget allowed for this type of technique. Hoover said that while the use was not illegal, it was unethical, and at the direction of the AG, any agent using it would be fired.

The AG reversed course again in January of 1931, giving the agencies under his direction, including the Bureau of Prohibition, its use in specific cases. In 1934, the method of wiretapping was used everywhere by police, federal agencies, private detectives, corporations, and private citizens. No specific law prohibited its use. And no one seemed to object, except the phone company.

It was easy to place a device that could listen in on a telephone call and record it. The United Press gave directions: scrape insulation from the phone line and attach the bare copper wires to another phone, "as easy as hooking up an extra reading lamp over the bed."

$ Wiretapping: as easy as hooking up a reading lamp.

The Communications Act of 1934 banned "the interception of telephone calls and the disclosure of their contents." Congress believed it had made wiretapping a crime. Hoover, ever the sly fox, interpreted "disclosure" to mean that wiretapping wasn't illegal if not used in court. It was, in effect, Hoover's own secret weapon, and as the Secretary of the Treasury, Henry Morgenthau, said, "Would anybody complain if we caught the Lindbergh kidnapper through wiretapping?"

FIRST FULL DAY OF CAPTIVITY, THURSDAY, OCTOBER 11

Early on, of course, the Division knew the identity of a least one of the kidnappers—or thought it did—thanks to the kidnapper's own ineptness. (Hoover described him as "a moral pervert.") They were waiting on a comparison of handwriting and photographs and wanted to know if Mrs. Stoll was alive before they made a move against him. This assessment would be overly optimistic on Hoover's part because the authorities didn't have any idea where the kidnapper was.

The authorities, as well as reporters, blanketed the Stoll estate, and SAC Connelley would try to clear them from the site but without much success. Even the Kentucky governor, Ruby Laffoon, made an appearance. Berry Stoll was hounded by reporters every time he left his house. "All I want is my wife back alive!" he would tell them, and he gave a radio plea asking for her safe return. His brother William was the family spokesman and told the press it was ready to deal with the takers. Hoover thought Stoll's broadcast was ill-advised, opening the flood gates to charlatans claiming the ransom.

Once the Division higher-ups were briefed, they took over media relations and asked police and family to refrain from providing any more information to the public. Hoover

$ Hoover, Assistant Attorney General William Stanley, and G-Man Purvis, a trifecta.

The G-men and the Heiress

💲 The drama outside converted the Stoll house into a parking lot.

was not a proponent of news organizations unless, of course, it suited his purposes. He knew that once a newspaper got the story, the rest would follow, as things were highly competitive in the print arena. He thought publicity did funny things to people, even law enforcement; there were always those who liked the limelight too much. Hoover could have been describing himself.

Ulric Bell, the *Courier-Journal's* Washington correspondent, asked about jurisdiction in the case, and Hoover explained that previously the Division couldn't be involved until the victim was taken across state lines and a ransom demanded. The updated law, though, made it a federal investigation after three days, and his agents weren't going to wait that long.

Hoover insisted the locals follow the Division's lead; otherwise, the Divison would work alone. He thought it was better to follow the ransom note's instructions quietly and secretly and let the investigators work discreetly. Hoover was overly optimistic that the Division would resolve the issue within five days.

Edward Tamm, an aide to Hoover's assistant director, Harold "Pop" Nathan, didn't want to take any chances. Tamm was responsible for getting men for the case, and he immediately contacted SAC Reed Vetterli of the St. Louis office and asked him to send three agents to Louisville. Vetterli sent four but only two were experienced. Tamm also called the Nashville office and asked for agents. And Nathan himself—Hoover's number two man—was on his way to Louisville. Any more agents, and it would have been a convention. It was the Division's process in its important cases: throw a wide net as quickly as possible, using as many investigators as possible. It was the agency equivalent of what the U.S. Army would do in WWII by throwing as much ordnance as possible at the enemy, rather than manpower.

$

CONNELLEY: HOOVER'S MAN

At 4 o'clock, early in the morning after the kidnapping, SAC Connelley had a conference with Louisville's police brass, including the mayor. The Division was taking over, which was its practice. But rifts were already showing within the Division; Hoover seemed to be losing patience with two of his top men, Connelley and Melvin Purvis, the Chicago SAC. Hoover wanted the Stoll case cleaned up, and he appeared to have lost faith in Connelly's abilities, and for whatever reason, he didn't want Purvis anywhere near the limelight. Purvis, of course, had presided over the elimination of both John Dillinger and Pretty Boy Floyd, which made him the legendary face of both captures. In Hoover's organization, however, there would be only one face—his.

Connelley, with his trademark pencil mustache (which somehow managed to survive Hoover's dislike of facial hair), headed up the New York City office from 1930-1932 where his initial management style exasperated his agents. He was a clock-watcher and a stickler for detail. He demanded agents be on time, to always sign in and out, to be *exacting*. Once, when he saw an agent reading a newspaper after the office clock had struck 9 a.m., he walked over to his desk and asked the embarrassed agent about his work. Connelley's men sometimes wondered whether they were in an investigative office or a grade-school classroom.

One of them complained to headquarters in Washington, calling Connelley harsh and undiplomatic, traits that didn't lead to loyalty by the rank and file. Hoover sent Connelley a letter denouncing his management style, but Connelley wasn't like other SACs, and he didn't take criticism particularly well. He told Hoover he'd appreciate Hoover advising him as to how his practices might be varied "to better suit conditions or your desires in the matter." Underneath Connelley's letter was the slightest hint of his own audacity, and while he had plenty of grit of his own, he managed—in spite of working some of the decade's high profile cases—to stay out of media's glare (which wasn't true of his compatriot Purvis).

The G-men and the Heiress

In time, Connelley would get better at running an office, and he *did* develop men loyal to him as he worked offices across the country (another of Hoover's institutional practices; he thought by moving his best operatives around it would test their loyalty, as well as improving the field offices). He had his detractors, who complained of his acerbic manner, and something called "Connelley's Rule," which was his directive that his agents spend less than ten percent of their work time on files and reports. And when field agents heard that Connelley was coming, they tended to brace themselves. Said one of his agents, "He was a little man by stature, but he had a very big voice. And it could be a very angry voice at times. We, the secretary and I, sat in on the conferences and really got an earful, too. He chewed out the agents very dramatically and sometimes maybe profanely. But he got a lot of results too."

$ Special agent in charge Earl Connelley, who was a man unlike all the others.

But the agents also recognized he didn't ask anything from them that he, himself, wouldn't provide. He was a workaholic, in the office—or field—on weekends, and he usually got his man. After his agents retired or left the bureau, some of them called him "the greatest boss we ever had."

Hoover made Pop Nathan the Division spokesman in Louisville, which left Connelley free to supervise investigative aspects and the dozen or so agents. (Privately, Hoover told Nathan he wanted him to oversee the Division efforts and make sure certain things were handled correctly. It was in keeping with Hoover's management style in which he liked to play his agents against one another. The competition may have sometimes made investigations more efficient, but it also kept Hoover firmly the alpha dog.)

Hoover wanted updates from Nathan several times a day, and he wanted the local police handled "with a firm hand." Connelley, meanwhile, kept an agent in the luxurious Brown Hotel, but he also asked for space in Louisville's U.S. Courthouse and Custom House, an enormous new six-story building that contained the city's post office and covered an entire city block. He'd have new phone lines installed there so he could be in constant contact with Division headquarters in Washington, in addition to the local lines.

Connelley got Thomas Robinson's fingerprints from the Nashville Police Department, made copies, and sent the original to the Division lab in Washington. The fingerprint card and a photograph of Robinson were combined to create a Division of Investigation identification order, which is essentially a small wanted poster. Details on Robinson were piling up: he had a cleft chin and odd earlobes or lack thereof, which was apparent to anyone who got a side view of him. His wife would tell the Division that when he smiled, a noticeable two-inch wrinkle ran down from the corner of his right eye, which occasionally twitched. The Division would soon know more about Robinson than Robinson himself knew.

The lab analyzed the ransom note and found Robinson's fingerprints on it. Technicians determined the letter came from a Corona typewriter with a black and red ribbon, used primarily to prepare bills and commercial documents. The paper for the note was Atlas bond, made by the Sheffield Paper Company of Cincinnati and Pittsburgh.

$

SECOND DAY OF CAPTIVITY, FRIDAY, OCTOBER 12

Hoover wanted to make sure his agents outnumbered the police at the Robinson Sr. residence and that the Division in all aspects of the investigation—surveillance, interviews, press contacts—"dominated the situation." Pop Nathan in Louisville and SAC William Rorer at Nashville were leading the field investigation from their respective locations.

Nathan, of course, was the Division's grand old man who carried the Number Two badge for years. He had joined the Division in 1917 at a salary of $5 a day and he was the only Jew to have any real rank. ("Jews," Hoover's aides explained, "are not attracted to law enforcement.") But even the goyim liked Nathan, probably even Hoover himself, for Nathan had the reputation of being the only agent who could talk Hoover out of some of his more far-fetched ideas. (In 1936, for example, he managed to dissuade Hoover from launching the agency into the film business where he wanted to make his own "G-Men" movies and compete with Hollywood.)

Rorer, like Nathan, had plenty of experience. He was one of the agents who captured Machine Gun Kelly in Memphis in 1934 when Kelly—without firing a shot—said, "Don't shoot, G-Men!" The statement didn't show up in the official reports, however, although a Philadelphia newspaper story months after the fact quoted Kelly as saying

The G-men and the Heiress

he didn't shoot because, "It was them Gs. Them Gs would have slaughtered me." The more accurate historical moment might have been when Rorer told the *Chicago American* immediately after Kelly's arrest that "Kelly's wife cried like a baby. She put her arms around [Kelly] and said: 'Honey, I guess it's all up for us. The 'g' men won't ever give us a break. I've been living in dread of this.'" Whatever was said, Rorer was present, and if Kelly *didn't* say "Don't shoot, G-Men!" it was still a good story. And good stories, as everyone knows, have a life all their own.

$

THIRD DAY OF CAPTIVITY, SATURDAY, OCTOBER 13

Early Saturday morning, Connelley met more Louisville brass at the Louisville armory where they talked about searching the Stoll estate. Connelley had forty-five policemen to conduct a search of the immediate area around The Cottage. The area would be split into four quarters, each examined by a group consisting of one Division agent, four county patrolmen, and seven Louisville police officers. Troopers with the Kentucky State Police were ordered to assist, and two thousand members of the Kentucky National Guard were on standby. The American Legion offered the assistance of its membership, and there were also horse patrols, motorcycle cops, and other officers looking for Alice Stoll. Even mules were put to work.

Connelley provided detailed instructions on how to search without missing a hidden body, and they would search until her body was found or she was released.

$ At the Stoll estate: how to find a policeman when you need one.

Manhunt: wanted by the Division of Investigation

$

Meanwhile, the Division monitored the Robinson family's telephones, and at approximately 11:20 p.m. operators picked up a telephone call to 7-5833J, the residence of Robinson Jr's father-in-law, Nathaniel L. Althauser, at the Sterling Court Apartments in Nashville where Robinson's wife was staying. The call was from Lincoln 0211, a pay station at Hook's Drug Store on North Illinois Street in Indianapolis.

The Division believed the call was from their suspect, Robinson Jr., who identified himself as John A. Ward, later verified as one of Robinson's aliases. When Mrs. Robinson answered the phone, he announced that he was Mrs. Stoll's kidnapper and said Mrs. Stoll's wedding ring and a letter of identification would be mailed to verify she was alive. "Make sure to do things right," he added. (While the record does not explicitly say, this directive appeared to be aimed less at the agents listening in and more at his wife; he was, in effect, telling her not to screw up.)

The bizarre nature of the conversation suggested to agents that Mrs. Robinson was likely involved, at least tangentially. At one point, the operator listening in had trouble hearing part of the conversation but thought the callers were joking with each other. And it was unclear why Robinson was calling his father-in-law's house with his ransom specifications.

Interviewed later by the Division, Mrs. Robinson said her father-in-law had told her that her husband was a suspect in the kidnapping, and the telephone call confirmed this.

In Indianapolis at midnight, Indianapolis SAC Reinecke and agent Bliss Morton arrived at Hook's Drug Store knowing there was almost no chance they'd find the caller. The drugstore was closed, and even though it was after midnight, the two agents conducted a neighborhood investigation with the suspect's photograph. They canvassed the streets, contacted nearby hotels, garages, and restaurants, and shortly after 3 a.m. they broke off empty-handed and returned to the Indianapolis office to meet with agents who had arrived from the Chicago office.

The agents were assigned to roam the downtown area on Illinois Street, canvassing the many "picture theatres, burlesque shows, hotels, rooming houses, and drug stores," on the off chance Robinson might show himself. Other agents combed tourist camps in the area.

Hoover said that if Robinson showed, he was to be followed. And if pursuit became difficult and agents even marginally thought they might lose him, said Hoover, "they should pick him up and give him a good working over." Both Assistant Director Nathan and Hoover thought Mrs. Stoll was probably dead.

The G-men and the Heiress

The forty year G-Man

Bliss Morton isn't a name you quickly forget, and it sounds like he could be either an outlaw or a lawman. He was, in fact, the latter in pursuit of the former, and he spent almost half of his long life as a Special Agent with the FBI. His early background was varied:

raised in Indiana, he was a schoolteacher, a drug company clerk, a railroad stenographer, and in 1908, began working for the Immigration Department.

Fearful for his job at the outbreak of WWI, he transferred to the Bureau of Investigation. In 1917, after only eight

$ Bliss Morton's Bureau credentials.

months as an agent, he was named head of the Cleveland office. In 1923, Ohio Republican Warren G. Harding took office. Political patronage in hiring was still very much a part of the BOI.

Bliss had to let a Democrat go and hire four Republicans with dubious experience as plasterer, bartender, section gang member, and of all things a politician. One of the new hires transferred to Washington, DC, and returned to Cleveland with a letter asserting that he was taking Bliss's place. Bliss merely shrugged it off and went back to investigating cases.

He served in Cincinnati and Indianapolis, retiring in 1956 at age 70, three years beyond mandatory, which had to be signed off by the director. He would reminisce that his most significant event was meeting Hoover in 1947. "He was one of the most wonderful men in the world." He described his career modestly, never having any "blood and thunder cases," nor being in a shootout.

His finest hour may have been when he filed a complaint in Indiana federal court charging George Barrett, a car thief, with the murder of fellow G-Man, Nelson B. Klein of the Cincinnati office, who was killed in a shootout in West College Corner, Indiana, in August of 1935.

It was a tranquil life for a man in a dangerous business, which perhaps allowed him to carry on until the ripe age of 94 when he died in Indianapolis.

FOURTH DAY OF CAPTIVITY, SUNDAY, OCTOBER 14, 1934

Division Inspector Hugh Clegg took an early Sunday morning plane from New York City, where he was on assignment, and landed in Louisville just before 3 p.m. Clegg was another of the legendary men of the Division, a courtly one-time Mississippi attorney who was known as "Troutmouth" because of his habit of pursing his lips when talking. (Because he was so well-liked, the nickname was said affectionately and never in front of him.) He was one of Hoover's favorite agents, so detailed in his work that he once informed Hoover that the briefcases used by the agency's accountants could be picked with a paper clip.

Clegg had just had a conversation with Norma Abrams with the *New York News* who was coming to Louisville to cover the kidnapping. Clegg thought Abrams was smart, that is, she had "something above her eyebrows." Hoover had met her during the Lindbergh kidnapping case and he, too, was impressed (which was unusual as Hoover typically found little to admire among the reporters). While the agency wouldn't give her any special treatment, they'd treat her very courteously (which, given the often adversarial relationship between the agency and the media, was in itself a courtesy). Nathan would meet her when she arrived.

$ Inspector Hugh Clegg, in the mold of Hoover, another taskmaster.

The G-men and the Heiress

Nathan had not been in touch with the Stoll family that day but would talk to them before he talked with Hoover again. He knew Connelley had begun his searches near the Stoll residence the day before, and he thought it was a good idea because it would keep the family busy.

Inspector Clegg and SAC Rorer would handle the case at Nashville, supervising the agents there. At headquarters, Edward Tamm was coordinating other agents coming in from Birmingham, Little Rock, and Charlotte. Hoover also wanted more men from Chicago. So much coordination also caused confusion, and Reinecke's Indianapolis squad came under fire for its eagerness—after the Hook's Drugstore phone call—in wanting a quick arrest. Nathan didn't want any agents going rogue and he told Indianapolis in no uncertain terms that "this is not a pick-up job." No one was to be grabbed until the victim was released.

Because the kidnapper had made his telephone call from Indianapolis, Reinecke and Purvis met with the president of the Indiana Bell Telephone Company to iron out telephone coverage. They wanted to make sure they received prompt reporting on any calls made from Indianapolis into their specified Louisville numbers. That evening, the telephone company began monitoring calls from Indianapolis to both Louisville and Nashville.

The telephones were covered around the clock by two experienced telephone employees who would alert the Division of any suspicious conversations. Bell employees were on the lookout for names and telephone numbers of twenty-one friends and family members of Mrs. Stoll, and four relatives of Robinson Jr.

Both the Stoll and Speed families were on edge, for they had no definitive word as to whether Mrs. Stoll was still among the living. What was the kidnapper—or kidnappers—waiting on? It was a high-tension waiting game for the family.

Since the kidnapping, both the Division and the police had invested heavily in human resources, and agents were working the case in Louisville, Indianapolis, Nashville, and to a lesser extent, Cincinnati. G-Men came in from Boston, Birmingham, Chicago, Cincinnati, Detroit, Kansas City, Pittsburgh, St. Louis, and New York. In time, more than one hundred agents would be involved. The Division had implemented various investigative techniques and spent plenty of money, not including the cost of agent salaries, lodging, and meals.

Would their efforts pay off with a released victim and captured kidnappers?

Nothing good had happened so far, and the clock was ticking.

Mr. Thomas H. Robinson
1716 Ashwood Avenue
Nashville, Tenn.

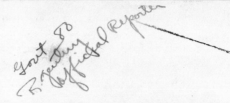

Dear Sir:

      I am the kidnaper of Alice Stoll. She is alive and well
in a place close to Louisville, and only has a small cut on her
head, which has healed.

      She is sending her wedding ring, on the side of which is
engraved her name and Berry Stoll's, to identify us. Also, she
is sending a letter in her own handwriting. You may identify her
handwriting, if necessary.

      MAYBE YOU HAVE TURNED THE MONEY OVER TO THE ONE WHO
APPROACHED YOU FOR IT.

      HOWEVER, IF YOU ARE NOT SURE THIS IS THE PROPER ONE, AND
YOU HAVE NOT ALREADY PAID THE MONEY, DO THE FOLLOWING:

      PAY THIS $50,000 over   to your daughter-in-law, who
lives in Sterling Court.

      We will give her instructions secretly. Have her walk around
her neighborhood so as thecontact with her can be made.

      <u>HAVE HER FOLLOW OUT EXACTLY THE PLANS WHICH ARE MADE KNOWN
TO HER.</u>

      SHE WILL HAVE TO MAKE A TRIP, so tell her this.

      This should be all the authority you need.

      Mrs. Stoll will never be seen alive, unless you do this,

ALSO SEE THAT YOUR DAUGHTER-IN-LAW IS NOT FOLLOWED OR WATCHED. IF SO,
well, you know what we threatened to do.

      This is all the identification that you need. So go ahead
and carry out the plan as soon as possible.

                             KIDNAPER

BE SURE AND TELL YOUR DAUGHTER-IN-LAW TO CARRY OUT HER INSTRUCTIONS
JUST AS THEY <u>WERE</u> GIVEN TO HER.

DO NOT GIVE THIS LETTER TO POLICE UNTIL YOU HEAR THAT MRS. STOLL HAS
BEEN RELEASED. ANY EFFORT TO SHADOW YOUR DAUGHTER-IN-LAW WILL MEAN
DEATH TO MRS. STOLL. YOU ARE A FRIEND OF THE STOLL'S. IF YOU WANT TO
SEE HER RETURNED ALIVE, DO NOT MAKE KNOWN THIS LETTER TO ANYONE UNTIL
SHE IS RELEASED.

The kidnapper's letter of October 13, 1934.

6 Kidnapper makes contact

"I know this is my last chance to be returned alive."

—Alice Stoll

$

FOURTH DAY OF CAPTIVITY, SUNDAY, OCTOBER 14

Robinson wanted the ransom money, but he didn't want to call the Stoll family directly. He suspected—accurately—that the phones were being monitored. No one had enough information: the Stolls thought Alice was still alive, but they weren't sure; Robinson wasn't sure about the money. And the Division operatives were having trouble keeping up with all the movement that seemed to be happening in several different cities.

Paying the ransom was never an issue because Alice's father, William Speed, made the decision the day after his daughter disappeared. That day, October 11, he'd begun gathering the $50,000, putting together a package in denominations of $5, $10, and $20 notes, which was assembled at the Fidelity & Columbia Trust Company in downtown Louisville. There, the bank president and six of his employees were preparing a list of the serial numbers before wrapping the cash in brown paper.

This, of course, was not known by Robinson, who was by now having his own case of nerves. Mrs. Stoll, in an apparent attempt to put him at ease (and to help herself get back home), suggested he call a friend of hers in Louisville, Miss Elizabeth McHenry. Robinson took her advice and made the call, saying his name was Henry Saunders—another Robinson alias. He said a stranger was forcing him, at gunpoint, to make the call. In the conversation, he mentioned a ring with sapphires and diamonds, and alligator shoes with gold buckles purchased at Saks Fifth Avenue. This was known property of Mrs. Stoll, which Robinson was using to convince the family she was alive and well.

Miss McHenry was directed to contact the Stoll family and tell them the kidnappers would mail an envelope containing a letter and Mrs. Stoll's ring for verification. They were aware that the police were watching the ransom money, making it difficult for an intermediary to deliver the money. The caller suggested to Miss McHenry that the Stoll family should correct that difficulty.

Louisville agents identified the call as coming from Riley 0808—booth eight at Indianapolis's Union Station. Indianapolis agents immediately headed to Union Station, which was only a few blocks away. They searched the station and surrounding area but came away empty-handed.

In Nashville, where SAC Rorer and his agents watched the residences of both Robinson's father and his father-in-law, a special delivery envelope arrived at the father's house. It contained two letters, one identified as in the handwriting of Mrs. Stoll, saying she was being treated well, although she had a small cut on her head. Her wedding ring was enclosed, verified by its inscription. The second letter was typewritten and addressed to Robinson Sr., telling him to turn over the $50,000 ransom money to his daughter-in-law. The daughter-in-law would receive further instructions.

$

FIFTH DAY OF CAPTIVITY, MONDAY, OCTOBER 15

The Division was still carrying the kidnapping case as "unsub/unknown suspect." That was for the files; the agents had a primary suspect who to the agents was more than a suspect—Thomas Henry Robinson Jr. The lab's handwriting examiner Samuel Pickering, one of the first members of the agency's technical laboratory, matched the writing on the ransom note with a sample from an application Robinson had filled out while working for the Stoll Oil Company. They were identical. Fingerprints on the note also matched Robinson's. Agents now had no doubt as to the identity of Alice Stoll's kidnapper.

From the beginning, SAC Purvis had been in Indianapolis with three of his best men. Three days later, he asked Hoover for additional men. Hoover agreed, thus the celebrated Dillinger Squad was on the case. So Purvis, who had lost the first round with Hoover in his original request for more men (it had been denied), had now won his second skirmish with Hoover. Purvis, however, needed to remember that it was only a skirmish, and a small one at that. There was only one person who was right all the time

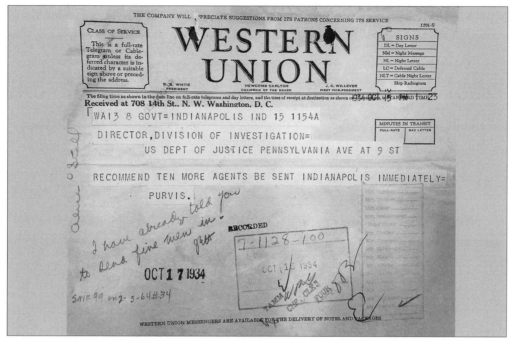

THE COMPANY WILL 'PRECIATE SUGGESTIONS FROM ITS PATRONS CONCERNING ITS SERVICE

1201-S

WESTERN UNION

CLASS OF SERVICE

This is a full-rate Telegram or Cablegram unless its deferred character is indicated by a suitable sign above or preceding the address.

NEWCOMB CARLTON
CHAIRMAN OF THE BOARD

R. B. WHITE
PRESIDENT

J. C. WILLEVER
FIRST VICE-PRESIDENT

SIGNS

DL = Day Letter
NM = Night Message
NL = Night Letter
LC = Deferred Cable
NLT = Cable Night Letter
Ship Radiogram

The filing time as shown in the date line on full-rate telegrams and day letters, and the time of receipt at destination as shown on all messages, is STANDARD TIME.

Received at 708 14th St., N. W. Washington. D. C. 1934 OCT 15 AM 5 23

WA13 8 GOVT=INDIANAPOLIS IND 15 1154A

DIRECTOR,DIVISION OF INVESTIGATION=

US DEPT OF JUSTICE PENNSYLVANIA AVE AT 9 ST

RECOMMEND TEN MORE AGENTS BE SENT INDIANAPOLIS IMMEDIATELY=

PURVIS.

MINUTES IN TRANSIT
FULL-RATE   DAY LETTER

I have already told you to send five men in! gkh

OCT 17 1934

RECORDED
7-1128-100
OCT 16 1934

SNIF 99 vn2-3-64#34

WESTERN UNION MESSENGERS ARE AVAILABLE FOR THE DELIVERY OF NOTES AND PACKAGES

💲 Agent Purvis inveigles the testy boss man, October, 1934.

and that was the Director. For Purvis, though, this simple dictum wasn't as easy as it sounded and it would ultimately lead to his downfall.

The kidnapper telephoned Elizabeth McHenry at 11:34 p.m.—number Magnolia 3310—saying he was willing to extend additional time for delivery of the money. Did Miss McHenry hear a note of desperation in his voice? He said he wouldn't release the victim until twenty-four hours had passed after the money arrived.

McHenry received a follow-up letter from the kidnapper, mailed special delivery from Indianapolis at 4 p.m. on October 14. It was in Mrs. Stoll's handwriting and addressed McHenry as "Dear Scat," a term they used as close friends so that McHenry would know it was from her.

The letter read as follows:

> Sunday
> October 14
>
> Dear Scat,
> The phone call to you was okay I asked the kidnapper to go somewhere and call you. He said he drove to Indianapolis to do so. He and I believe that Berry delivered the money to Mr. T. H. Robinson, the intermediary, in good

Kidnapper makes contact

faith. However, the kidnapper knows that the police are watching the intermediary. The kidnapper now wants the intermediary to deliver the money to Mrs. Frances Robinson, his daughter-in-law. She will, or already has, received instructions. She is the only person from whom and the only way by which the kidnapper will agree to accept the money. This is final. Don't attempt to try and call the person who called you or trace it in any way. The person who called is a friend of the kidnapper, who will receive the money. Therefore, instruct all my family to be sure that this daughter-in-law is not followed or interfered with in any way. If these instructions are followed, I will be released unharmed within twenty-four hours. Get my family to use all their influence to withdraw the law from this case until I am returned. This is imperative.

Love from A.

The Division verified with family members that it was Mrs. Stoll's handwriting, although they believed that the letter was dictated to Mrs. Stoll by the kidnapper. The Division laboratory dusted the notes for prints and found Robinson's fingerprints on the letter.

The second letter was mailed from Indianapolis three hours later and addressed to Mr. Berry Stoll, in care of Mr. W. S. Speed of 2828 Lexington Road, Louisville.

It read as follows:

Sunday
October 14

Dear Berry,

I only had a small cut on my head, and it has healed. I am otherwise all right and being treated nicely. The kidnapper found out last night that the intermediary, Mr. T. H. Robinson, and his daughter-in-law, were being watched and that he couldn't give the money to his daughter-in-law because of the police. Both the kidnapper and I believe that you meant to deliver the money in good faith, but that you are being double-crossed by the police. My life depends on his daughter-in-law not being shadowed so she can deliver the money. The kidnapper will not accept any other persons other than this daughter-in-law to deliver the money. Will you, for my sake, see that this girl is not interfered with or followed to our destination? I sent a letter with my wedding ring to Mr. T. H. Robinson because the law is double-crossing us the kidnappers refuse to release me until twenty-four hours after they receive the money from the girl. I know this is my last chance to be returned alive. If the money is delivered all right, I will be released unharmed.

Much love,

Alice

In reading the letters, Nathan, Hoover's assistant director, noticed the second letter mentioned both "kidnapper" and "kidnappers." Hoover thought Mrs. Stoll wrote them under duress, and because there were two letters, the kidnapper might be getting nervous about when—and if—he was getting his payoff. Later, the investigation determined Robinson *did* dictate the notes to Mrs. Stoll. She would say more than once that she thought her kidnapper had trouble planning things, so she had provided her own input.

Hoover had unrealistic expectations of what his men could accomplish and vented his displeasure in a telephone conversation with Indianapolis SAC Reinecke. The Director thought the telephone calls and letters mailed from Indianapolis's main post office should have been covered by surveillance. If the agents had witnessed the mailing of the second letter, he said, they would have captured the kidnapper. In theory, Hoover was right, but examining every piece of mail in the massive flow that went through the Indianapolis post office every day was quite another matter. Agent Herman Hollis was working the post office even on a Sunday, but in the deluge of mail he simply missed it. (The Division agents didn't initially advise postal clerks what they were doing or why, and they didn't request help; that would soon be corrected.)

Reinecke felt the agents were doing everything humanly possible. Hoover stressed that he didn't want any more letters or telephone calls coming from Indianapolis without being traced. In other words, he wanted an *inhuman* response. Reinecke said he needed between three and five more agents, and Hoover agreed, but he also demanded more of the current agents.

$ Thomas Robinson Sr., night-time athlete.

THE SEEDY SIDE OF LIFE

In Nashville, SAC Rorer and his agents did a workup on Robinson's parents. The year before the kidnapping, Robinson Sr. had been working for the Nashville Bridge Company, and he was known to frequent prostitutes where he used the aliases of T. C. Robertson or J. H. Johnson. Madam Bess Hosse told the Nashville police that Robinson Sr., using the name "Arnold," was a regular for years at a number of the cathouses, where he usually arrived drunk. (The madam identified him as Robinson Sr. after seeing a picture about the kidnapping in the newspaper.)

Prostitutes described him as tall and handsome but "a natural born freak," which was amplified by a description of one of them tattooing her initials onto his penis with a needle. They considered him a hall-of-fame degenerate, as he also liked having Lysol poured on his privates. After exhausting all the girls at one location, he might ask then for "a well-built man."

Nashville police arrested Robinson Sr. at least twice in 1929, charging him with disorderly conduct and loitering about a disorderly house. The first arrest took place at Carrie Richmond's bawdy house, in which officers took into custody "J. H. Johnson," five prostitutes, and a second "client." The girls knew that Johnson was Robinson Sr., employed with the Nashville Bridge Company, and police recognized him as well. (His reputation had obviously preceded him.) The second arrest came at Madam Billy Perry's house where detectives found a nude man using the last name of "Robertson" being beaten by two prostitutes with a whip.

Prostitutes, in police interviews, described Robinson Sr.'s masochistic activities as follows: beaten with stick, burned with a hot stove poker, and hit by board with protruding nail while performing a sex act. Officers described him as having an abnormally large penis, and one of the prostitutes who had performed for him over a decade or more said regular intercourse was impossible as his penis was too big.

(It seemed that Robinson Sr. was an *athlete*; it was not difficult to see that when he entered one of the local *maisons de tolérance*, a shiver ran through what may be called "the serving staff." Preceeded by his, shall we say, enlarged reputation, even the most experienced of them might wonder what unsanctified pleasures he might be after *this* time.)

During the agents' investigation, SAC Rorer contacted Western Union Telegraph and the Postal Telegraph Company in Nashville, asking them to watch for wires sent or received at both the home and business addresses of the Robinson family, their associates, and attorneys—nine individuals and fifteen locations.

Shadowing

Most of what we know about following a criminal suspect comes from the popular cultural forms, movies and television, in which  clichés abound. A bored guy slouches in a car parked forty yards from the suspect's house but is never spotted. Or he tails a subject at night, headlights blazing down a deserted country road, and *he* is not spotted. The truth is, though, that much of surveillance *is* a cliché because often the cliché is what works.

There are, of course, the modern techniques of advanced electronic surveillance, but, again, the most productive work is often boring but time-tested work in which the agent must fit unnoticed into the environment. Much of it is simply common sense, equal parts patience, cunning, and boredom. Or as one agent advises: "Fit in. Don't look. Drive a nondescript car." (The

$ The evolving technique of snoopery.

latter quality has inspired a movie trope in which the boring car is *so* boring that it stands out, thus outing itself.)

There's also the matter of what can be euphemistically called "personal business"—the bathroom break, for agents can't be seen getting in and out of parked cars. The answer: "Bring a pee bottle" (or creativity, as one agent was reported to have used a box of Kleenex, which prompted one on the next shift to ask, "What in God's name is *this*?").

GPS tracking has changed the game totally. *The Yale Law Journal*, for instance, figured costs of the standard surveillance procedure at $275 an hour and GPS tracking as little as thirty-six cents. And last year the San Pablo, California, police began using a GPS tagging system on its cars to avoid high-speed chases. The technology uses an air cannon which shoots a glue-capped GPS capsule "about the size of a mini-Coke can" to mark the car.

The time-tested methods thus fall to the forces of modernity, although in the movies, at least, the car surveillance—and subsequent chase—will remain, a theme as eternal as the western and its chase-by-horse.

By now, William Speed's bank had prepared the ransom package and—ostensibly—copied the serial numbers. Overseen by bank president Menefee Wirgman on October 12, it ended up in the safe on the Number 3 Louisville & Nashville train, addressed to Thomas Robinson Sr. Two agents went along, safeguarding the package to Nashville's Railway Express Office. From there, it went to the office of attorney Ferris Bailey who transferred the money to Robinson Sr. (Bailey was Berry Stoll's cousin, and C. C. Stoll, Berry's father, had paid the $125 in expenses to see that the seven-pound box of cash was delivered to Bailey. It was old C. C., fearful that Robinson Jr. might kill his daughter-in-law, who'd wanted Robinson Sr. to be the intermediary.)

Robinson put the money in a suitcase and went immediately to his own attorney, J. G. Lackey, less than a block away in the Stahlman Building. Lackey's nephew, Carver, who'd been a Vanderbilt friend of Robinson Jr., stowed the suitcase in the rumble seat of his sports coupe, and headed to his uncle's home on Elmwood Avenue. There, Mrs. Robinson Jr. was waiting, per instructions sent to Elizabeth McHenry, which specified that she, Mrs. Robinson, was to make the ransom delivery.

Carver drove her fifty miles north to Guthrie, Kentucky, a tiny place just across the state line, where she would catch a train north to Indianapolis. It worked splendidly for the Robinsons because it was so small that a trailing agent may as well have had his photograph on the Goodyear blimp. The agents seemed to be having difficulties coordinating, even before Guthrie. Agent Bliss Morton was working undercover, unshaven and looking homeless, and his job was to shadow Mrs. Robinson but he didn't know what she looked like. The agents seemed to be uncertain as to exactly where Carver was taking her, and they didn't make it to Guthrie before the train left.

Pop Nathan, in an attempt to get ahead of the game, sent agents to Evansville where they were to board and watch Mrs. Robinson. She was in Car 44 for a trip that usually took two-and-a-half hours. All she carried with her was a borrowed nightdress from her mother-in-law and the suitcase. She asked the porter to make the bed, then went to sit in the lady's room. Even though she hadn't opened the package, she knew it was ransom money and she was frightened. The vast responsibility of all that money weighed on her. Not wanting it out of her sight, she brought it along with her.

She went to the dining car (the porter carried her suitcase, probably regarding her as just one more peculiar white woman), but she had no appetite. She returned to her compartment where she lay on top of her bunk, unable to sleep.

Meanwhile, the Division had the serial numbers from the ransom bills sent to all the Division offices, ready for distribution to the banks. Some time later, however, agents

The G-men and the Heiress

found out an error had been made in copying the serial numbers, which made tracking the bills impossible. It would be the most significant reason Robinson Jr. was able to elude capture for so long, for the thousands of dollars he would spend at hotels, race-tracks, and nightclubs went undetected. It was, literally, free money, although he would pay in other ways.

$

SIXTH DAY OF CAPTIVITY, TUESDAY, OCTOBER 16

Some asked why the Division didn't have an agent accompany Mrs. Robinson. After all, she was frightened about carrying so much money. The most likely plausible answer is that the Division could say it was not its decision to pay the ransom, nor did it want to jeopardize the delivery and preclude Mrs. Stoll's release. The Division would win no matter the outcome, or at least until the press learned agents surveilling Mrs. Robinson had lost her, calling the agents "Keystone Kops." (They were the comically inept police-men of the silent film comedies made by Mack Sennett for the Keystone Film Company.)

At midnight, Mrs. Robinson got off the train at Terre Haute. Already nervous about carrying so much money, she was not helped by spending midnight in a near-deserted train station. She told a cabbie some men were following her and she wanted out of the area. He suggested taking her to Clinton, Indiana—fifteen miles away—where she could get a bus into Indianpolis. But when they got to Clinton, she changed her mind again and told him to just drive her to Indianapolis, another ninety miles.

Actually, Mrs. Robinson wasn't being unnaturally paranoid, for she *was* being shadowed in Terre Haute, and she may have caught a glimpse of the uber-cautious agents. They reported that she seemed "hysterical," and while they could have stepped in and escorted her the rest of way, they were suffering their own form of paranoia. The agents were stuck in the middle; if they helped her, they would have been open to criticism by Hoover who was, as usual, difficult to please. If they maintained surveil-lance and lost her—and the cash—they would have been pilloried not only by Hoover but by *everyone*.

Once in Indianapolis, Mrs. Robinson had the cabbie drop her at a Shell Station on the outskirts of the city. From there, she took two more cabs, eventually getting out at Central and 28th streets. After taking a streetcar and yet another cab, she reached the Lincoln Hotel around 7 a.m. Such circuitous movement easily led to the conclusion that Mrs. Robinson was either frightened out of her wits or had professional training in the avoidance of surveillance (which was known in the trade as "dry cleaning").

Kidnapper makes contact

Even before Mrs. Robinson's peripatetic journey, Alice Stoll had asked Robinson what would happen if the person delivering the cash was robbed. Robinson said his wife was terrific, knew how to be elusive and, if suspected of being followed, would change cabs four or five times.

Hoover wanted to know how she got away from the Division agents in Terre Haute. Reinecke had talked with SAC Purvis, who was leading the surveillance team, who said the town was small, and at that time of night it was challenging to watch anyone without being seen, so they had just called it off and headed back to Indianapolis.

When agents located Mrs. Robinson's hotel, the bellboy who had taken her to her room said she was nervous and asked if it was possible to leave the hotel through the freight elevator, without being observed. The bellhop told her that was against hotel policy. The hotel, however, was filled with women attending the Pocahontas Lodge Convention, most of them dark-haired, and Mrs. Robinson was able to lose herself in the assemblage.

Again, agents missed her. And they'd forgotten to give the desk clerk Mrs. Robinson's description. Reinecke sent three cars up North Meridian to try and locate her.

$ Home away from home: Robinson's Indianapolis back door.

The G-men and the Heiress

Meanwhile, she stopped and had a breakfast—chili, toast, and coffee—then hailed a taxi that let her out a few blocks from the apartment complex where her husband had stashed Alice Stoll.

$

ALICE DOESN'T LIVE HERE ANYMORE

It was 8:30 a.m. when she knocked on the apartment door. Robinson opened the door and greeted his wife. Alice Stoll heard him call his wife "honey." Mrs. Robinson went immediately to the bedroom and tossed the brown paper-wrapped bundle she was carrying on the bed (it contained the money and her nightgown). She said the police were following her and he should leave immediately. Alice, wearing a dress of Mrs. Robinson's, was lying on the bed, tied. When Mrs. Robinson walked over to her, Mrs. Stoll said, "Turn me loose, please, turn me loose," and she began to cry.

The couple went into the living room to talk and Robinson, still in his bathrobe, dressed while urging his wife to leave with him. The original plan, after all, had been for the two of them to depart, leaving Mrs. Stoll in the apartment and a letter for the janitor who could release her and receive any reward.

Mrs. Robinson said she couldn't go, that she'd had enough of the whole sordid affair. Mrs. Stoll pleaded with him to let Mrs. Robinson stay with her, and as his wife seemed determined to stay behind, he finally agreed. But he insisted Mrs. Stoll be held for twenty-four hours. He said he would kill her if she left before the time was up.

He placed Mrs. Stoll on a chair in the living room closet, tied her hands and feet to it, then closed and locked the door. Robinson took "clean" money from his wife's pocketbook and threw $500 of the ransom money at her. He said the $500 was to get Mrs. Stoll home. He asked his wife to get his car for him, but she refused. He placed the ransom, tightly wrapped in brown paper, in a grip, kissed his wife goodbye, and said he would probably never see her again.

As for Mrs. Stoll, she was glad Mrs. Robinson had happened along, for she couldn't stand confinement another day. Mrs. Robinson, obviously, wouldn't leave Mrs. Stoll in the closet. She made Mrs. Stoll a breakfast of boiled eggs, toast, and coffee, and afterward started straightening things in the littered apartment. She told Mrs. Stoll she was free to leave, but Mrs. Stoll appeared to be glad for her company.

At 3 p.m., the two of them walked two blocks to a drugstore where they hailed a taxi which took them to North Capital Street, the residence of Reverend Eugene Arnold Clegg and his wife, who was a relative of the Stoll's. Mrs. Stoll had never met them but

Kidnapper makes contact

71

she knew the wife was related to her husband, and she knew their address from reading about them in the newspaper.

From the Clegg residence, Mrs. Stoll telephoned her friend Elizabeth McHenry in Louisville and asked her to call her husband and tell him she would return home that evening. (No one thought of asking why she, herself, didn't call her husband.) The telephone company was monitoring the telephones and this information was relayed to the Division office in Indianapolis and thus to Louisville agents. Pop Nathan himself, and SAC Connelley, with other agents, staked out Lime Kiln Lane in both directions in the off chance the kidnapper was bringing her home, which seemed highly unlikely.

Tipped off by the phone call, Purvis and Reneicke and three of their agents went to the Clegg residence where they observed Mrs. Stoll and the Cleggs leaving. They didn't approach, because they didn't know if Alice Stoll was still with her kidnapper. Or kidnappers. They feared if they approached there might be shooting and, above all, they

$ At the Harrods Creek Post Office (and grocery store), overrun by the swarming press.

The G-men and the Heiress

didn't want Mrs. Stoll harmed. The Reverend Clegg drove his new Studebaker sedan, and the women sat in the back.

The evening edition of *The Herald-Post* would print a story which revealed that neither its reporters nor Berry Stoll had any idea Mrs. Stoll was about to be free later in the day. At noon, Berry Stoll met with the press where he appeared cheerful, waiting on the telephone call saying his wife had been released, even though the family had received no information that she was still among the living. Stoll appeared refreshed, not haggard, which had been previously reported, and he was well-groomed, wearing a double-breasted suit.

For six days, gawkers had been driving by the entrance to the Lime Kiln Lane residence. The area was not only teeming with agents and police, but newspaper staffers as well. The nearby Harrods Creek Post Office and grocery store was inundated with visitors and reporters fighting over the pay telephone, and snacks or drinks.

But now Mrs. Stoll was on her way home and the Division could say, at a minimum, that their lack of interference with the money exchange hadn't hurt. That was the positive side of things. On the negative side, Hoover was livid because he had declared the ransom money must not get into the hands of the kidnapper. Mrs. Robinson had seemingly outmaneuvered his agents, and bank employees had somehow contaminated the numbers on the ransom money.

Hoover and his agents needed a face-lift, and so far, fortune had been on the side of the kidnapper. That wouldn't last forever, but for a time, it seemed it might. And what happened next was as improbable as any case the Division would ever have.

Kidnapper makes contact

73

THE WEATHER:
Cloudy, probably rain tonight and Friday. Slightly cooler tonight.

SPRINGFIELD DAILY NEWS

HOME EDITION

NRA CODE

PRICE TWO CENTS

SPRINGFIELD, OHIO, THURSDAY, OCTOBER 18, 1934.

Associated Press, United Press and International News Leased Wire Service.

VOL. LXXXI, No. 196.   18 PAGES

KIDNAPER'S AUTOMOBILE FOUND IN SPRINGFIELD

Postponement Of B-L Trial Is Granted

DEFENSE PLEA OF ILL HEALTH IS SUSTAINED

Motion Is Heard By Outside Judge Temporarily Assigned To City

CASE TO GO OVER FOR AT LEAST TWO MONTHS

Decision Is Given After Testimony Of Physicians

New trial in the case of Charles E. Betliowe and F. A. Schaeffer, Associated Building and Loan Association officers, charged with embezzlement of Association funds, which was to have been held beginning the week of Oct. 29, has been postponed at least two months due to the illness of the defendant, Betliowe.

A motion for continuance of the case on the ground of ill health was sustained Thursday in the Clark County Common Pleas Court by Judge Harley M. Whitbarth, of Hocking County, who had been assigned to the local court to hear the local motion. The hear...

SEES BANKRUPTCY FOR AIR CONCERNS

FUGITIVE AND PLACE WHERE MACHINE WAS FOUND

THOMAS H. ROBINSON, JR.

MONEY PAID WOMAN FOR ROOM IDENTIFIED AS PART OF RANSOM

Police and Federal Agents Pick Up Trail of Thomas H. Robinson, Jr., Here

An automobile definitely identified as one used by Thomas H. Robinson, Jr., fugitive kidnaper of Mrs. Alice Speed Stoll, of Louisville, Ky., was found in a garage on W. Main st. Thursday by Springfield police.

Identification of the car was made through the license-plates and the motor number. The driver of the machine, who answered to the description of the kidnaper, was in Springfield Tuesday afternoon, it was learned.

In addition to these facts, police located a $5 bill which was identified as part of the ransom paid to Mrs. Stoll's abductor by her millionaire husband, Berry V. Stoll.

The man believed to be Robinson drove into Springfield from the east Tuesday shortly after 1 p. m., police were told.

License Issued to Robinson

(INDIANAPOLIS, Oct. 18. UP) Department of Justice officials said today there is no doubt but that the automobile found at Springfield O. today was that of Thomas H. Robinson, Jr., sought as the kidnaper of Mrs. Alice Speed Stoll, of Louisville.

At the department offices here it was said the lead was being checked "post haste."

A check at the State Automobile License Bureau here...

The headlines scream—Springfield Daily News, October 18, 1934.

Stockholm Syndrome, anyone?

"You must think me a criminal."

—Thomas Robinson to Alice Stoll

Director Hoover's best men were escorting Alice Stoll home, but it was no triumphal procession. The man in charge, actually, seemed to be an obscure minister who'd been brought into events only because the victim—who had never met him—saw his name in the newspapers and remembered his wife was somehow related to her husband's family.

The Reverend Clegg was driving, sitting up front like a chauffeur while his charges—Alice, Frances Robinson, and the reverend's wife—sat primly in the back. Agents Purvis and Reinecke headed south to intercept, while Nathan sent agents Francis Hurley and Horace Maynor north from Louisville. After driving about forty miles, Hurley turned around and set up on the side of Highway 31, heading south. Around 7 p.m., they picked up the Clegg vehicle, unaware that Clegg was being trailed by Purvis and his men. Purvis, for his part, seemed unaware of Hurley, and he pulled his car around Hurley's and forced Clegg off the road.

Maynor, one of the agents from Louisville, his gun drawn, demanded Clegg's weapon, and pulled him from the car. The reverend, armed only with righteous indignation, decided his best course of action was to turn the other cheek. There was, of course, no weapon in the car.

Agents separated Frances Robinson and Alice Stoll, placing them in different cars; Mrs. Stoll was upset at the separation. Purvis had them reunited and talked with them alone where Alice seemed sympathetic to Frances Robinson, intimating Frances had

$ The Indianapolis garage of Robinson's hideaway.

saved her life. Alice seemed perturbed about the authorities whose actions, she thought, had kept her from being released sooner. She indicated that Frances did more for her release than anyone, eluding the agents to deliver the money and, as she put it, "getting through the lines." Alice felt she owed her life to Mrs. Robinson.

Purvis tried to explain to Mrs. Stoll that, at that time, no one had been following Mrs. Robinson. The G-Men and authorities had backed off, they said (in truth, their surveillance had lost her). That fact wouldn't be lost on media critics; The *Memphis Commercial Appeal*, for instance, said in an October 23 editorial that it found "nothing particularly creditable" in the Division's case.

"Somebody bungled and the kidnapper got away," the editorial read. "And to make it worse they did not even know he had escaped until they found out that the victim was well started on her way to home and safety....When capture is made, however, pursuing

The G-men and the Heiress

forces should avoid any show of self-congratulation. They lost the right to do that somewhere between Nashville and Indianapolis."

Purvis tried to gain information from Mrs. Stoll, but she did not want to talk any more. She would not even answer basic questions like where she had been taken and held, the number of kidnappers, and the location of the chief kidnapper. She could not describe the kidnapping vehicle. She did say that she could have escaped several times but felt it was too dangerous because the kidnapper had threatened to kill her.

Mrs. Stoll may have been suffering from an alliance with her captors—which in 1973 was named the Stockholm Syndrome by a Swedish criminologist and intimated that hostages sometimes had sympathy for their abductors—or perhaps it was as she said: she was simply exhausted from her ordeal.

Purvis drove her home to Louisville where Berry Stoll came out of the house and met his wife on the lawn. They spoke a few words, then went inside. After a few minutes, Berry came out and thanked the agents.

Agent Earl Wynn, who'd been the first agent on the case, was one of those who remained at the residence for security, but others remained, too, at least for a time. It was a precaution because Robinson was still at large, and agents were uncertain what an erratic personality such as Robinson's might do.

Berry talked to his wife about what had happened to her in Indianapolis, and she said other than being hit twice before she'd been taken from The Cottage and having her mouth taped, she'd been otherwise treated considerately, and she denied being a victim of sexual assault. Berry was highly agitated and came downstairs to tell SAC Connelley that his wife had been beaten and treated "in a brutish manner."

Mrs. Stoll was more forthcoming the next day, and when interviewed by Connelley and Nathan, she related the kidnapping. When she was placed in the back of the kidnapper's automobile, she had pretended to be unconscious and kept repeating the Indiana license plate number—504-519—over and over so she would not forget it. (Unfortunately, when she was later shown the kidnapper's vehicle, she was unable to identify it.)

$

ALICE IN BLUNDERLAND

At their destination, he parked in a row of garages and said, "We are now in Indianapolis." Mrs. Stoll thought she heard whispering and, upon reflection, figured it might have been Mrs. Robinson, but she wasn't sure. Robinson said he had to check to see if

Stockholm Syndrome, anyone?

any of his friends were in the apartment. Then he locked her in the vehicle and told her if she made any attempt to scream or attract attention, he'd kill her.

When he returned, he said his friends were still in the apartment, and they must wait. He drove her to a secluded part of town, removing the tape from her mouth and taking the restraints off her ankles, then he placed her upright in the front seat. He untied her wrists as well. While driving, they talked and debated the material value of capitalism and communism, religion, and higher math. She said he appeared knowledgeable on these subjects, as well as others. She still found him "maniacal." Around 11 p.m., they went back to the garage, which was in an alley at the rear of the North Meridian Street apartment Robinson was using as a hideout. It was unit number two, located on the first floor of the complex. There was no explanation for Robinson's curious behavior.

They walked down an alley and entered the apartment kitchen through the back entrance; the front door access was through a courtyard. Once inside, Robinson tied a belt from his bathrobe around her hands, and "he got cold towels and placed them upon my head and bathed the wound and got me something to eat."

She asked if he would put mercurochrome on her wounds, which he did. She found the place dirty, used dishes everywhere, although the refrigerator and cupboards were stocked with eggs, potatoes, oranges, coffee, and bread.

The apartment was what one might expect: kitchen, bathroom, living room, and one bedroom with twin beds. There was a grocery in the basement of the apartment building, and Robinson bought food there, and Patrick Henry beer, which upon occasion they drank together. (Robinson and his father shared the middle name of Henry. They were supposedly descendants of Patrick Henry, the founding father who shouted: "Give me liberty, or give me death!" Robinson considered himself the reincarnation of Patrick Henry and drank his namesake beer, found in Illinois and Indiana. Mrs. Stoll was happy to have at least one beer a day, perhaps finding some irony in the quaffing of an ale named after the man whose influence helped create the Bill of Rights which, among other things, guaranteed personal freedoms, although, apparently, not hers.)

She spent much of the time either tied to the bed, or—when he left the apartment—locked in the living room closet, sitting on a chair, hands and feet tied with adhesive tape over her mouth. Robinson left every day to make telephone calls to his father or wife, mail letters, and buy food and beer. He would say later there were times, when he was gone for just a few minutes, that he let her have the run of the apartment, but that didn't seem to be true.

The G-men and the Heiress

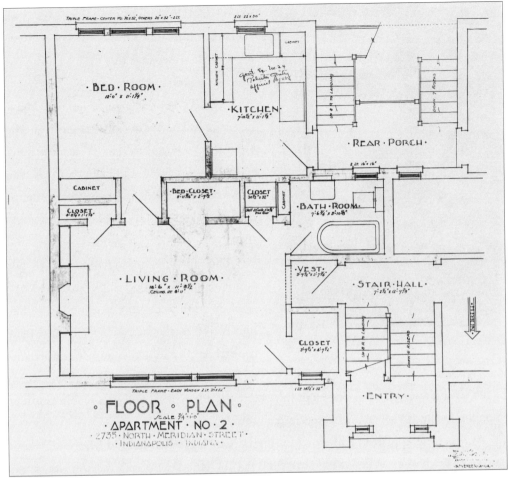

·FLOOR·PLAN·
·APARTMENT·NO·2·
·2735·NORTH·MERIDIAN·STREET·
·INDIANAPOLIS·INDIANA·

$ A diagram of Robinson's hideout apartment.

Their time was filled by reading, listening to the radio, and Robinson expostulating another of his crazy theories. He told her how three men were involved with her kidnapping; two of his cohorts in Louisville would bring the money and another in Indianapolis would signal when it arrived. She thought it was a concocted story but pretended otherwise.

On the second day of her kidnapping, he came back from making a telephone call and said everyone now knew his identity. He said he was going to release her, without receiving the money. Then he changed his mind. He was apologetic, started crying, and said he was sorry he had taken her. During her time with him, Mrs. Stoll tried to keep him talking when he became quiet or inactive because his sullenness worried her.

The first three days in the apartment, he read the newspapers, which seemed to make him anxious, then he paced up and down, concerned about whether the money would come or not. He alternated from anger to excitement when he read something

Stockholm Syndrome, anyone?

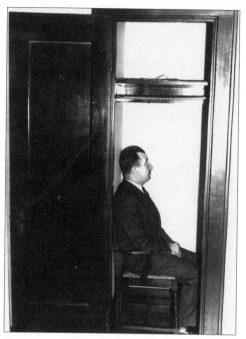

$ The apartment closet: an exercise in claustrophobia.

he regarded as false information. Mrs. Stoll reassured him that erroneous reports were a good thing because this indicated the authorities weren't close.

"Oh, if you only knew, if you only knew, if you only knew the circumstances of why I did this," he said to her. "You must think me a criminal." He said his father and wife knew nothing about the kidnapping, that if they knew he was responsible, it would break them.

The sleeping arrangements were not conducive to a good night's rest. They slept on twin beds, in the same room, her hands tied to the boxsprings. He strung a rope under her mattress over to his bed, attached to his wrist, so any significant move by her would awaken him. She slept fully clothed, under her overcoat. Robinson slept in pajamas, but he never undressed in front of her.

At times, he appeared frustrated, or angry, which is when he told Mrs. Stoll about getting rid of her, as well as the entire Stoll family. He said the only person who knew the location of the Indianapolis apartment was his wife. "Suppose your wife wouldn't go through with this?" Mrs. Stoll asked. He said then his father would bring the money. It was obvious that Robinson was unstable. In one moment of frustration, he even suggested to Mrs. Stoll that perhaps he should just stop everything and go to a hotel. Maybe he could get treatment for his mental health. It appeared to Mrs. Stoll that Robinson was creating an alternate reality for himself.

Most of their meals consisted of shredded wheat cereal and eggs. At various times, she cooked, did the dishes, and made the beds. She took it upon herself to try and motivate Robinson to make the contacts to arrange her release, instead of sleeping until noon. At times she had to guide him or think for him as he dictated the ransom letters she wrote out, making suggestions and adding information. He talked about escaping with the money to some place where he would not need a passport, and Mrs. Stoll suggested Cuba and Bermuda. Ironically, she had inadvertently segued into the domesticity of a kind she'd never known in her otherwise privileged life.

The G-men and the Heiress

ROBINSON FAMILY IN THE HOT SEAT

Upon Mrs. Stoll's release, the Division interrogated those closest to Robinson Jr. Hoover had a telephone conversation with Nathan and asked him about who was to be taken into custody. "I intend to place the whole crowd in jail and question them vigorously," Nathan said. Good as his word, he detained Robinson Jr.'s parents, Nathaniel and Martha Althauser (Frances Robinson's parents), Mr. and Mrs. Ernest M. Warner (Robinson Jr.'s aunt and her husband), Mrs. Martha Sandmann (Frances Robinson's sister), Mr. Joseph Carlton Loser (a Davidson County attorney), as well as J. G. Lackey and his nephew, Carver Lackey, both attorneys.

Agents grabbed Robinson Sr. and took him to a hotel to have him tell his side of the story. Mrs. Robinson Sr. had a broken hip and was confined to her home. Questioning her provided nothing of value. Agents also interviewed, at the Divison's temporary office at the post office, the Althausers, the Warners, and Martha Sandmann. They were released a short time later. Agents were posted with each of those families, to monitor telephones and watch for Robinson Jr., no matter how unlikely it was for him to turn up in Louisville. Agents also brought in the three attorneys for what was called "a friendly

chat." Being as they were only tangentially involved (and because they were attorneys), they weren't in custody long.

The G-Men didn't have to round up Mrs. Robinson Jr.; she was in room 336 of the Kentucky Baptist Hospital. She told SAC Reinecke that apartment number 2 at 2735 North Meridian Street in Indianapolis was part of a complex in an exclusive neighborhood a few blocks from the governor's mansion. Robinson had rented the unit under the name Thomas W. Kennedy, telling the landlord he was the area representative for the United Mix Asphalt Company of Louisville. They had rented the apartment three weeks earlier, but on October 1, Mrs. Robinson was needed in Nashville to care for a sick relative and left for home.

$ Thomas Robinson Sr., the tree from which the apple fell.

Stockholm Syndrome, anyone?

Indianapolis agents went to the apartment and found the lights on but no one was home. It smelled of cigarette smoke, stale beer, and women's perfume. They found the gray suit Robinson was wearing in his 1932 photograph (and used in the Division Identification Order). Agents also found a Corona portable typewriter and the letter Robinson had left for the janitor. The Division lab verified the ransom letter came from the Corona, and the janitor's note contained latent impressions belonging to Frances Robinson.

Frances Robinson gave the Division plenty of information during questioning, even though she was nervous, worried, and cried intermittently. She denied having any prior knowledge of the kidnapping or any involvement, and said she only found out about it from the newspapers. The doctors and nurses came in her room at various times and told agents she was in a state of hysterics and needed to rest.

Mrs. Robinson explained to agents that as soon as she reached the Indianapolis apartment, Robinson blurted out, "Why did I do it?" When she tossed the money on the bed, he didn't even look at it. He hurriedly dressed, kissed her, and left. She told SAC Reinecke that she was afraid of him because he had once gone into a rage and shot her in the thigh—and she had the scar to prove it. She had no idea where he was going, but he had talked about buying a ranch in Nevada or Canada.

The most important question the agents asked her was why, once she knew her husband was involved and his location, did she not tell someone? Mrs. Robinson said that the process was so far along and there was so much notoriety that she didn't know what to do. She was also afraid that her husband might possibly kill Mrs. Stoll. In her mind, doing nothing was her best option.

$

THE OLD MAN TELLS A TALE

In Nashville, SAC Rorer interviewed Robinson Sr. for the second time. He said he'd learned of his son's possible involvement on Thursday, October 11, when he received a telephone call from Attorney J. G. Lackey of Nashville, and learned that his son, Thomas, was the prime suspect in Mrs. Stoll's kidnapping. The operation of the kidnapper, pretending to be a telephone repairman, seemed eerily similar to Robinson Jr.'s 1929 pretense of posing as a deputy and entering the homes of two Nashville women.

On Saturday morning, October 13, Robinson Sr. received a letter from the kidnapper, who instructed him to accept the ransom and await additional instructions. The

The G-men and the Heiress

second notification directed him to give the money to his daughter-in-law, and she would receive instructions on how to deliver it.

By this time, agents were highly suspicious of Robinson Sr. He had not told them that his daughter-in-law mentioned her husband was driving a Ford V-8 in Indianapolis. Indeed, he had previously told agents his son didn't have a car. Then he told agents that he would rather see his son killed than involved in the kidnapping.

At first, Robinson Sr. planned to accompany his daughter-in-law while delivering the money. After consultation with the Stoll family, though, he was persuaded that following the kidnapper's request of having Frances Robinson deliver the money was the prudent course. She would go alone, and the kidnapper wouldn't suspect a trick.

The Railway Express office delivered the money in Nashville in a package to attorney Ferris Bailey, a relative of the Stolls, Robinson transferred the cash to a suitcase, and went to see his attorney, J. G. Lackey. There, Lackey's nephew took the suitcase to meet Frances Robinson and drove her to the Guthrie, Kentucky, train station where she left for Terre Haute.

Late Monday morning, Robinson Sr. received a telephone call and immediately recognized the voice of his son.

"This is our last chance; we have to have the dough. When will your daughter-in-law get here?"

"Tomorrow," Robinson said.

"You called off the law?"

"Yes, I do not want anything to happen to me."

"You will get your share if this thing goes through," said Robinson Jr.

It was, ostensibly, a most damning statement, as it implicated Robinson Sr. in the kidnapping. That it did not seem to become part of the official record—although obviously obtained through Division wiretaps—might have been due to the complicated and evolving use of wiretaps themselves. After all, they had been "narrowly affirmed" by the Supreme Court in 1928, but contention surrounding their use lingered for some time, and the Court itself vacillated. Hoover's policy was duplicitous: he conveyed to agents that they use wiretaps but not to let anyone *know* they used wiretaps. This may have been what happened to Robinson Jr.'s incriminating statement. Agents would find other proof. But now they *knew*.

After his daughter-in-law left for the train, Robinson Sr. had no more involvement, nor did he receive any updates from either her or his son. He said he had no idea where his son was or what his plans were after receiving the money. He was concerned that if

Stockholm Syndrome, anyone?

$ Frances Robinson: long-suffering wife or brazen accomplice?

his son's apprehension didn't happen in the short run, he would be killed by authorities in the long run.

The Division employed various techniques: mail cover (monitoring the post office for mail going to a designated addressee) on Robinson family members and close associates and wiretaps on the family. (Agents even watched the home and office of Dr. Joseph Fenn, who had treated Robinson Jr. for gonorrhea and syphilis.) The Division also monitored incoming calls to the Stoll and Speed families, as well as Alice Stoll's friend, Elizabeth McHenry. (Once again, given Hoover's loose wiretap protocol, it's doubtful that all those monitored knew they were being surveilled.)

The agency also updated Robinson Jr.'s Identification Order—No. 1233—with a new photograph, and thousands of them would be sent to the various Division offices. A portion of the first batch went to Nashville's 180 police officers and thirty city detectives, as well as one hundred county deputy sheriffs.

$

AGENTS STACK THE DECK

Back in Indianapolis, the press had somehow found out the location of Robinson's hideout apartment where photographers had already shown up. The media also knew SAC Purvis was in Indianapolis and working the case. He met with them outside the Division office in the Fletcher Trust Building and, essentially, said, "No comment." To his perturbed boss, Hoover, that was still one comment too many. He told Purvis he didn't want any of the Division offices making statements to the press. The attorney general would make any further public comments on the Stoll investigation. (Hoover's standard line was always the same when he, himself, wasn't getting the publicity or, more important, didn't want anyone else to.)

The G-men and the Heiress

Hoover wanted Purvis out of Indianapolis. (In truth, he probably wanted Purvis out of the agency.) He told Purvis to return to Chicago. After all, there was a good chance Robinson, who'd lived there before, might show up there again. Purvis planned on leaving immediately on one of the agency's leased airplanes.

In Louisville, Agent Murry Falkner was assigned to the house of Robinson Sr. where he happened to notice a drawing of a garage with a street intersection. When he asked Robinson Sr. about it, Robinson Sr. denied knowing what it was, then finally revealed to Falkner that it was a drawing of Mrs. Stoll's location in Indianapolis. He said he drew it the day his daughter-in-law left with the ransom money. The note had the street number in a code Robinson Sr. used in making building project cost estimates. He said his daughter-in-law gave him the street address because he was initially going to deliver the ransom funds.

The G-Men had had enough, in patience as well as in conflicting statements and out-and-out lies. So SAC Connelley, after meeting with United States Attorney Thomas Sparks, swore to a federal complaint before U.S. Commissioner Eugene Dailey in Louisville in which Robinson Jr. and Sr., as well as Mrs. Robinson Jr., were charged with Alice Stoll's kidnapping and aiding and abetting each other in the kidnapping.

Frances Robinson was served by Nathan, Connelley, and Reinecke in her hospital bed, and her bond was set at $50,000 (the amount of the ransom itself, although the number was probably nothing more than a tabloid coincidence). She remained at the hospital for two more days, then was taken to the Jefferson County Jail in Louisville, unable to make bail.

Stoll family members were all being guarded, courtesy of the Louisville Police Department, at their various residences. There was some concern that Robinson might return and perhaps seek vengeance upon them. Mrs. Stoll was resting at home in bed, her husband keeping a watchful eye. Her brother-in-law William Stoll was there, as were her parents, who had brought their daughter fresh milk and flowers. She also received a single rose and note from the neighbors, the James Clark family, who lived across Lime Kiln Lane.

Even by today's standards of a major Federal Bureau case, "STOLNAP"—its agency codename—was a massive effort involving, ultimately, hundreds of agents. Every field office would have a role to play in trying to capture Robinson. The title of the case was changed to add the subjects—Thomas Henry Robinson Sr.; Mrs. Frances Natalie Robinson, alias Catherine Beech; and aliases of Robinson Jr., Thomas W. Kennedy, and John Ward. A passport stop was placed on Robinson and all his aliases, in case he tried

Stockholm Syndrome, anyone?

Division flyboy

Murry Charles "Jack" Falkner was a two-hitch serviceman and three-time FBI Special Agent. Mississippi-born, he would early on—unlike his famous Nobel-Prize winning brother, William—keep his grandfather's spelling, who'd omitted the "u" from his family's last name. In May of 1918, he trained with the Marines at Parris Island and Quantico and was shipped off to France where he would say the Marines made a fighting man out of a little boy. He arrived in Brest, France, in August of 1918, and marched off to the front near St. Mihiel carrying a fifty-pound pack and a firm sense of himself.

§ Special Agent Falkner, famous in his own right.

On November 1 near the Argonne Forest, a sergeant yelled, "Keep your heads down," advice he perilously ignored. He was severely wounded in head and knee and fell into his trench, landing in three years of accumulated muck. His war was over and he was left with a Purple Heart, a French Brigade Citation, and the shrapnel, which he gave to his mother.

Once back home, he graduated from the University of Mississippi and in 1922 obtained a law degree. After practicing law, he moved to Washington, DC, in 1924, and ended up working for the Division of Investigation. He was one of the agents outside the Biograph Theater in Chicago when Dillinger was shot, and the bonus he earned for his work on the 1934 Bremer kidnapping case he spent on flying lessons, becoming the only agent during the 1930s who was an authorized pilot. He had his own plane and, on some occasions, flew Hoover himself.

He served again during WWII, wanting to fly but learning that he'd aged out, and thus he ended up as an Army Counter-Intelligence Officer in Algiers where—while attending his only ballet—he met a beautiful French ballet dancer who became his wife. After the war, he returned to the FBI and retired after thirty-five years, writing a memoir, *The Falkners of Mississippi*, which is known as a significant and basic source into the life of his family.

$ Springfield officers find Robinson's getaway vehicle—but no Robinson.

to leave the country, and because Robinson had mentioned to Mrs. Stoll the possibility of traveling to Havana or Bermuda, agents covered all sailing and airline flights to either location, as well as the Caribbean cruises.

PURVIS AND HIS AGENTS GET THE LIMELIGHT

As for Robinson Jr. himself, he was in the money, and for the moment, no one was the wiser. An almost impossible chain of providential—for him—circumstances had allowed him to be on his way, unencumbered at least momentarily and in possession of what would today be almost a million dollars.

He headed first for Springfield, Ohio, about four hours away, and rented a room on Main Street, registering as Jerry Dobson of South Bend, Indiana—yet another

Stockholm Syndrome, anyone?

alias—and telling the landlady he was traveling for a correspondence school. He paid her $11, which covered his rent for the week. At some point, he told the landlady his car was burning oil and he was going to Columbus in a friend's car and would return for his car.

After two days passed, the landlady called the Springfield Police Department, which happened to be at the same time Robinson sightings were reported in the area. Springfield police called Division agents who blanketed the area but found only Robinson's abandoned 1934 Ford V-8 sedan with the yellow wheels. He'd changed the license plates but never returned it to the unhappy managers of the Mid-West Drive It Yourself Company in Chicago.

The landlady described Robinson as wearing a gray suit, black derby hat, and glasses. In a search of the car, police found a loaded magazine from a .45 automatic handgun, the weapon Mrs. Stoll's maid described during the kidnapping. Robinson also left behind an imitation leather suitcase with his gray overcoat, a Chicago newspaper, his toothbrush, and a single pencil. A dragnet was set up on U.S. 40 around Springfield for twenty-four hours but nothing was gained but overtime hours.

Agents interviewed a taxi driver who said that around mid-afternoon, he'd taken Robinson to the Chicago and Eastern Illinois Railroad Station in Springfield. From there, he went to Toledo, where he had another unnervingly close call: on Wednesday, October 17, an old boss, Frank Butler, who knew him at the Wayne Lumber and Manufacturing Company in Nashville where Robinson was a timekeeper, saw him leaving the Commodore Perry Hotel. Butler reported the information to the Division office in Detroit, which was the closest office, and gave the same description as the Springfield landlady—gray suit, black derby hat, rimless wire glasses. As befitting his new station as someone who had come into money (even if it wasn't his), Robinson was staying at the best place in town, and he'd bought new clothes and a travel bag.

The next day, he took a taxi to the train station and bought a ticket to what his pursuers thought was Cincinnati. Agents searched the train a half-dozen times but to no avail. Robinson had, in fact, gone to Cleveland, and his incredible good fortune continued to hold. His picture was in all the newspapers, but no one in the dining car recognized him. He was reading a newspaper article about himself while a porter was talking to him, and the porter didn't notice, either.

Hoover was not happy with the Detroit office's efforts, certain that agents there hadn't responded quickly enough. The G-Men spread out across Ohio—some of their energetic movement caused by the hunt for Robinson and some of it from trying to stay out of Hoover's crosshairs. Agents contacted Robinson's great-aunts, Nora and Anna Preston, in Marietta, Ohio, but they hadn't seen him since 1913. Cincinnati agents interviewed a dozen or so members of Robinson's family living in the Cincinnati area and others in Ohio, but turned up nothing of substance. The investigation was an endless merry-go-round of useless information, none of it bringing them any closer to Robinson.

At the moment, Robinson was a ghost, and one that was haunting the Division.

Stockholm Syndrome, anyone?

IDENTIFICATION
ORDER NO. 1273
October 16, 1934.

DIVISION OF INVESTIGATION
U. S. DEPARTMENT OF JUSTICE
WASHINGTON, D. C.

Fingerprint Classification
21 27 W
15 rW 20

WANTED

THOMAS H. ROBINSON, JR.
alias T. H. ROBINSON, JR.

KIDNAPING

Photograph taken in 1932.

DESCRIPTION

Age, 22 years (1929); Height, 6 feet;
Weight, 140 pounds; Build, slender;
Hair, black; Eyes, gray; Complexion,
fair; Occupation, Attorney's Clerk.

RELATIVES:

Mrs. Frances Althauser Robinson,
wife, Sterling Court Apartments,
Nashville, Tennessee
Thomas H. Robinson, Sr, father,
1716 Ashwood Avenue, Nashville,
Tennessee
Mrs. Jessie P. Robinson, mother,
1716 Ashwood Avenue, Nashville,
Tennessee
Mrs. Ernest M. (Bertha) Warner,
sister, 2 East Jackson Boulevard,
Harding Place, Nashville, Tennessee
N. L. Althauser, father-in-law,
Sterling Court Apartments,
Nashville, Tennessee

CRIMINAL RECORD

As T. H. Robinson, Jr. #3488,
arrested Police Department, Nashville,
Tennessee, June 6, 1929; charge, impersonating an officer; committed State
Insane Asylum, Nashville, Tennessee,
July 4, 1929, for 30 day period observation, released; charge dismissed.
As T. H. Robinson, Jr. #3488, arrested Police Department, Nashville,
Tennessee, April 22, 1934; charge,
robbery from person; pending.

RECORDED

7-1128-1226
DIVISION OF
JAN 15 1935
U. S. DEPARTMENT OF JUSTICE

FILE

Thomas H. Robinson, Jr. is wanted in connection with the kidnaping of Mrs. Alice Speed Stoll at Louisville, Kentucky, on
October 10, 1934.
Law enforcement agencies kindly transmit any additional information or crimnal record to the nearest office of the Division
of Investigation, U. S. Department of Justice, Washington, D. C., or
If apprehended, please notify the Director, Division of Investigation, U. S. Department of Justice, Washington, D. C., or
the Special Agent in Charge of the office of the Division of Investigation listed on the back hereof which is nearest your city.
(over)   Issued by: JOHN EDGAR HOOVER, DIRECTOR.

Robinson hits the big time: his own Identification Order.

Time for a grand jury

8

"They have made up their minds to electrocute him, and nothing will stop them. I don't give a damn."—Mrs. Robinson Sr.

The shuffling of agents from different locales into the Stoll case was about to affect—adversely—the agency's other investigations. On Thursday, October 18, Inspector Samuel Cowley, who'd been sent from headquarters to Chicago to oversee its investigative efforts, was finding it impossible to cover all the leads on Lester Joseph Gillis, aka Baby Face Nelson, the current Public Enemy Number One. Most, if not all, of the Chicago agents were in Indianapolis and Louisville on the Stoll case.

A month later, Cowley and Chicago agent Herman Hollis would be killed in a shootout with Nelson at Barrington, Illinois. There was not a direct correlation between their deaths and the dearth of agents in the Chicago office, but agents in charge felt their housework was piling up, their manpower stretched dangerously thin. And it was all because of the superstitiously good fortune of kidnapper Thomas Robinson Jr., who had somehow managed to drop so cleanly out of sight.

On Friday, October 19, Alice Stoll and her husband were seen mid-morning, sitting on the front patio of their home, holding hands and talking. If she was worried about testifying before the upcoming grand jury—the first step in determining the fate of the Robinsons—she wasn't showing it. The only outward sign that something might be amiss was the black turban covering her head wounds. As if on cue, her Scottish Terrier came around, and she tied a ribbon on his collar and, with a stick, began playing fetch with him. Noticeably absent was Hector, the Great Dane, who had been purchased for security but was most likely still in the doghouse for not confronting the kidnapper.

Agent Dependable

In early 1934, Samuel Cowley was sent from Division headquarters to the Chicago office on an unusual assignment: Director Hoover had lost faith in SAC Melvin Purvis's leadership to capture John Dillinger. Hoover, a prolific memo writer, was impressed with Cowley's ability to pare voluminous file information into concise reports. Thus Cowley became overseer of the case, Purvis, and the Chicago agents—and one of Hoover's most trusted men.

The mild-mannered Cowley was destined for service since age 17 when he went to Hawaii on a four-year mission for the Mormon

church, then after obtaining a law degree in 1929 and joining the FBI, he served in half a dozen agency offices. After John Dillinger was killed in July 1934, Cowley was promoted to Inspector, although Purvis got the limelight while Cowley stayed in the shadows completing the follow-up tasks. It's a credit to Cowley and Purvis that they made the Chicago situation work, Cowley covering for Purvis after the botched

§ Nelson's care, riddled by the guns of Cowley and Hollis.

Dillinger raid on Little Bohemia Lodge, which sent Purvis off on a drinking spree.

There was a fracture in Cowley's formidable armor, though: he neglected the shooting range and he wouldn't wear a bulletproof vest. Thus when he and agent Herman Hollis happened upon Baby Face Nelson's car and a gunfight ensued, Cowley was helplessly underdressed. Hollis was shot in the head by Nelson and Cowley mortally hit in the side; he died early the next morning in a rural hospital. Nelson's body was found in a ditch, hit at least nine times. The coroner's report indicated the round which ultimately killed him was from Cowley's Thompson.

Ironically, as Bryan Burrough wrote in *Public Enemies*, "A desk man his entire career, the squat, jowly Mormon was the last man Hoover would have wanted facing off with Nelson." His aversion to publicity overshadowed his inestimable value to the agency, for his demeanor and expertise made him a primary figure in ending the great crime wave of the 1930s.

That same day, Nashville agents were headed to Louisville to testify at the upcoming federal grand jury. Robinson Sr. was in the company of agents who had picked him up for questioning, and he ended up sequestered away in a hotel where the rumors of him being given the third degree by Division agents were patently untrue. Momentarily anyway, Senior was on easy street: nice hotel room, good food, plenty of sleep. The agents seemed to be applying the old adage of catching their flies with honey as opposed to vinegar.

When Robinson Sr. was escorted into the U.S. Marshals office in Nashville by SAC Rorer for the arraignment, he was smoking a pipe Rorer had given him, which he planned on keeping as a souvenir of how well the agents had treated him.

Then when the Department of Justice sought Robinson Sr.'s removal to Louisville to stand trial, the U.S. Commissioner in Nashville found no probable cause for the government's charges and refused to send Robinson Sr. to Louisville. Count one for the home boy, which is what Hoover was afraid of. He said it was "the maudlin sentiment for Robinson at Nashville."

Hoover was concerned, too, about Mrs. Stoll's testimony regarding Frances Robinson, fearful that Alice Stoll looked upon Frances as her "savior" and might be sympathetic to her on the stand. Hoover told SAC Connelley to advise her husband, Berry, "that she should by no means indulge in any sentimentality…I can understand why she may not want to go the limit against Mrs. Robinson but it must be done."

Connelley told Hoover he thought Purvis would be needed to testify before the grand jury, most likely about the money Mrs. Robinson had given Mrs. Stoll. Purvis, though, thought it would be better to have another agent testify, and Hoover agreed. Hoover told Purvis he would rather have him in Cincinnati. (Perhaps Hoover thought Purvis would be out of the public eye in Cincinnati.)

For whatever change in command, however, Purvis did testify before the grand jury, even as Hoover seethed at every mention of Purvis by the press. After the grand jury concluded, Hoover told Connelley to ship Purvis back to Chicago. Even Cincinnati was too close. Purvis reluctantly headed north with what was known as "the Chicago Wrecking Crew"—agents Samuel McKee, Bud Hopton, and Thomas Connor.

Purvis fumed over the removal, but stopping in Indianapolis on his way home to Chicago, he had an idea and telephoned Hoover. What if he and his agents operated from a hotel on the outskirts of Cincinnati, working separately from the local office, because any publicity about them would be non-existent?

Hoover agreed.

$

ROBINSONS, A BOXED SET

On Saturday, October 20, a special federal grand jury in Louisville indicted all three Robinsons on charges of kidnapping and conspiracy. The entire process took less than two hours. The judge, Charles Dawson, called it "the most heinous crime conceivable" (which seemed a bit of hyperbole by a federal judge showing, perhaps, the lack of his own imagination). Dawson, however, was incited enough by what he heard to say that if he could, he'd hold them all without bond.

Alice Stoll, wearing a close-fitting hat that concealed the mark on her forehead inflicted by the kidnapper, testified in a composed and straightforward manner. She did not indulge in any sentimentality, although it was most likely not for Hoover's benefit but because of the lawyers' questions and her own reticent nature.

In Frances Robinson's defense, her attorney quoted Alice Stoll's famous uncle, Frederic Sackett, former senator and ambassador to Germany, who had requested that Mrs. Robinson deliver the ransom money.

"Send that girl," Sackett had said.

The jurors did not wish to be photographed, causing a commotion among the photographers. They pleaded with the judge that the case was the first federal grand jury impaneled under the new Lindbergh Law, and they were duty-bound to capture the historic moment. The judge was not impressed, and when Alice Stoll was leaving, a photographer tried to take her picture only to be wrestled to the ground by her attorney. Mrs. Stoll stooped down, removed the lens from the camera, and as she walked away she turned and rolled the lens back down the sidewalk. History thus moved on, absent any defined imagery.

The trial was scheduled for June of 1935, then postponed, finally taking place in October. And so history had an entire year with which to amuse itself. Among those not amused was Director Hoover. Robinson Jr. was still on the lam, with reports of Robinson sightings coming from all over the country which necessitated what seemed to be half of Hoover's men chasing specious leads. Also on the list of the definitely-not-amusing was an article that appeared in the *Louisville Herald-Post* reporting that Hoover hadn't known about the kidnapping because no one dared wake him up. (Because of his notable dictatorial methods, Hoover was often referred to by his employees as "Kid Napoleon." But never, of course, to his face.)

"This is a damn lie," Hoover fumed. "Tell Connelley to blacklist this paper."

The G-men and the Heiress

Golden boy

Director Hoover wanted all his agents to play ball, at least metaphorically, but none more than Thomas John Connor, who was in actuality a professional. Born in Washington, DC, in 1906 to Irish parents, he was a public school standout in both baseball and basketball, entered Columbia Law School at seventeen, then in 1929 landed a gig playing third base for the Boston Braves Triple-A team. It was fortuitous for Director Hoover, or perhaps as with the professional teams, he was recruited. He began with the Bureau of Investigation in 1931 in a clerical position and, after receiving his law degree, rose to become a Special Agent.

Hoover, it seemed, had needed a special coach more than a special agent, and he had Connor organize the office baseball and basketball teams where he was player-coach, winning the 1932 Government League Championship in both. Connor became a favorite of Hoover and, as a result, spent an hour a week in the boss's office talking sports. Good things never last, and the next year when the team finished in second, Connor was transferred, his bat replaced with a Thompson submachine gun.

$ Thomas Connor in his Bureau uniform (once a third baseman, always a third baseman).

A move to Chicago put him in the middle of some of the agency's most famous operations. In 1934, he was in an alley near the Biograph Theatre when John Dillinger was killed where, mistaken for Dillinger, he, himself, was almost shot. He also helped hunt down Baby Face Nelson (who killed his good friend Agent Carter Baum), Pretty Boy Floyd, and the Barker Gang.

He left the FBI in 1935 after many sleepless nights, wearing the same clothes for days on end and popping antacid tablets like candy, looking for a less stressful line of work, which would be the war. He served with Naval Intelligence and later joined the Central Intelligence Agency where he spent eighteen years, retiring in 1966. He served in New York City, supervising Radio Free Europe personnel and interviewing business people who traveled overseas.

Compared to the FBI, the CIA work was a yawnfest.

HOOVER SLEEPS DURING SEARCH

"Foolproof" System Bars Justice Chief From News of Kidnap.

By DAVID R. SCOTT.
Herald-Post Bureau.

Washington, Oct. 11—A victim of his fool-proof system to prevent his official slumbers being disturbed by government business and reporters, J. Edgar Hoover, much publicized as the super-efficient director of the Federal Bureau of Investigation, found himself in the predicament today of directing a kidnaping investigation he knew nothing about.

Hoover reported that all available resources of the government are being thrown into the search and bureau agents are in full cry after the abductors. Directing the case from here, Hoover made no indication he would leave for Louisville.

Hoover, sometimes called "Kid Napoleon" by his employes because of his dictatorial methods, slept all night long without learning of the kidnaping of Mrs. Berry V. Stoll in Louisville. This happened because no bureau employe or official had dared wake up Hoover to inform him of the Stoll case and that his bureau was active in the search for Mrs. Stoll's abductors.

With the far flung federal investigation of the Lindbergh kidnaping case concluded but last night, Attorney General Homer S. Summings today was mobilizing anew the forces of the United States Department of Justice to investigate the latest extorting outrage, the abduction of Mrs. Stoll.

The bureau is preparing to throw its entire resources if needed into the hunt for Mrs. Stoll's abductors. Cincinnati regional headquarters of

Continued on Page 3, Column 6.

$ The *Herald-Post* on its way to being blacklisted.

Melvin Purvis was also about to turn up again, back in the headlines, and it was partly Hoover's fault. The day after the grand jury, Purvis received a noon telephone call at Cincinnati's Hotel Alms from Acting SAC Howard Harris of the Cincinnati office. The Division had information that Charles Arthur "Pretty Boy" Floyd—current Public Enemy No. 1—might be near Wellsville, Ohio. Adam Richetti, a cohort of Floyd, had been arrested by the Wellsville police chief, and a posse was chasing another man thought to be Floyd.

Purvis telephoned Hoover in Washington and then, with his agents in a rented airplane, took off for eastern Ohio where they shot Floyd in an East Liverpool cornfield. He died in a clump of grass beside a dirt road, and his last words were, "Who the hell tipped you?" After shooting Floyd, Purvis jumped in his car and streaked off to find a telephone and call Hoover. "Floyd has been mortally wounded," he told the Director.

Even that made the headlines, beneath a larger one in the October 23 *Akron Beacon Journal* that screamed, "Government guns make corpse of nation's No. 1 outlaw." Next to the photograph of Floyd's body was one of Purvis, described as "collegiate-looking." Purvis did not take credit for shooting Floyd, and when pressed by reporters on who did the actual shooting, Purvis said, "We all did." He even made sure the slugs from Floyd's body weren't matched to the gun of any single agent. And

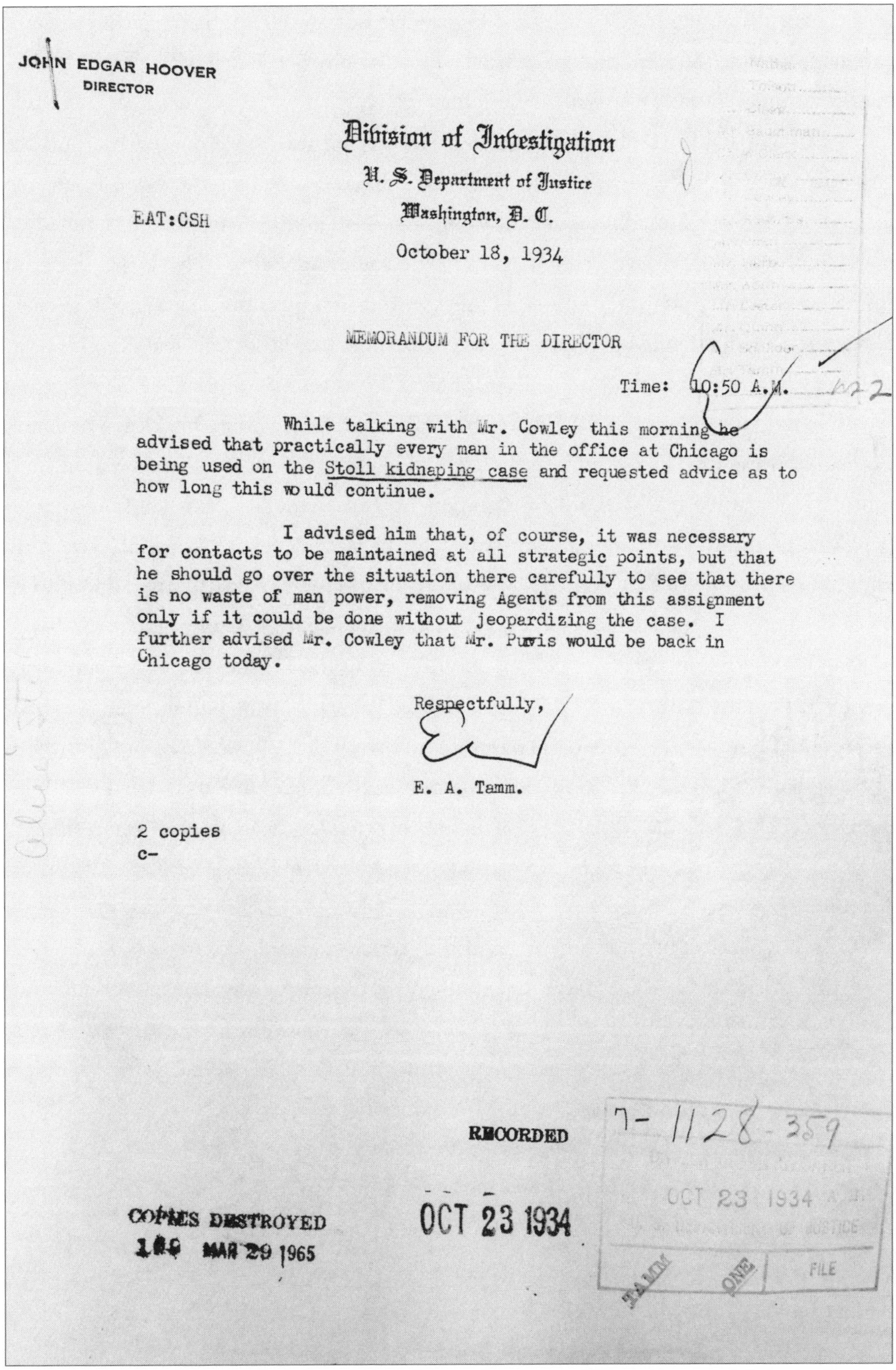

JOHN EDGAR HOOVER
DIRECTOR

Division of Investigation
U. S. Department of Justice
Washington, D. C.

EAT:CSH

October 18, 1934

MEMORANDUM FOR THE DIRECTOR

Time: 10:50 A.M.

While talking with Mr. Cowley this morning he advised that practically every man in the office at Chicago is being used on the Stoll kidnaping case and requested advice as to how long this would continue.

I advised him that, of course, it was necessary for contacts to be maintained at all strategic points, but that he should go over the situation there carefully to see that there is no waste of man power, removing Agents from this assignment only if it could be done without jeopardizing the case. I further advised Mr. Cowley that Mr. Purvis would be back in Chicago today.

Respectfully,

E. A. Tamm.

2 copies
c-

RECORDED   7-1128-359

OCT 23 1934

COPIES DESTROYED
180 MAR 29 1965

OCT 23 1934

FILE

$ Memorandum to Director Hoover on officer depletion in Chicago office.

Time for a grand jury

yet he had still outvied both Floyd *and* Hoover. It was as though the cheering throngs gathering outside the local mortuary where Floyd's body was taken were cheering Purvis, even though little of it was his own doing.

If Purvis back in the headlines peeved Hoover, he was more peeved by the U.S. Commissioner in Nashville who ruled Robinson Sr. could not be removed to Louisville for his trial. Hoover was convinced that Robinson Sr. shouldn't be tried in his hometown because of what he, Hoover, called "sugarcoated sentimentality." The Department of Justice would not stand for the ruling, Hoover vowed, and this time he was right: in early November, a federal judge in Nashville overturned the first order and sent Robinson Sr. to Louisville to stand trial.

In early November of 1934, Hoover had already begun scaling back the Division's Louisville presence. The provisional squad of agents there were soon released, and future investigative leads would be handled by Indianapolis agents making a road trip. Before the month was out, wiretaps had been scaled back, as well. The only ones left were those of Robinson Sr. and his sister-in-law, Bertha Warner. There were agents monitoring the Althausers (Frances Robinson's parents), and one at the home of Martha Sandmann, Frances's sister. In addition to the Warner wiretap, there were two live-in-agents, which sorely displeased Mrs. Warner, but she had made the agents' list by complaining. She wanted to complain further, if only she could figure out where to make her complaints. "They expect our hospitality, then knife us in the back," she lamented. The Division also had four agents staying at the Robinson Sr. residence working in pairs, day and night, even though it was probably the last place Robinson Jr. would show up.

Before long, the Division did an administrative review of resources committed to Nashville. Assistant Director Nathan recommended the release of two agents conducting surveillance of Robinson Sr. and four others who were monitoring the Althauser residence. The agents at the home of Mrs. Warner were left in place, as well as the agents on the telephone taps of Robinson Sr. and Mrs. Warner.

The agency had the added benefit of Nashville agent Reuben Peterson, who happened to live next door to the Warners. A hedge hindered his view but he did his best, watching while at home, at all hours, which would have pleased the Director, who tended to view his agents in a proprietary manner.

The G-men and the Heiress

$

TRAVELING TRANSVESTITE

On Saturday, December 15, Fred Willey, president and general manager of the Tri-Cities Yellow Cab Company in Davenport, Iowa, had an unusual visitor. That afternoon, a tall, slender woman with a marked southern accent, wearing a brown coat with a dark felt collar and dark gloves, appeared. She had a fair complexion, no indication of a beard but a predominately male voice. She said she didn't have references but had plenty of money, showing him a wad of bills she pulled from a large handbag. It all seemed rather odd to him, so much so that he refused to rent her a car. He was later notified by Tri-Cities' Moline, Illinois, office that a similarly-described person had rented a car at its location.

Walter Snider, who'd been formerly affiliated with the Davenport Police De-

$ Robinson Jr.'s softer side—the agency's depiction of him disguised as a woman.

partment in Iowa was visiting, saw the person, and went to the police station where he picked out Robinson Jr. on his Identification Order. An agent in the Omaha office showed both Willey and Snider an artist's depiction of what Robinson Jr. might look like as a woman, and both confirmed that this was the person they saw. The eyes and the dimple in the chin were identical.

Sightings of women look-alikes happened all across the country, including one in California near where Robinson and his girlfriend were hiding. They read about the story in a Los Angeles paper and had a good laugh. His girlfriend later told the FBI that it was absurd he would dress as a woman. For eighteen months, he had a mustache and hair on the back of his hands. Robinson pointed out that at six feet tall, 170 pounds, a full mustache, and 11½ size shoes, it would have been almost impossible to pull off that kind of disguise. The agents were undeterred, spending numerous working hours chasing down leads of a womanly Robinson.

Time for a grand jury

Thomas McDade, undercover scribe

Thomas McDade was a City College of New York graduate with a law degree from St. John's University where he wrote for the law review, an early act that presaged his second career as a diarist and mystery writer. He arrived in Nashville in 1935 to assist with the Stoll case and was given instruction on wiretapping, which in his analysis didn't help investigations much.

$ A smiling McDade escorts Robinson (far left) who is not.

Earlier, McDade and agent William Ryan had chased Baby Face Nelson, resulting in the death of Nelson, but also that of agents Samuel Cowley and Herman Hollis. Even then, he demonstrated his literary side, writing in his journal, "A day I will never forget…"

The agents were typically close-mouthed, but McDade was unusual in that he kept a pocket diary of his time with the agency. And while his career as an agent was relatively brief, his diary provided "a rare first-person window into the daily life of the 1930s G-Man."

In 1961, he published his encyclopedia of crime, *The Annals of Murder*, a bibliography of American murder trials that *The New Yorker* called "the indispensable guide to early American murder." McDade had a formidable collection of trial publications in his personal library, which he called "Scotland Yard," and from which much of his writing was taken.

His *Annals* was a hit with audiences both popular and academic. *The New York Times* called it "a great value to collectors" and a legal journal hailed McDade's work as filled with "memorable information about arsenic, drunkenness, insanity, and the legal rights of murderers as interpreted by our fathers."

McDade, it seems, remained an agent to the end; it was simply that as a writer, he always had the last shot. Given the hazards of his earlier work, it was the enviable position.

The G-men and the Heiress

In the third week of December, Agent Murry Falkner went to the Jefferson County Jail to talk with Mrs. Robinson Jr. about the possible whereabouts of her fugitive husband. To Falkner's chagrin, the jailer, Mark Connors, who ran the prison, would not allow the visit because her attorney, Clem Huggins, wasn't present.

The next day, Falkner returned and this time Connors said she was ill with a cold. Falkner knew the jailer was close to the defense attorney, and he wasn't happy about the situation. He went to the U.S. attorney, who sent the U.S. Marshal to the jail to retrieve Mrs. Robinson and bring her to the federal building. The jailer, however, wouldn't allow the marshal to take custody of her. The attorney then contacted a federal doctor who examined Mrs. Robinson, reporting that while she did not have a cold, she was a nervous wreck.

SAC Reinecke reported the incident to Division Headquarters and Director Hoover said, "Have her removed from jail where jailer is obviously hostile to government." However, Judge Charles Dawson, who'd presided over the special grand jury, was fearful of being open to criticism if he moved her. The judge instructed the jailer to allow agents in, although being present was all they were likely to achieve because Mrs. Robinson had already said she wouldn't talk with them.

Her trial—and that of Robinson—was now set for February 11, 1935. Her son, Jimmy, was finally allowed to visit on Christmas Eve, and Frances would spend more than another month in jail before her bond was reduced to $5,000 and she was released. She returned home to Nashville to live with her parents at the Sterling Court Apartments. She had spent four months in jail.

At about the time Frances Robinson was released, the Nashville SAC Rorer told Division headquarters he'd talked to a local judge who was following the case and had observed the actions of the federal prosecutors in the Robinson case. He said their efforts were "pitiful," and he found them incapable and incompetent. If the government prosecution continued down this same road, he said, the case would be lost—a prophetic statement that would come back to haunt the prosecution—and the Division. Hoover, for his part, suggested to the attorney general that a more aggressive attorney be assigned, but the files did not reflect any change in prosecutors.

$

ENEMY OF THE PEOPLE?

On Tuesday, March 19, 1935, a wiretap of a telephone conversation between Mrs. Bertha Warner and Jessie Robinson (Thomas Jr.'s aunt and his mother) was overheard by agents. The sisters were discussing an article in the newspaper about the postponement of the trial until later in 1935. (In the conversation, "Daddy" is Robinson Sr., "Frances" is Mrs. Robinson Jr., and "Cummings" is the attorney general.)

Jessie Robinson: "They will build two separate electric chairs for Frances and Daddy; they are certainly going to electrocute Daddy; they call everybody liars; they won't believe a word anyone else says; they are going to electrocute Daddy. The government can do anything; they have made up their minds to electrocute him, and nothing will stop them. I don't give a damn. Daddy said this morning that he doesn't give a damn, and I feel the same way; neither of us gives a damn what they do. This drive Cummings is making against attorneys, it's a damn disgrace; it's worse than the Inquisition; they do anything they want to."

Bertha Warner: "Cummings ought to have his teeth knocked down his throat."

Jessie Robinson: "Somebody ought to take him for a ride. The government is full of crooks."

Bertha Warner: "It is like any other organization; you will find crooks in any business."

Jessie Robinson: "Well, Daddy said this morning that he doesn't give a damn what happens to him. I don't have anything to live for, and we don't care if we don't live; we just don't give a damn."

The agents learned that Robinson Sr. told his wife he was concerned that the government was lumping his son with the likes of John Dillinger to sway public opinion. Mrs. Robinson Sr. thought the government was nothing but "low-down sneaking liars." They were of the mindset that the government should be "catching genuine criminals" instead of prosecuting their son.

But Robinson, although not a killer, was a real criminal with a pattern of criminal behavior against women that had escalated to ransom kidnapping. He was fortunate

The G-men and the Heiress

that the blows he had inflicted on Mrs. Stoll had been largely superficial, or murder could easily have been added to his crimes.

As for Hoover, he was inventing America's modern crime-fighting institution. He was probably a zealot because the work required zealotry. History might have the final say, but in the moment, Hoover himself would have it.

A decade before, the smart money may have been on Robinson Jr.

But no longer.

WANTED FOR KIDNAPING

THOMAS HENRY ROBINSON, JR., with aliases: T. H. ROBINSON, JR., JOHN WARD, JOHN WARD, JR., JOHN E. WARD, JOHN W. WARD, THOMAS W. KENNEDY, JERRY DOBSEN, HENRY SAUNDERS, MR. KNAPP.

DESCRIPTION

Age 28, (born May 5, 1907); Build, slender; Height, 6'; Weight, 149 lbs.; Hair, dark brown; Eyes, gray; Complexion, sallow; Occupation, attorney's clerk; Beard, heavy and dark; Ears, no lobes; Chin, prominent cleft in chin.

Thomas Henry Robinson, Jr. is wanted in connection with the kidnaping of Mrs. Alice Speed Stoll of Louisville, Kentucky, on October 10, 1934.

If you are in possession of any information concerning the location of Thomas Henry Robinson, Jr., please communicate by telephone or telegraph collect with the undersigned, or with the nearest office of the Federal Bureau of Investigation, U. S. Department of Justice, the local addresses of which are set forth on the reverse side of this notice.

October 7, 1935.

JOHN EDGAR HOOVER, DIRECTOR,
FEDERAL BUREAU OF INVESTIGATION,
UNITED STATES DEPARTMENT OF JUSTICE,
WASHINGTON, D. C.
TELEPHONE, NATIONAL 7117.

Thomas Robinson Jr., man of the hour, on his FBI wanted flyer, October 7, 1935.

9 Wanted public enemy

"We were living in a fool's paradise."—Thomas Robinson Jr.

The fugitive Robinson was on the run, pursued by what seemed to be Hoover's entire contingent of G-Men. Close behind or not, Robinson surely felt the heat because the Division had a complement of agents from more than half a dozen field offices in a full-court press on him, wherever he was.

The term "Public Enemy" had been around for a long time, but it wasn't until 1930 when the Chicago Crime Commission came up with a Public Enemies List of twenty-eight names, popularizing the modern use of the term. (Early on, it seemed that to make the list one must first commit a capital crime, then acquire a good nickname: Tony "Mops" Volpe, for instance, or William "Three-Finger Jack" White, and the most famous of all, Alphonse Gabriel "Scarface" Capone.)

The commission suggested that the Department of Justice compile a list. United States Attorney General Homer Cummings must have liked the idea as unofficially he referred to John Dillinger as "Public Enemy No. 1," which caught on with the press. Some thought the 1931 Warner Bros. film, *The Public Enemy*, starring James Cagney and Jean Harlow, may also have had something to do with the proper use of the term by the government. In the film, Cagney met his end killed by gangsters, his body left on the family doorstep.

Director Hoover was not at first keen on the idea of an enemy list, because he felt it brought felons too much attention and fed their own self-importance. But his public relations man, Assistant Director Louis Nichols, put the term to such good use, both before and after an "enemy's" capture, that Hoover relented, and by 1934 the Division was using "Public Enemy No. 1" both internally and publicly. So were newspapers and "true crime" magazines, all of it brought about by the public's fascination with big-time gangsters.

In 1935, the Warner Bros. film *G Men* starred James Cagney—who was now perpetuating the myth of how Hoover wanted his agents portrayed—standing tall and wearing a white hat. Radio serials like *Gang Busters* and the comic strip, *War on Crime,* continued to promulgate the FBI Special Agent as a wholesome, incorruptible, devoted crusader who always got the public enemy, whether he did or not.

$

HIDING IN PLAIN SIGHT

In mid-October, two days before he was indicted in Louisville by the special grand jury, Thomas Robinson arrived in New York City by train and took a cab to the swanky New Yorker Hotel where he would stay until December 10. He registered as Thomas M. Wakefield of Waukegan, Illinois, purporting to be a representative of the Johns-Manville Corporation. He remained in total seclusion for just one day, receiving meals in his room and reading the newspapers, all of which seemed to be devoted extensively to him, his mug plastered across the front pages; he was almost giddy, both at the exposure and the fact that no one had recognized him.

The next day, he went out and bought some suits and full-dress evening clothes, pleased to see his name in lights near Broadway where it appeared on the electric sign strip of the *New York Times* building near Times Square. He saw films nearly every day, changing out $20 ransom bills with the ticket agent. In the movie houses, he saw himself again in the newsreels, enshrouded by the protecting darkness.

Emboldened, he went out sight-seeing. At Battery Park on the southern tip of Manhattan, he asked a man about the ferry to the Statue of Liberty, then noticed the man was wearing a police badge. He told Robinson that before he left he should see the Aquarium. These close encounters seemed to entertain and stimulate Robinson, a naughty boy checkmating his elders.

On December 10, he changed hotels, moving to the Lexington in midtown where he registered as Ted M. Warner (Warner was his aunt's married name) of Lake Forest, Illinois where he worked with the Chicago Board of Trade. (In a sudden burst of creativity, Robinson had kept the initials—T.M.W.—of his previous alias so the laundry marks in his clothes were the same.)

One evening, he met a woman in a nightclub, let his guard down, and got drunk. She may also have drugged his drink, for he passed out in his room and slept for sixteen

The G-men and the Heiress

hours. She had taken $500 from his wallet, courteously leaving him a five-spot, but she had overlooked the $48,000 in ransom money in his travel bag. To honor his great good fortune, he immediately moved to the Waldorf-Astoria on Park Avenue, keeping the name Warner.

If he had died, he would have chosen Manhattan as his final reward. His new life-style was profligate, and before Christmas of 1934 he was running up weekly bills of $200 (nearly $4,000 in today's value). He was deep into nightlife, hitting all the hotspots of Greenwich Village, the Pepper Pot Inn on Fourth Street, the Open Door on McDougal Street, and the Greenwich Village Inn.

$ Jean Breese, Robinson's cross-country paramour.

At Sheridan Square, it was the El Chico and the Nut Club, Sully's Showboat on lower Seventh, Jimmy Kelly's on Sullivan Street and the Village Barn on Eighth.

$

ROMANCE ON THE RUN

On New Year's Eve, he met Jean Gordon—birth name Jean Breese—a captivating party girl. He was about to ignore part of John Dillinger's famous advice: "Never trust a woman or an automatic pistol." Breese had been orphaned by age eight, and by her own admission she wasn't from the wrong side of the tracks but she may have crossed them a few times.

They became constant companions, frequenting Elise's on Forty-ninth Street, Eddie's on West Fifth, and Harlem's Ubangi Club. Their basic work seemed to be reducing the available supply of champagne in Manhattan. After their excursion into Harlem, they took a taxi and she dropped him at the Waldorf, which he quickly recognized might have been a mistake. To rectify that possibility, he moved back to the Lexington, stopped seeing her, and began a migration across the island, from the Lexington to the Ritz-Carlton, and from there to the Hotel St. George. (Once again, he managed to keep his initials, this time using the alias of T. Morton Wallace.) All of this was in January.

Ubangi Club

An African name with a voodoo touch, the Ubangi catered to everyone: black, white, straight, gay. It opened in 1934, an avant-garde scene rivaling those in the European capitals. Playboys and playgirls from radio, stage, and screen flocked to the location, as well as others from all across The Big Apple. It employed crooning waiters who harmonized between shows, hired both for their vocals and their ability to handle a service tray.

💲 The lure of club life—and Gladys Bentley—proved irresistible to Robinson.

Black entertainers like Avon Long, a Broadway actor and singer; Mabel Scott, a R&B singer; and tapdancer Bill Bailey (first to do the Moonwalk, which he called the Backslide), performed. Earl "Snakehips" Tucker—known also as "the Human Boa Constrictor"—who got his nickname by popularizing the dance of the same name, was the headliner.

But none could top the most sought out entertainer, curvy, mannish Gladys Bentley. She was a 250-pound Black lesbian cross-dresser who appeared in top hat and tuxedo. She played the piano, sang raunchy songs, shamelessly flirted with women in the crowd, and was backed up by a chorus of drag queens. (Her prize number was "Nothing Perplexes like the Sexes because When You See Them Switch You Can't Tell Which from Which;" her male wardrobe occurred after she learned the Clam House was looking for a male piano player.) Bentley was not only a great musician, "but a linguist and composer who performed in French, Spanish, and Yiddish." Even though she weighed nearly 300 pounds, she was a nimble dancer.

Clubs with the same name sprang up in Baltimore, Philadelphia, Los Angeles, and other cities. Unfortunately, a local law prohibiting cross-dressing went into effect, and along with a minor liquor infraction, the Ubangi closed its exotic doors. It ended its run in 1937, reopened in a different location in the 1940s, but its time had passed.

The G-men and the Heiress

His last stop was to find a swimming pool and the Turkish baths, as he was trying to "snap out of it." He even stopped drinking for a few days, but he couldn't get her out of his mind. He was lonely, and he was infatuated. He went back to The Village Tavern looking for her because he knew she was friends with the pianist, Harpo, and Primo the bartender.

Once he found her they were together a lot, although at first she was suspicious of him. He always paid restaurant bills in five- and ten-dollar bills and never tipped proportionately. It suggested to her that he was unaccustomed to having money, and she thought he must be a fugitive of some kind. (It made her think of the 1934 Rubel Ice Corporation job in Brooklyn, in which an armored car had been robbed of almost $500,000, the nation's biggest heist.)

Robinson told her that because of a divorce in Chicago, he was hiding from his wife. She didn't believe him because he had a southern accent, and all his clothes had New York labels. In Breese's mind, though, it was better to let a fugitive dog lie, at least for the time being, something she had learned from her dealings with the criminal underworld.

For once, Robinson—who had vast experience in bamboozling women—may have met his female match. Breese had her own kind of experience, not all of it immediately observable. In the middle of January, Breese called him and said she needed to talk to him about something she couldn't discuss over the phone. When she got to the St. George, she said she knew he was a fugitive, but she had a criminal past, too.

She said the New York police had put up a "pink slip" at its Center Street Station and both their pictures were on it. She also said two G-Men had turned up at the Open Door club a few nights before looking for him. He wasn't sure about either event, but he was unnerved. Breese, meanwhile, was going to stick close; she'd found herself a meal ticket. They were now a couple, in spite of the lingering atmosphere of mutual suspicion.

$

GO WEST, YOUNG MAN

Robinson took at least some of what she told him as true, and he immediately decided to move, not across Manhattan this time, or to Brooklyn, but across the country. They flew to Los Angeles and leased a house in Santa Monica, just blocks from the Riviera Country Club. They hired a maid. Robinson rented a car and hired a chauffeur to drive him to the motor vehicle office where he took his driver's test, supervised by a state police officer. He even joined the Auto Club of Southern California (he was now Leslie King Burgess).

Wanted public enemy

109

💲 Robinson's 1935 Packard sedan, what every kidnapper was driving that year.

Next, he bought a not-so-subtle robin's-egg blue Packard sedan for $3,200 (paid for in hundred-dollar bills). Even Breese understood this wasn't the kind of car one drove while being pursued by the authorities. In her mind, Robinson was being impulsive (see Hare Psychopathy checklist: "impulsivity"), and had too much money to spend. (Robinson was pleased with the purchase, partly because the salesman had once worked for the Department of Justice; Robinson was always buoyed by these chance encounters with policemen or other authorities who might have recognized him.)

Romance was still present, although it was likely enhanced by the aphrodisaic of the ransom money. They took long moonlight drives on Roosevelt Highway alongside the ocean. They mingled with a wealthy crowd and went to parties and dances at the Del-Mar Beach Club. They showed up at The Cotton Club and dined at the Trocadero Café on Sunset Boulevard, mingling with film stars.

Robinson loved California and began a tranquil life in a quiet neighborhood, enjoying the balmy weather. They had a beautiful home, lounged in the sun on its patio, and watched the evening breeze off the ocean ruffle the Australian sweet peas growing on a backyard fence. They had a Japanese gardener. They took long horseback rides in the mountains. "We were living in a fool's paradise," Robinson would say later, not yet aware of how high the rent was on such a place.

The G-men and the Heiress

Robinson's set of mind, by his own admission, was back to normal, whatever that might have meant for someone like him. His dream was to purchase a ranch, and as early as 1933 he had read an article in the *American Magazine* about obtaining government land out west for a mere $200. He had tried to borrow money from his in-laws, but they had refused. Now, he had plenty of cash. Finding a job was out of the question because people would ask too many questions. So for the next year, the purchase of the dream ranch would be foremost in his mind.

$

BACK TO GOTHAM CITY

In March of 1935, the couple decided to go back to New York City to continue exchanging the ransom money for "clean" money, so they might purchase a ranch. They were already having some success "cleaning" the money (even though most of the serial numbers were never recorded properly and thus they had little to worry about). For the time, it actually appeared quite ingenious, if time-consuming: they exchanged the money by wiring the "hot" money to Western Union or Postal Telegraph in another city in amounts of, say $500, and waived any payee identification. Then they reclaimed it, using a code word. Robinson said it was Breese's idea, perhaps another mark of her earlier—and unorthodox—street education.

They drove their flagrantly blue Packard across country, no more conspicuous should they have been in a blimp, stopping first in Vegas where Robinson gambled away more of Alice Stoll's money. Then Salt Lake City, Cheyenne, Omaha, and Chicago. And finally into Philadelphia and on to Newark where Breese went into New York by herself to find an apartment, leaving Robinson at the Douglas Hotel.

Days later, she picked up Robinson at his hotel and drove to a Manhattan apartment on 66th Street where she introduced a new wrinkle: her brother, Steve, and his wife Ingeborg. Steve had a criminal record and was apparently involved in various rackets, thus who better to help exchange the "hot" money?

Robinson's first act back in New York was to ditch the Packard, which was like driving a large billboard. He got $1,750 for it from a dealer on Columbus Circle in New York City. He replaced it with a much less conspicuous black Plymouth sedan for $750.

Robinson helped Steve Breese by paying to get some of his belongings out of hock from a pawn shop, as well as paying off a debt to the owner of a Brooklyn bar and grille. Robinson went to The Chase National Bank and acquired Federal Reserve wrappers, which he used on the ransom money. He made new packets of bills, and he placed

$10,000 in a filing cabinet at a storage facility. He thought of it as money for his criminal defense, should he be caught. In early April, the trio spent days going to the various banks, trading $500 at more than a dozen banks. Robinson also washed the currency in a sink and dried it, eliminating any fingerprints.

$

HOME IS WHERE THE HAT IS

Robinson kept up with the Nashville newspapers, knowing that charges of conspiracy in the kidnapping had been brought against his father and wife. He also knew their home was heavily mortgaged, and his father needed money to defend himself. His wife, Robinson thought, could get funds from her father. Robinson was worried about his father and felt guilty. He told Breese his father had nothing to do with the kidnapping. Some of the ransom money was now clean cash, and the time was right to take the dangerous trip to Nashville, even though he knew the authorities were watching his parents' home.

He and Breese left New York City a few days before Easter of 1935, arriving in various towns late each evening to avoid contact with anyone, and Robinson carried two five-gallon gasoline cans to limit the times they had to stop. They arrived in Nashville on April 20 at 10 p.m. and drove by his parents' house on Ashwood Avenue, seeing nothing amiss. Filled with regret about hurting his parents, Robinson had the urge to run into the house and console them. He found it ironic that he was outside with $10,000 and didn't know how to get the money to them.

Their plan was to have Breese go to the house and bring his father back to the car parked several blocks away. Breese made it into the house, talked to his parents for a few minutes, then a vehicle pulled up. His mother recognized the sound of the engine as the vehicle of one of the G-Men who had previously stayed at the house. Breese went out the back door, and she and Robinson left hurriedly.

Back in New York City, they moved from the Flushing apartment to one on Long Island and with Steve, made a new plan to get $1,000 to Robinson Sr.—and $500 in expenses for Steve. On April 30, Steve left by train for Nashville, left the money with Robinson Sr.'s attorney, and returned to New York. The attorney kept half, and Steve returned saying he'd been followed by G-Men the entire time. Because G-Men did not invade Long Island, Steve was apparently suffering a bout of paranoia.

Robinson and Breese headed back to California, taking the northern route and driving through rain most of the way to Chicago, then they headed to Omaha, and

The G-men and the Heiress

Jean Breese, moll

Jean Breese was eight when orphaned, raised begrudgingly for a short time by her grandmother, then her older sister. Breese had only a grade school education but was working as a department store clerk (and later in a theatre) when she was barely a teenager. She was married at age 20 to a traveling salesman, divorced four years later, then remarried the same man because, she said, she wanted revenge for the first time, and the only way to really hurt a man was through his wallet.

She worked as a nightclub waitress until she found herself broke, then turned to shoplifting, learned from her waitress friends. She escalated to stealing expensive furs and said she earned enough to last her months, even an entire year. She would tell Robinson about doing time in a New Haven jail for ripping off furriers on Fifth Avenue in New York City.

The story was that she had earned the confidence of a man named Kroll, who had been arrested with her brother, Steve, in a check scheme. Kroll was eventually convicted and got three years at Sing Sing,

$ Ms. Breese, looking like the actress Gene Tierney, prominent 1940s star.

a maximum-security facility at Ossining, New York. She visited him while he was in prison, and once he was out and his parole up, she, along with Steve and cohort Jack Harris, took him for a ride, killed him, and disposed of his body in a New Jersey swamp.

In 1929, Breese married Harold Leans, a former sailor with the British Navy. She told Robinson he was a big-time gangster, had committed many crimes, even killed a policeman in a holdup. This marriage lasted only a year, at which time she left him because he was, she said, "of low moral principles." He'd wanted her to participate in the old badger game, tricking mutual acquaintances who were supposedly people of affluence and good reputation, then blackmailing them. (A girl must have her principles.)

If boyfriend Thomas Robinson had moved from being a petty grifter into the big leagues, Breese may have already been ahead of him. In their oddball relationship, it would be difficult to know who was scamming whom.

then to Denver, moving farther south through New Mexico and Arizona. Arriving in San Diego at the end of May 1935, they stayed a few nights at the Pickwick Hotel before going on an excursion to Agua Caliente where Robinson gave away more money in one of the casinos.

On their way up to Los Angeles, the Weyerhauser kidnapping broke in the newspapers, and Robinson was considered an initial suspect, then eliminated. The victim was a nine-year-old boy, almost the age of Robinson's own son. The kidnapping spooked them and, fearing roadblocks and other scrutiny—even though the Weyerhauser case happened much farther north in Tacoma—they turned around and headed back to New York.

Breese rented an apartment in Queens so Robinson could hide out while his father's trial was going on. In early June, the couple moved into the apartment with Steve and Inge. Robinson stayed in seclusion for two weeks straight to remain invisible. Inge was sick and needed an operation, and Robinson paid the bill, then he gave Steve $1,500 to set him up as a bookmaker.

At first, Steve operated out of the Aqueduct racetrack, then with a partner he branched out to Empire City and Saratoga. Breese's sister, Ethel Haney, who lived in Brooklyn, had three children to support and was in financial difficulties, so Robinson gave her money, too.

The developing irony of Robinson's expatriation was that he seemed unable to see he was being bled by the Breese family. In one notable way, they were about to inflict upon Robinson his most grievous injury. But, first, another relative would be heard from, if he was related to them at all. He was Breese's uncle and the story was that he had disapproved of her lifestyle but now she wished to reconcile with him.

Breese and her sister met their uncle at Michael's Restaurant in Brooklyn, whereby they made up, then gave him a large brown envelope containing $2,000 cash (apparently the going rate for reconciliation). And they asked him to make a deposit whereby either sister could withdraw funds, if and when needed. Robinson observed the transaction from another table, none the wiser.

He had become the butter-and-egg man to the entire Breese family. The Breese clan were predators, a pack of cash-starved wolves, and Robinson was the surrounded prey. Breese and her brother Steve were not only helping Robinson clean the money; they were cleaning *Robinson*. If he suspected what was going on, he wasn't admitting it to anyone, perhaps not even to himself.

The G-men and the Heiress

$

AT THE BEACH, IN A FAMILY WAY

The trial of Robinson's wife and father was postponed, so in July the couple, along with the omnipresent Steve and Inge, rented a beach house in Rye, New York. Breese had been pregnant for about three months and wanted to have the child. Her reasoning was if something happened to Robinson, i.e., captured by the authorities, they would have something to bind them together forever. Robinson was vehemently opposed to bringing a child into the world under their current circumstances. He wasn't divorced from his second wife, and he already had a son he wasn't able to see. He didn't want another child to become a social pariah because of his illicit behavior. Besides, they both had had sexually transmitted diseases in the past, and the state required a blood test.

Breese was 35 and had been married at least twice before but had not wanted to have a child with either husband, or so she said. But now she wanted one with Robinson because she loved him. She didn't care about Robinson's logic and began ranting, threatening to kill him, then commit suicide. This occurred as they were driving. Robinson said she was selfish and wouldn't be a fit mother because of her criminal record, past and present debauchery, and injudiciousness. This made her more disturbed, and she grabbed the handbrake, pulled it back hard, and almost caused an accident. Finally, she relented and found a Manhattan abortionist who terminated the pregnancy. Their relationship seemed never the same. It appeared that Robinson had inadvertently sown the seeds of his own destruction.

In September, with his father's trial coming up, they decided to find another house where he could hide. They got help from a man named Jack Harris, one of Steve's cohorts. Harris was a former boxer, and he and Breese, representing themselves as man and wife, rented a house in Queens Village. She bought some cheap furniture (it included a punching bag for Harris), and they played ping-pong and pinochle to pass the time.

Steve had not been doing well as a bookmaker and decided to return to the food business; he'd previously run restaurants and was an excellent chef. Robinson, of course, was available to finance him. He'd already given Steve $1,500 for his race track enterprise, and now he kicked in another $3,000 for a restaurant in Knoxille, Tennessee, where Steve had previously been in business.

He explained to Robinson that this would also put him closer to Robinson Sr., and better prepared to get funds to him. The Idle Hour Café opened in the fall, although not long after, Robinson got word that both Steve and Inge were ill and having trouble

Wanted public enemy

Going the limit

Jean Breese found herself a woman apart during the mid-1930s, as her escapades with Thomas Robinson put her in the company of any number of period gun molls such as Billie Frechette (Dillinger's girlfriend), Beulah Baird (Pretty Boy Floyd), and the infamous Bonnie Parker, Clyde Barrow's moll. (Parker was killed by Texas Ranger Frank Hamer, who looked down upon her bullet-riddled form and said without irony, "I hate to bust a cap on a woman, especially when she was sitting down...") Although suffering the label, Breese didn't really seem to possess the attributes of the classic moll.

The term had been around for some time but achieved real popularity in the 1930s with the rise of Depression-era banditry that assumed a romantic aura. While some thought of the moll as merely another hustler, a closer look showed she tended to have her standards: devout, observing in effect the old Italian code of silence, and as one crime writer reported, "the crooked woman is loyal to her man, as a rule, and gets a perverse pleasure out of refusing to answer questions even when she knows the agents have the answer."

💲 Those scandalous women of the 1930s: working the other side of the street.

They were "socially marginal" but they weren't prostitutes, and as one astute observer said, "They imagined a new realm of home and family in an outlaw world that emphasized female honor rather than social obligation, romance rather than domestic security."

So these women, reinventing themselves in a perilous decade that had little use for even their men, gave rise to an adventurous liberation that disturbed the prevailing order. Said one writer, "It is their very familiarity which makes them disturbing. They are uncomfortably ordinary." Jean Breese's ordinariness, though, came from the fact that, at heart, she had few of the virtues of molls like Billie Frechette—but all of the liabilities.

paying the overhead. He forwarded another $500 through Western Union to help them, even as the ransom money continued to dwindle. Another $1,000 was given to Harris for his help in hiding Robinson.

The trial began on October 7, 1935, and Robinson listened to the radio day and night for any news, beside himself and unable to bear the thought that either of them might be convicted.

Mrs. Robinson Jr. with her uncle, Edwin Sears (in middle) and her attorney Clem Huggins.

10 Jekyll or Hyde, on trial in absentia

"He hit me with an iron pipe." —Alice Stoll

By early March 1935, the Division was using the Federal Bureau of Investigation nomenclature on office stationery, even though the new designation wouldn't be official for months. A name change, however, wasn't going to modify the fact that the Division's performance in the Stoll case was less than stellar. It was not the agency's finest hour, and the press was having itself a field day pointing it out.

In one editorial titled "It Comes Of Bungling," in the Memphis *Commerical Appeal*, the paper suggested G-Men not only lost the kidnapper but they lost the money—and none of them knew where to look. Agents were well aware of the mistakes they made, and they knew the pressure was mounting: they had to do a better job with the Robinson fugitive investigation. And surely they would, for in 1934 agents in the field had located 928 federal fugitives. The only problem was that Robinson wasn't one of them.

By this time, they had gathered a tremendous amount of personal information on Robinson Jr., conducting nearly a hundred interviews and compiling a trove of knowledge about his personality, habits, and proclivities. They found Robinson to be a complex personality: spoiled, arrogant, lazy, violent, boastful, and even his own father said he had a Jekyll-and-Hyde personality.

Frances Robinson told agents her husband always bought Hart Schaffner Marx conservative-colored suits off the rack (irregular long). He wore white shirts, gray or dark blue ties, and black oxford shoes. Identification Orders were sent to retailers that sold Robinson's brands, and notices were sent to doctors in Chicago where Robinson had resided, in the off chance he needed treatment for syphilis. Thousands of Identification

💲 The cherubic appearing Robin-son: how looks can deceive.

Orders and wanted flyers of Robinson were circulated to every conceivable outlet: bus stations, amusement parks, transit bureaus, gas stations, telegraph offices, barber shops and beauty parlors.

Hoover was still pondering the reports that Robinson had been seen masquerading as a cross-dresser—two New Yorkers said they'd seen in a Harlem nightclub a woman whose face resembled Robinson's. The G-Men—in spite of their boss—dismissed such reports as frivolous, but Hoover, imagining his quarry gallivanting around the country as "a dashing merry widow," as one report had it, circulated posters with six photos of Robinson, one showing him as a woman. He/she was wearing a "smart turban-type hat placed rakishly upon his permanently-waved wig, and a coat with a higher fur collar concealing the Adam's apple."

The agency even compiled a list of places Robinson might have his Hamilton seventeen-jewel wristwatch repaired and contacted them before distributing copies of the Identification Order to the Hamilton Watch Company itself (and its distributors).

Robinson's picture appeared everywhere, in magazines from the familiar (*Journal of the American Medical Association*) to the obscure (*Masonic Home Journal*), in countless stories and articles, and thousands of leads poured in from across the country, either as walk-ins to FBI offices or through the U.S. mail or telephone contacts.

HOT POTATO

At the time of the Stoll kidnapping, the Louisville Field Office of the Division of Investigation was non-existent. It had been opened in 1924 and closed nine months later when the Indianapolis office opened and began to handle federal law violations in Kentucky. In 1934, however, the Divisions' budget increased, and by 1935 an additional six offices would be added to the existing twenty-four. The Louisville office reopened in June of 1935—a direct result of the Stoll investigation. (Another example, it might be said, in which Robinson Jr. aided the local economy.) Its offices were in the Starks

$ The Starks Building in downtown Louisville, landmark place for a landmark case.

Jekyll or Hyde, on trial in absentia

Building, a fourteen-story downtown landmark, under SAC Orville Dewey, who had an office staff of seven agents and jurisdiction over the entire state.

Thus far, Reinecke and the Indianapolis office had jurisdiction over the Robinson case, but as investigators were fond of saying, "Big cases, big problems; little cases, little problems; no cases, no problems." Given the basic truth of that remark, Reinecke was delighted to get it off his desk, and he didn't waste much time doing so. His file—a thousand-plus pages—was delivered a few days after Dewey's office opened. Given all that had gone wrong—and Hoover's constant irritation at the media, various officials, and his own agents—it had become Reinecke's personal albatross, which he could now hang around Dewey's neck.

On Thursday, October 3, 1935, Frances Robinson arrived for trial in Louisville with her mother, Martha Althauser, and an uncle, Edwin Sears. (A few months before, Frances, her mother, and her young son, Jimmy, had moved about eighteen miles from Nashville to a small house in Pegram, Tennessee, off U.S. 70. It was owned by Sears, who was a mail carrier and lived nearby.) A photographic collage appearing in *The Courier-Journal* showed her smiling. Her father-in-law arrived a few days later, and his attorneys released a statement saying there would be a lot of character witnesses vouching for him. He expected nothing less than a ringing exoneration.

The entourage of lawyers for the Robinsons was so large it seemed there might not be any room at the defense table for the defendants. There was Clement "Clem" William Huggins, representing Mrs. Robinson Jr. He was a graduate of the University of Louisville Law School, a colorful orator, and at the top of his lawyerly game. He was the elder statesman of the defense, scarred and decorated from previous combat. *The Herald-Post* described his role as that of a sniper, his shots forcing the prosecution to keep their heads down. He never missed a chance to object or interject, which made them wary. The papers described him as "pink, abiding, and jovial, with a preference for pearl gray suits." It was his last big case, and he wanted a good send-off, for his client, of course, but also for himself.

Robinson Sr.'s lead attorney was Montague "Monte" S. Ross, who had been the Nashville city attorney and ran for Congress in the 1930s as a Democrat. Ross, with a flair for the dramatic, said his client was "innocent as a newborn baby." (How the evening ladies back in Nashville must have smiled at that.) He was described as "a spare, pale man with a thin, bitter mouth and confused black hair." His physical presence was startlingly energetic, for he might fling his hands to the ceiling, use his forefinger as an exclamation point, and pirouette like a dancer. His voice was a bit harsh, but his occa-

The G-men and the Heiress

sional smile, wrote the *Herald-Post*, "has the effect of a magical illusion. Until it actually appears, you wonder if it could, and when it has gone, you wonder if it did."

There was Ira Maynard Tipps, a University of Tennessee graduate who during WWII would serve in the U.S. Army Legal Divison, and Ewing Cannon Baskette, lawyer and librarian who would own the largest private collection on civil liberties and freedom of expression in the United States. Another was Jack Norman, from Nashville, bright and handsome with great appeal to the motherly types in the gallery (as well as their daughters). The athlete of the team was Charles Akin "Slim" Embry, a one-time pitcher for the St. Louis Browns who traded his glove for a law degree and another Vanderbilt graduate.

 Mrs. Alice Stoll, representing Kentucky's best pioneer stock—and herself.

TRIAL (AND ERROR)

On October 7, 1935, the trial opened on schedule with Judge Elwood Hamilton, new on the bench—and soon to be elevated to the United States Court of Appeals for the 6th Circuit by President Roosevelt—determined to stay on schedule and instituting night sessions to speed things along.

The twelve jurors were middle-aged men, mostly from small cities and towns in Western Kentucky, and among them were a blacksmith, a postmaster, more than one farmer, and a bank president. Alice Stoll testified for an hour and a half in the afternoon of the first day—three days shy of the anniversary of her kidnapping. She appeared as stylish as she usually did (discounting the kidnapping itself when Robinson Jr. dragged her out of her house in little more than a kimono). She was wearing a brown turban, a grayish wool suit, a velvet blouse, and brown gloves, and she related the events of her traumatic occasion as she might have been narrating a museum house tour.

A *Courier-Journal* columnist wrote that she spoke in a clear, unhesitant tone, "in a dignified manner that made you remember she comes from Kentucky's best pioneer

Pulp Fiction

Tom Robinson's favorite reading material, the pulp magazines of the 1930s, had a great run, from early in the century until they were eclipsed by WWII paper shortages, the rise of comic books, and the advent of television. And while their basic readership was largely "the socially and economically marginal," they attracted a vagabond audience that was said to include President Harry Truman, Al Capone, and even J. Edgar Hoover himself, who wrote the occasional editorial for *G-Men Detective*.

$ The shameless pulps of the 1930s helped build the FBI's reputation.

There were several "G-Man" titles—*Ace G-Man Stories*, the Special Agent Dan Fowler stories of *G-Men* ("four new gun-blazing cases!"), and one called simply *Feds*. *G-Men* was first out of the gate, cashing in on the rising popularity of Hoover's agents and a boon to the new agency, its jazzy covers featuring lantern-jawed feds, ties askew, blazing away at various public enemies.

Robinson had found them when they were at the peak of their popularity, for in 1934 there may have been as many as 150 titles, and the best of them might sell a million copies an issue. They were pure expediency, their highly acidic paper so cheap they were yellowing while still on the newsstand. The edges were untrimmed, there were no illustrations, and no color except the cover which often featured a damsel in distress (who appeared to be distraught while looking for her bra).

Writers were paid by the word and like Robinson himself, used a panoply of aliases. (Upton Sinclair was said to write 8,000 words a day while employing two stenographers.) They left behind an indelible mark, relentlessly shaping all the popular cultural forms. Or as one writer felicitously observed, "their purple blood runs in the veins of every hero of film, television, and paperbacks, and the pulp magazines have proven to be the wellspring of the American mythology."

The G-men and the Heiress

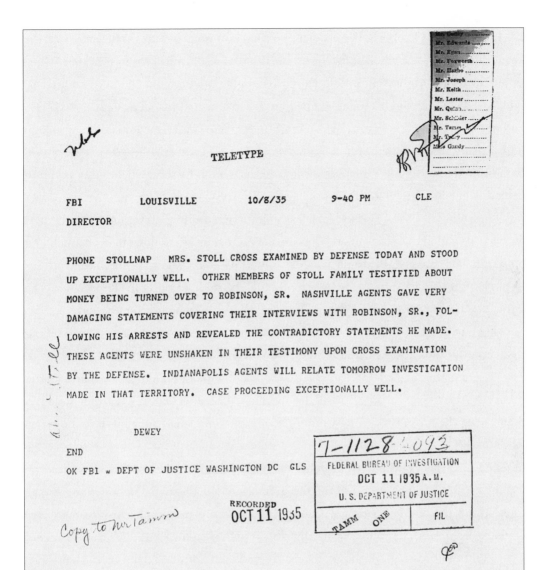

TELETYPE

FBI   LOUISVILLE   10/8/35   9-40 PM   CLE

DIRECTOR

PHONE STOLLNAP   MRS. STOLL CROSS EXAMINED BY DEFENSE TODAY AND STOOD
UP EXCEPTIONALLY WELL. OTHER MEMBERS OF STOLL FAMILY TESTIFIED ABOUT
MONEY BEING TURNED OVER TO ROBINSON, SR. NASHVILLE AGENTS GAVE VERY
DAMAGING STATEMENTS COVERING THEIR INTERVIEWS WITH ROBINSON, SR., FOL-
LOWING HIS ARRESTS AND REVEALED THE CONTRADICTORY STATEMENTS HE MADE.
THESE AGENTS WERE UNSHAKEN IN THEIR TESTIMONY UPON CROSS EXAMINATION
BY THE DEFENSE. INDIANAPOLIS AGENTS WILL RELATE TOMORROW INVESTIGATION
MADE IN THAT TERRITORY. CASE PROCEEDING EXCEPTIONALLY WELL.

          DEWEY

END

OK FBI w DEPT OF JUSTICE WASHINGTON DC GLS

7-1128-4093
FEDERAL BUREAU OF INVESTIGATION
OCT 11 1935 A.M.
U. S. DEPARTMENT OF JUSTICE
TAMM   ONE   FIL

RECORDED
OCT 11 1935

Copy to Mr Tamm

$ Teletype giving Hoover an agent's eye view of the trial's progress.

stock." Describing the scene in her bedroom that day, she said—calmly and perfectly composed—"He hit me with an iron pipe." Then he forced her into the back seat of his car and covered her with newspapers and a blanket. She said she was eager to go with her captor because she was afraid that Robinson would kill her husband, who was soon to arrive home.

Once in the Indianapolis apartment where she was held, she even made scrambled eggs for Robinson, her attempt, she said, to keep the mercurial Robinson on an even keel. Thus her existence settled into a bizarre parody of domesticity, that is, if your domestic life included intervals of being tied up and locked in a closet.

Jekyll or Hyde, on trial in absentia

On Tuesday, October 8, the prosecution used testimony by SAC William Rorer, the former head of the Nashville office, to show discrepancies in Robinson Sr.'s statements. In one interview, Robinson Sr. told Rorer his son had an automobile but in another he said he did not. He said his son could be found at either the Lincoln or Claypool Hotels, and never mentioned the North Meridian Street hideout Apartment location, although he'd already drawn a diagram of it. Agent Murry C. Falkner testified that Robinson Sr. admitted to receiving a telephone call from his son on October 15, another fact he'd denied to agents in previous interviews.

The young defense attorney, Jack Norman, at one point gave an eloquent rebuttal for what he called the government's circumstantial evidence. "I don't believe any living human outside an asylum would have permitted his crazy son to name him as an intermediary if he had an agreement beforehand," he said, wagging his forefinger at the jurors and bending over for emphasis, his voice ringing through the courtroom.

Then he pleaded for Mrs. Robinson's innocence: "No woman, unless she was telling the truth, the facts as they actually were, would have stood up under such a barrage as was leveled on her by Federal agents at the hospital, without breaking down and telling the truth," he shouted. "They blame her because she succeeded in what they failed to do—saving the life of this young woman," pointing to the chair previously occupied by Alice Stoll.

The next day, Wednesday, October 9, agent John Madala testified about finding five magazines during a search of the Indianapolis hideout apartment: *Sensational Kidnap Cases, Master Detective, Real Detective, Startling Detective,* and *Screenplay*. They were, it seemed obvious, Robinson's handbooks on what to do and not do in pulling off a successful caper, and the prosecution said as much. (New York City mayor Jimmy Walker once said, "No woman was ever ruined by a book," which is generally accepted as a truism, but Alice Stoll might have had her own thoughts about how much harm a pulp magazine might cause a girl.)

If nothing else, the collection of magazines showed the disconnect between Robinson and the world most people actually lived in—and consulting the Hare Psychopathy checklist, we find the item, "Do you lack realistic long-term goals?" The Thomas Robinson Jr. National Library of Kidnapping would, no doubt, consist of mostly pulp magazines of the 1930s.

The G-men and the Heiress

Gangbuster

Special Agent John "Johnny" Madala said at the inquest that it was purely accidental when Inspector Samuel Cowley and Agent Herman Hollis came upon the vehicle occupied by Baby Face Nelson, his wife, and John Paul Chase; the agents were not even surveilling them at the time. But such happenstance led to the death of both agents, as well as Nelson.

When Cowley and Hollis encountered Nelson outside Barrington, Illinois, all parties recognized each other and a gun battle ensued. A fusillade of gunfire hit both agents; Nelson was also shot. Hollis died there, Nelson died that night, and Cowley died the next morning. ("Nothing would bring Nelson down," he told Purvis before he died.) Something had, though, and the incident became famously known as the Battle of Barrington.

Madala also testified at the 1935 trial of the seven charged in the kidnapping of Edward Bremer, and one subject, James Wilson, claimed that Madala and agent Ralph Brown elicited a confession by hammering it out of him on the ninth floor of the FBI office in Chicago, leaving him with a perforated eardrum. The agents denied the charge, and the judge ruled in their favor.

BEHIND THE SCENES AT GARDEN STATE
John Madala learned his job with Uncle Sam

John Madala, Safety Director at Garden State Park, is a graduate of the world's greatest detective school—Uncle Sam's own F.B.I. It's his job to direct the men who watch over your safety and protect your property while you enjoy a day of sport at the track. Director Madala and his men also cooperate closely with the Thoroughbred Racing Protective Bureau, racing's own nation-wide organization of former F.B.I. men set up to help management protect the public. The T.R.P.B. is the greatest self-policing effort in the history of sport.

FIRST POST-TIME 2 P.M.
DAILY DOUBLE CLOSES 1:40

Racing PLANNED FOR PLEASURE

GARDEN STATE PARK ROUTE 40, NEAR CAMDEN
TRAINS AND BUSES DIRECT TO TRACK

§ Johnny Madala appears in advertisements as safety director at Garden State Park.

Hungarian-born, Madala grew up on the south side of Chicago, graduated from Fenger High School, then attended Illinois University. In 1930 he began a fifteen-year career with the FBI as a file clerk, becoming ultimately Assistant SAC in the Miami office. He left the FBI in 1946 to become safety director at Garden State Park racetrack in Cherryhill, New Jersey, where he was known for being tough on track hustlers, con artists, and pickpockets.

The job was also tough on him, for in 1959, he was shot at the front gate of the Hialeah Race Track in Miami by Maxim Gay, a tip sheet seller barred from the premises. Gay, using a silver-plated .38 revolver, shot Madala three times in full view of track patrons. Badly injured, Madala still finished, spending nearly another quarter of a century at the tracks before dying suddenly in 1983.

Jekyll or Hyde, on trial in absentia

PURVIS: ACE INVESTIGATOR

On that same Wednesday morning, the defense called former SAC Purvis as a witness, and the judge consented. Purvis had talked with both women, and the defense was probably angling to find sympathy evoked by Alice Stoll for Frances Robinson. This, of course, would accrue favorably to Mrs. Robinson. It was also precisely what the prosecution feared. It did not want the slightest amount of sympathy for her.

Hoover was already highly doubtful about Purvis testifying at all. He had resigned from the agency in July, most likely because of Hoover, who was jealous of Purvis's popularity with the press (after he and his men killed John Dillinger the year before, Purvis got marriage proposals in the mail), and Hoover was increasingly critical of him.

The Director was, as usual, concerned about saving face, and he blamed Purvis for losing track of Mrs. Robinson in a midnight train station when she was on her way to Indianapolis with the ransom money. Yet the Division's policy was to "surveil loosely," and if the intermediary suspected she was being followed, then break it off. Hoover wrote in the margins of one memorandum, "We lost the woman at the time, and it was due to Purvis's inefficiency in handling it…"

Now Hoover was concerned that if the attorneys interviewed Purvis about his testimony ahead of time, they could get accused of tampering with a witness. If the other side brought him in, it would give the defense the benefit—and the appearance of "a sort of a halo around Purvis's head." Hoover wrote in the margin of one memorandum, "Of course we won't interview Purvis as he could and probably would write an article on our attempts to tamper with him…He should be called by the defense. Facts are facts, and if he distorts them, then testimony of the truth can be introduced."

A subpoena for Purvis's testimony, though, had already been issued. The U.S. Marshal in Chicago had telephoned the Chicago FBI office to obtain Purvis's home telephone number. "This is outrageous," Hoover wrote, again in the margins of another memorandum. "It looks to me as if Purvis has the U.S. Attorney and our men at Louisville completely on the run."

When Purvis came into the courtroom on Thursday, several of the agents approached him and greeted him warmly. He testified for no more than fifteen minutes, all of it favorable to the government. It demonstrated that Purvis was a better man than Hoover gave him credit for, and it made Hoover look even more self-serving than usual.

Mrs. Robinson, in her testimony, denied any prior knowledge of the conspiracy; she said she learned from her father-in-law that her husband was the kidnapper, and

Erased from the record

They called Melvin Purvis "Little Mel" because he was short (5-foot-4) and slight, but that overlooked his personality, which was anything but small. He made his bones on some of the biggest man-hunts of the 1930s decade: Baby Face Nelson, John Dillinger, and Pretty Boy Floyd. The press loved him, and in late 1934, after his men killed Baby Face Nelson in a furious shootout, *Literary Digest* named him one of the ten outstanding personalities in the world.

The boss man, Hoover, had made Purvis, at age 27, special agent in charge of the Cincinnati bureau—his youngest office chief, and in 1932 he was transferred to Chicago. He was smart, hard-working, and through the media readers saw what his secretary, Doris Rogers, saw: "a dapper and elegant dresser, a soft spoken gentleman, charming, young, and handsome."

Charm, though, was not high on Hoover's list of notable agent attributes. And neither was publicity. In a sense, Purvis's personality—and Hoover's almost irrational antagonism to a man who was perhaps one of his best agents—became his undoing. He seemed unable to stay out of the headlines, and he never got out of the doghouse after losing Frances Robinson in a midnight train station. There were extenuating circumstances but Hoover remained irate. "We lost the woman at the time, and it was due to Purvis's inefficiency in handling it," he wrote.

Not long after the safe return of Alice Stoll, Purvis was gone. He was a colonel in WWII, practiced law, and ran a radio station, and he stayed loyal to the agency. Not so, the agency. Hoover seemed to do everything in his power to erase Purvis from the agency record, and his name failed to appear once in the Bureau's authorized history.

He died mysteriously in 1960 by a gunshot wound that was either suicide or an accident (it appeared he could have been trying to remove a tracer round from a .45). It was an unkind ending yet softened by the many book and movie treatments, most of which hailed his career, both with Hoover and without him.

💲 *Et tu*, Hoover? The truth becomes legend.

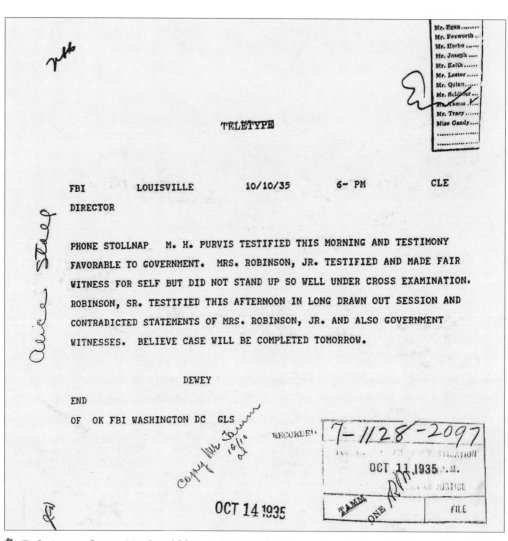

TELETYPE

FBI   LOUISVILLE   10/10/35   6- PM   CLE

DIRECTOR

PHONE STOLLNAP M. H. PURVIS TESTIFIED THIS MORNING AND TESTIMONY
FAVORABLE TO GOVERNMENT. MRS. ROBINSON, JR. TESTIFIED AND MADE FAIR
WITNESS FOR SELF BUT DID NOT STAND UP SO WELL UNDER CROSS EXAMINATION.
ROBINSON, SR. TESTIFIED THIS AFTERNOON IN LONG DRAWN OUT SESSION AND
CONTRADICTED STATEMENTS OF MRS. ROBINSON, JR. AND ALSO GOVERNMENT
WITNESSES. BELIEVE CASE WILL BE COMPLETED TOMORROW.

                    DEWEY

END

OF OK FBI WASHINGTON DC GLS

RECORDED 7-1128-2097

OCT 11 1935

OCT 14 1935

$ Teletype from Louisville SAC to Director Hoover, October 10, 1935.

everything she did from then on was to assist Mrs. Stoll's release. She never discussed the kidnapping with her husband, she said. She didn't hold up well under cross-examination by Oldham Clarke, who asked her why she moved to Chicago with her husband. "I can't say," she said, then slumped back in the witness chair and began to cry, unable to continue.

The judge tried to move things along by telling her she could inform him, but counsel said she needed to speak to the jury. Weeping, she tried explaining that she always wanted her husband to be successful, even when he was spiteful, or choked her—even shooting her above the knee with a handgun. She was unable to fully answer the question. Finally she said, "I went to Chicago to try to give him a new life. I suppose I loved him."

$

THE VERDICT

On Saturday, October 12, the judge gave defense and prosecution three hours each to present closing arguments to the jury. Attorney Clarke opened arguments with a fifty-five minute summary of the government's case, which included more than half a dozen reasons attesting to Robinson Sr.'s guilt. Clarke did the same with Frances Robinson, providing seven points towards *her* guilt.

Then the defense came on, with Monte Ross performing as himself, complete with various dramatizations, concluding with Ross's poetic parody of Hoover's G-Men, spoofing the hunt for Robinson Jr., and the number of men employed by the case.

Forward the G Brigade,
Headlines their names displayed,
Pompous in gay parade,
They strutted and blundered.
Tyros appearing sly,
They never made reply
What they meant or why—
None of the six hundred.

The jurors received the case at 4 p.m. and deliberated nearly six hours. With over a hundred spectators waiting for a verdict and the evening nearing an end, they found themselves deadlocked, at which time they adjourned to the Brown Hotel until 9 a.m. the next day. On Sunday morning, the judge said, "I hope you had a good night's rest. If you need me at any time, call me." After another hour and a half of deliberation, the jurors simply wanted to go home.

Before they returned, however, the judge calmly gave instructions to the courtroom spectators. He wanted everyone quiet and orderly, and he suggested the courtroom be treated as a sacred place; no undue emotion would be tolerated, and anyone violating his policy would be cited for contempt. When the twelve men had formed a semi-circle around his raised wooden desk, the judge asked, "Have you reached a verdict?"

"Your honor," replied foreman Louis Bauer, "we have."

He walked toward the bench and handed the clerk a piece of paper. Mrs. Robinson Jr. was biting her lip and turned her head towards her mother, then back to the clerk. When the not guilty verdict was read, she buried her face in her handkerchief.

Jekyll or Hyde, on trial in absentia

ESTABLISHED 1896

STOLL OIL REFINING CO.

INCORPORATED

·REFINERS and MARKETERS·

PETROLEUM PRODUCTS

·REFINERY AND GENERAL OFFICES AT LOUISVILLE·

227 WEST MAIN ST.

LOUISVILLE, KY.

October 15, 1935

ADDRESS ALL COMMUNICATIONS
TO THE COMPANY

FOR ATTENTION OF

Berry V. Stoll

Mr. Harold Nathan
Federal Bureau of Investigation
Department of Justice
Washington, D. C.

Dear Mr. Nathan:

When anything goes wrong in our organization, I never
worry much about it but worry a great deal about preventing it from happening again.

Being only a layman, I hesitate to make suggestions to
an expert, but I have sat on a number of juries and wish
to make the following suggestion: The Department of
Justice should put out a book of instructions to judges
in instructing juries, or for fear that I be ruled in
contempt of court, I would term it a book of definitions
of legal phraseology, so that the ordinary, average juror
could understand it.

First, I would define reasonable doubt as follows:
when a juror feels that the odds are 98% reason and
2% doubt, that is not enough to be called reasonable
doubt; when the odds are 50% either way, that would be
a little more than reasonable doubt and the benefit should
be given to the defendant.

Second, I would define circumstantial evidence as being
like a rope or a wire cable made up of a number of small
cords and interwoven; and while one cord in itself would
not be strong enough to convict, as it would not be
stout enough to carry the weight of the evidence, yet
a number of such small cords woven together into a rope
would make a strong and substantial rope, each bit of
circumstantial evidence being one small cord, and the
rope would be strong enough to support the evidence of guilt.

VISCOYL
MOTOR OIL

GOLDEN TIP
ETHYL

GOLDEN TIP

RECORDED
NOV 1 1935

7-1128-2169

OCT 1935

INVESTIGATION

JUSTICE

ALL QUOTATIONS SUBJECT TO PRIOR SALE AND IMMEDIATE ACCEPTANCE AND CHANGE WITHOUT NOTICE. UNLESS ACCEPTED. NOT RESPON-
SIBLE FOR INABILITY TO SHIP DUE TO FIRE, FLOOD, STRIKES, FAILURE OF THE USUAL SOURCES OF SUPPLIES OR MATERIALS, OR OTHER
CAUSES BEYOND THE CONTROL OF EITHER PARTY. UNLESS OTHERWISE SPECIFIED ALL QUOTATIONS MADE F. O. B. LOUISVILLE REFINERY

$ Berry Stoll dissects court proceedings in letter to the FBI.

"So say all you gentlemen?" asked the clerk.

Foreman Bauer nodded vigorously and gave the clerk a small salute.

"Thank God," said Robinson Sr., his eyes full of tears. He seemed aware of how close he had come to conviction, a notion validated by one juror who, afterward, talked to Berry Stoll about the case, saying that had Robinson Sr. been tried separately, he would have been unanimously convicted. The disagreement among jurors was that two of the jurors would not convict him unless Mrs. Robinson was *also* convicted.

Two other jurors thought that Mrs. Robinson "was not the kind of woman to do this unless she were forced to do so." These two thought she was "entirely too nice-looking to be a very bad woman in any way," thereby implying cosmetic surgery might be useful as a defense strategy.

Unable to reach any other accord, the jurors simply freed them both. There was no doubt, however, that Robinson Sr. owed his daughter-in-law his freedom. No one—except the Robinsons—would know whether she was a consummate actress or was actually telling the truth.

"Please let me go home," Mrs. Robinson said as photographers pressed around her at the entrance to the Federal Building. "I am so tired."

Berry Stoll gave credit to the FBI and the prosecutors for their efforts but didn't believe justice got served, and neither did Hoover's men, who'd just taken another shot. The two people prosecutors felt certain were Robinson's confederates had just been found not guilty, and Robinson himself was still nowhere in sight.

Justice, it seemed to them, wasn't blind; sometimes it was simply cross-eyed.

TWA
THE
LINDBERGH LINE

TWA

G-MEN SEIZE KIDNAPER OF ALICE STOLL

Thomas H. Robinson, Jr., Is Captured in Glendale, California

LAST OF THE 'RATS'

Hoover Announces Success of Drive Against Public Enemies

G-Men seize Robinson; the cross-country odyssey ends at long last.

11 Lovebirds on the lam

"Betrayal and dishonor is usually an inside job."
—T.F. Hodge

Robinson would say that he went through pure torture while hovering over the radio, waiting for news of the trial. It was something he never wanted to experience again. When the not-guilty results finally arrived by a radio news flash, Robinson was ecstatic. He would tell the FBI in 1937 if his father had been convicted, he would have surrendered to provide new evidence for a second trial, which seemed self-serving. (See, once again, the Hare Psychopathy checklist: "psychopaths don't care about the truth.")

Robinson wanted to head back west, but first he wanted to give his father money to help his financial situation. Before the trial, Steve—then living in Knoxville—drove to Nashville and, through a prearranged third party, met Robinson Sr. on a streetcar and gave him $250. They arranged that Robinson Sr., if found not guilty at his trial, would visit his son in New York. He would meet Jean Breese at the Thomas Jefferson Hotel in Richmond, Virginia, under the name "Miss Holbrook," where she would be waiting from November 5-8.

On November 5, Robinson Sr. met Breese at her hotel, and they drove in Robinson's Plymouth back to New York City. Father and son hadn't seen each other for more than a year, and tears flowed on both sides. Robinson Sr. thought he would never again see his son alive, and he needed two bromides to calm himself. It was a happy reunion.

Unfortunately for Robinson, their get-together turned maudlin when Senior became intoxicated. Robinson worried that if his father went on an alcohol bender, he might wash away any money given to him. He knew of Senior's habit of lavish spending

135

when he had a snootful. Robinson decided it was better to give his father only a smaller amount—$500 sewn in his underwear—for the trip back to Nashville. (Mrs. Robinson Sr. later told the FBI that when Senior arrived back in Nashville, he didn't have the $500; and there was no explanation about what happened to it.)

In early December of 1935, Robinson Sr. contacted the chief deputy of the U.S. Marshals office in Nashville to facilitate the surrender of his son. He said his motive was his son's safety and the return of the ransom money. Perhaps this might get Junior into a mental hospital instead of a prison. (Senior may have had his eye on a cash reward, as well.) The marshal asked how long it would take. Robinson said it might be a matter of days or longer.

He told the marshal that for over a year the FBI had him under surveillance, and it would depend upon whether he could lose them. (If the agency *was* tailing Senior, they weren't doing a very good job of it, because they hadn't noticed he'd just met his son in New York.) The FBI had a rather unflattering portrait of Senior in its files, where he was described as square-jawed, with thin grayish-brown hair and stooped shoulders. The file said he had a dissipated look, like that of a heavy drinker.

Robinson Sr. and his attorneys made other overtures to both police and the FBI. Robinson's attorney Monte Ross met with the FBI, asking for a written guarantee that neither he nor Senior would be charged with harboring. The FBI declined. Desperate by now, the agency would have worked with almost anyone, and its refusal to work with Senior was a testament to the amount of distrust—and enmity—it had for the Robinsons. Not surprisingly, agents still had wiretaps on the office and home of Senior, as well as attorneys Ross, Jack Norman, and Charles Embry.

On November 12, Robinson Jr. and his paramour, Breese, left New York City, driving west. They met his mother in St. Louis, bringing her to a studio apartment they'd rented for the occasion. (The visit had been prearranged during his father's visit to New York.) Mrs. Robinson Sr. was glad to see her son, but Junior thought she hadn't fared well under the strain of events around her. She was happy to help cook for them during their short visit, and he told her he was going west to buy a ranch, and he would send for her and his father.

Junior washed money ($4,000) with soap and water to remove any fingerprints and hung it on the bathroom mirror to dry; his mother was fascinated by it all. But when he told her it was for her, she was shocked and didn't want to take it. When he showed her that he had plenty of money left for himself—and wouldn't have to commit another crime—she appeared relieved and agreed to accept it, sewing it into her corset. (She later told the FBI that she funneled a majority of the $4,000 back to Breese, thinking it was for her son's legal defense.)

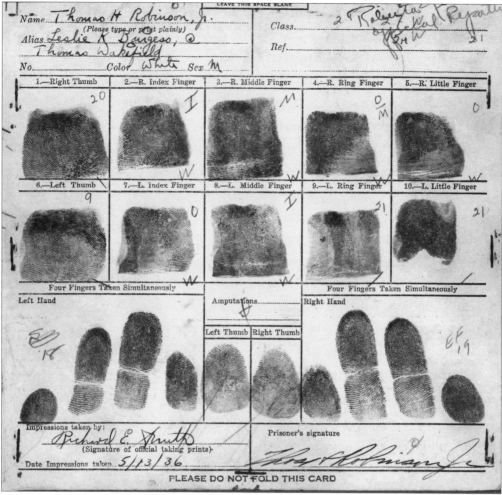

$ Thomas Robinson: leaving his fingerprints behind him.

In Junior's mind, his parents' house would now be safe from foreclosure, and the rest of the money was payment for all the grief he'd caused them. Mother and son had four days together, a short visit to keep family members (and the authorities) from questioning her short absence. He kissed her, and Breese walked her to the train station. Half a block away, she turned towards him, both waving. His mother then turned to Breese and said, "I've lost my boy." It was a prophetic statement: fathers know best, but the real wisdom belongs to mothers.

$

TOMMY TWO HATS

The couple left St. Louis on Saturday, November 23, heading west on Route 66. In New Mexico they met William Warner, a broker working for a St. Paul Bank, and they started looking at land around Tyrone, a small town of less than two hundred people. During a four-day stay, Warner took them to see a ranch on the upper Gila River, which had a twenty-room ranch house and several hundred acres.

After the showing, they drove thirty miles southeast to the Silver City Elks Club bar for cocktails where they met the sheriff of Silver City, Owen "Slim" Matthews, a towering picturesque westerner in cowboy boots. There, they also met the visiting Tucson police chief, Christopher A. Wollard. The drinks were flowing, the party lively, and Breese took Wollard's stetson and placed it on Robinson's head. She wanted to see how Robinson looked wearing the ten-gallon hat of the lawman who once caught John Dillinger. (Wollard was in charge when Dillinger got nabbed in Tucson in January of 1934 after firemen at a hotel fire identified Dillinger by checking his photograph in *True Detective Mysteries* magazine and called the police. It was such an event in Tucson that for years, the gang's guns were on display at the police department, and a jar full of gum chewed by Dillinger is still part of a University of Arizona collection.)

It wasn't the smartest move by Breese, but once again Robinson had walked among his possible captors and come away unscathed; his immense good fortune remained uncannily in place. Still, he was shaken by the incident and left town quickly, without retrieving the $300 deposit placed with Warner on the Upper Gila ranch land. His plan of growing alfalfa, raising chickens and cattle, and building a kennel so Breese could raise dogs proved fleeting.

Heading back to Los Angeles, they stopped at an Arizona border patrol station at Duncan, a town of over a thousand, where they saw wanted flyers on the building, including a prominent one of Robinson. Back in California, they rented a house in Van Nuys for $45 a month, on a hillside overlooking the San Fernando Valley. They bought maps of California, Oregon, and Washington. Breese went to the Department of Agriculture and obtained brochures on poultry breeding. She bought books about breeding dogs and read publications on growing fruit. Robinson sent away for a correspondence course in agriculture and placed an ad in the *Los Angeles Examiner* about the kind of ranch he wanted. A quarter of a century later, they might have appeared as a couple of hippies on a back-to-the-earth jag.

Then Breese became pregnant and, all over again, they had the same arguments about having a child. Breese worked herself into hysterics, and Robinson finally called Dr. Gerald Sprague, who gave her a complete examination and said Breese would not be able to bring the baby to term—she had too many adhesions from a previous operation.

The G-men and the Heiress

Breese refused to accept Sprague's view and one evening, after a heated exchange, she told Robinson he was a sucker if he thought she was going to move to some "wild and woolly" place. She wasn't interested in sharing his dream and wanted them to move back to New York City, where she could be near her friends. She had also begun to use morphine.

They had purchased two .25 caliber handguns, and Breese had one under the pillow of the chair she was sitting on that evening. She pulled the weapon and threatened to kill both of them. Robinson grabbed her, they struggled for the gun, and he finally managed to get it from her, locking it in a strongbox. Dr. Sprague was called back to the house and gave her a shot of morphine.

Robinson wanted her to see an abortionist in Hollywood, one of the best in the area, but she refused. She was going to have the child with or without him. Robinson finally told her she could have the child if having it might restore whatever feelings she previously had for him. But Dr. Sprague's earlier diagnosis proved accurate: she lost the baby. "A just God must have presided over the destiny of the child which Jean had conceived," Robinson would say afterward.

$

A COOL BREESE

Breese, wanting to get away, took a Union Pacific train to New York City to visit her sister where Robinson wrote her, begging her to come back. For whatever reason, Breese decided to return. In early February of 1936, she did. But Robinson was drinking again and indiscriminately running around Los Angeles and Hollywood with gamblers, bookmakers, and nightclub owners. She demanded they move to a new residence, and they moved south into Los Angeles where Breese bought an Old English Sheepdog which, she explained, she could use for breeding purposes when they had their ranch.

The dog was female, weighing around seventy pounds, and Robinson allowed Breese to spoil it. (Perhaps it was from a sense of guilt over her lost baby.) It slept in their bed, on the sofa, and chewed up expensive shoes and clothing. He thought the dog shouldn't have the run of the house, with access only to the porch, kitchen, basement, and yard. Breese accused him of mistreating the animal, and the deterioration of their relationship appeared to continue unrelieved.

A month later, they moved again, to Manhattan Beach where they were now the Milners. While there may have been a sense of forbidden freedom to a life of the perpetual quick exit, it was also taking a toll on their nerves. One evening they heard a police siren in front of their house, and Breese saw two uniformed cops confronting a man. She

Lovebirds on the lam

woke the sleeping Robinson and, thinking his arrest was imminent, he loaded one of his handguns. He was headed outside but Breese persuaded him not to. The police left the area, but Robinson felt that maybe their location was under surveillance.

Breese wanted Robinson to either get California plates for the Plymouth sedan or—in case it was too hot to drive—sell it. They were concerned that the authorities in New Mexico might have seen the plates and passed the numbers along to the FBI. When the new plates arrived, Robinson hired a messenger to go to the postal box, then saw a black sedan pulling to the curb, certain it was coming for him. It wasn't. Not this time, anyway. The pulp crime magazines he was always reading may have given him some instruction in how to pull off a kidnapping, but they tended to emphasize the same moral instruction, which was that crime didn't pay. (It *did* pay, of course, but Hoover's G-Men were making serious inroads into its wages.) And the life Robinson had chosen had created for him a claustrophobic sense of paranoia.

Early in 1936, the FBI publicity machine wasn't saying much about the Stoll/Robinson criminal investigation, only providing an occasional remark that the case was on-going. (There was simply no positive spin that could be applied to a manhunt that had been going on for well over a year.) When Robinson wasn't feeling paranoid, he must have been delighted at his fame, for he was being seen all over America. Sightings came from the Atlantic seaboard to the Pacific Ocean, the Gulf of Mexico to the Canadian border.

He had turned up in an Ontario hotel; a Lima, Ohio, garage; and in airports on the West Coast where he was trying to catch a liner for the Orient. He was seen hitchhiking in Tennessee and Pennsylvania, and a counterman had served him in Buffalo. The international bridges at Port Erie and Niagara Falls were guarded and every auto scanned. And yet, Thomas Robinson Jr. remained a ghost.

The Robinson case, said a Tulsa newspaper, "was one of the strangest on record." The paper also pointed out that even though Robinson had once been judged mentally unbalanced, he was the only kidnapper who'd managed to avoid what it called the G-Men's "vigil." Said the article, "They know his name. They have his picture. They have everything but Robinson." Woe betide the poor agent who brought Hoover *that* particular copy of the *Tulsa Daily World*.

$

WANTED: EXPERIENCED AGENTS

In March, Director Hoover sent a letter relating to the Hamm, Bremer, Weyerhaeuser, and Stoll kidnapping cases to all FBI Special Agents in Charge. He addressed the prac-

The G-men and the Heiress

Public Creep Number One

What's in a name? Alvin Karpis said the cops gave him his nick-name of "Old Creepy" or just "Creepy." More than likely, it was those that knew him best, the fellow Barker-Karpis gang members who provided the handle because he walked stealthily like a cat and had an eerie laugh. By the age of ten, he was consorting with pimps and bootleggers and moved up from there.

$ Alvin Karpis, 1539, whose number was up.

Joining the criminal "Bloody Barkers," the asso-ciation created one of the most menacing gangs of the era, robbing banks and mail deliveries, kidnapping, and caring little about the collateral damage they left behind. Their first bank job was in a sleepy Missouri town and they got away with $7,000, sprink-ling the road with two-inch roofing tacks as they passed.

Their turn to kidnapping, though, would prove their undoing, and eighteen agents were at the scene of his apprehension in New Orleans. There were two versions: The FBI said Hoover reached into Karpis's car and grabbed him before he could reach a rifle in the back seat. The other version—which was Karpis's—said Hoover only came out after he'd already been grabbed by the other agents. For all his braggadocio at being a tough guy, Karpis sang like a bird. When asked by the Washington press if he led the arrest, Hoover replied: "I did, but it was a 'we' job and not an 'I' job."

Karpis continued to aggravate Hoover by saying that he alone had made the reputation of Hoover and the Bureau, a narcissist (and sociopath) to the very end. But he was the last of the big-name gangsters of the Depression and his capture ended the Public Enemy era.

Karpis would spend twenty-six years at Alcatraz, its lon-gest-serving inmate. In 1969 he was paroled and deported to his native Canada, then moved to Spain. He died in 1979, age 72, of ei-ther natural causes, suicide, or murder, depending on the source, and he left, no doubt, with the sinister smile still on his face.

tice of offices assigning leads in important matters to their newest agents. He wanted the method stopped because, he said, these agents didn't have enough investigative experience.

Perhaps it was coincidence but in May of 1936, over eleven days, agents captured the fugitives responsible for the Hamm, Bremer, and Weyerhaeuser kidnapping cases. Alvin Karpis, the last of the big-name Depression-era Public Enemy Number Ones, was arrested on May 1 in New Orleans, wanted for the Hamm and Bremer matters. On May 7, William Dainard was grabbed by agents in San Francisco for his part in the Weyerhaeuser kidnapping. On the same day, agents caught Harry Campbell, a Barker-Karpis gang member. The G-Men had arrived at an apartment in Toledo, Ohio, rented by a Campbell under an alias. He never got to the .45- caliber Colt automatic under his pillow. Karpis would plead guilty and receive a sentence of life at Alcatraz. Campbell acknowledged guilt in the Bremer kidnapping and received the same penalty. Dainard received two concurrent sixty-year sentences, housed first at a mental hospital, then at Alcatraz.

$

O WHAT A TANGLED WEB

Robinson's life on the lam was what he had made of it, and he enjoyed himself for much of it. But he was still a wanted man, always suspicious, imagining the G-Men were one step behind, when unbeknownst to him they hadn't been close. Yet in his mind, he knew it was just a matter of time. He was apprehensive and couldn't sleep, and even Breese thought he needed some kind of professional mental health assistance.

In the first week of May, 1936, a telephone call gave the FBI its first big break in the case. Breese wouldn't initially provide her name, address, or telephone number, but she told Los Angeles agent Murray Meyerson she was residing with Robinson in the Los Angeles area. She said she'd become afraid of him, that he was heavily armed, and had said if apprehended he'd resist. She would give specific information only under appropriate circumstances, afraid of being shot during any arrest attempt at their residence. She told Meyerson to expect a call soon with an address.

The man who had victimized so many women was now about to be victimized by one. (For those who suffered at his hands—including, first of all, Alice Stoll—there seemed to be a God, whether Thomas Robinson believed in Her or not.)

Breese's original plan for his capture was for the FBI to grab Robinson during one of his frequent trips to the dentist because when going to the dentist, he never carried his .25 automatic. But the arrest of Karpis, Campbell, and Dainard spooked him, and he stopped going to the dentist. The FBI's recent arrests of such high profile fugitives

The G-men and the Heiress

renewed his paranoia. As a result, he rarely left their residence, allowing Breese out for only short periods. This made it difficult for her to get to a telephone, but on her third call to Meyerson—Saturday, May 9—they set up a meeting at the Los Angeles office for Monday morning with Acting SAC John Bugas.

At the appointed time, however, she telephoned Bugas and said she was unable to come to the office; she wanted to meet at the downtown Los Angeles Biltmore Hotel, in the Mezzanine Room at 2 p.m. She knew the hotel well because she and Robinson had stayed there upon their arrival in Los Angeles. She told the agents her name was Jane Hughes from New York City, currently married but separated. She wouldn't provide an address and said she was a shoplifter by trade. The agents thought she was around 35, 5-7", 150 pounds, with dark brown hair and eyes. They described her language as somewhat slangy and short-clipped. When Bugas and Meyerson showed her photographs of various FBI subjects, she quickly identified Robinson.

To test the integrity of information the FBI believed it was going to receive from her, Bugas mentioned a reward for information leading to Robinson's arrest. Breese said while she needed the money, she wasn't going to accept any. She told the agents that after leaving the meeting and not being shadowed by any of them, she would telephone the office within an hour or so and give them Robinson's location. They received her call at 3:30 p.m. She gave them an address, which was listed as the address of Captain Ernie Smith, a pilot who was an acquaintance of another agent in the Los Angeles office.

She made sure she would be out of the house; even the dog wouldn't be there. A team of agents led by the tough westerner Bugas left their offices at 4 p.m. loaded for combat. It was May 11, 1936. Breese's information had said Robinson would resist, and they planned accordingly: in addition to their service revolvers, agents carried two Thompson submachine guns, a tear gas gun, one shotgun, and two spotlights.

They took two vehicles, one with four agents set up a few blocks from the residence. Bugas, Edward Merritt, and Thomas Billings were in the other. It was a narrow street with only three other homes on the block, and Robinson's house second from the corner. The house had three entrances, front and side doors, and the garage entrance at the back of the house. Teams were at the front and rear of the home, each with a Thompson submachine gun.

Agent Bugas, after he had taken his jacket and tie off to look like just another pedestrian passerby, approached the bungalow, and rang the doorbell. When Robinson opened the smaller eye level door—part of the more solid and locked main front door— Bugas asked if Captain Smith was in. Robinson said Smith had moved but he'd get the landlady's address and telephone number because she might be able to help him.

$ Robinson's Los Angeles pied-à-terre: where the music died.

The agents knew right away they had their man, even though his face was plumper than his photos and he had a mustache. The cleft chin was there; so were the odd earlobes. When Robinson returned to the front door, Agent Merritt reached through the smaller door and grabbed Robinson with his left hand. He stuck an automatic in his face, told him they were federal agents, and to open the door.

"All right, all right!" Robinson said. "I knew you were; I'll open up—just a minute!"

Robinson was taken out of the house and to a Bureau vehicle. A limited search found a loaded .45 automatic in his pocket and $2,300 in cash. He was brought back into the house and strip-searched. Robinson provided the key to a strongbox found in the bedroom, and it held stacks of $5 bills still in bank wrappers. He had $4,687 left from an initial haul of $50,000. Agents also found a shotgun, two .25 Colt automatics, and a revolver, all loaded.

$

THE END OF THE RIDE

Robinson was taken to the Los Angeles office, and Bugas telephoned Assistant Director Nathan, telling him that Robinson's identity was confirmed by fingerprinting. Robinson voluntarily signed a removal order back to Louisville, and Hoover told Bugas to get Robinson on a chartered airplane to Louisville as soon as possible.

The G-Men had worked hard trying to find Robinson, but all their efforts had been inconsequential. The help they needed came from what some in the organization

The G-men and the Heiress

thought was its bread and butter, a good source. It was a time-honored method, but it didn't assuage Hoover's ego, who liked to think the work of his developing organization was procedural and scientific. The source, Breese, in the parlance of the pulp magazines her boyfriend loved, had dimed him out, all the angles figured in her favor. The G-Men hadn't really brought their man down, *she* had.

Breese had become increasingly aware that the gig was almost up, and if there was an ice floe out there—which there was—she wanted a lifeboat and not a deck chair. She had read about John Dillinger's girlfriend, Billie Frechette, who in 1934 got two years at the Federal Correctional Farm at Milan, Michigan, for harboring a fugitive. Agent Bugas had offered Breese money for her help and she had been offended—or pretended to be—and politely declined. But she *did* want some things for providing Robinson's whereabouts, notably custody of her dog, Shep. She wanted the FBI to ship the animal to her in New York City, along with two of her handbags, and the agency agreed. She also wanted to be allowed to correspond with Robinson, to be able to visit him, and last, that he not be housed at Alcatraz. Bugas explained that the FBI could not make those promises.

Like Frechette, who toured with the Dillinger family in a show called *Crime Didn't Pay,* Breese had her own gig. She appeared at Nashville's Princess Theatre, her performance described by an ad in *The Nashville Tennessean*: "Hear Jean Breese tell from her own lips how she met Robinson, their enthralling adventures together, why she turned him over to the G-Men, and her plans for the future." Whatever those plans were, it was likely she would be spending more time at home now.

A plane with Bugas, three of his agents, and Robinson left the Grand Central Air Terminal at Glendale at 9:30 p.m. Flying east under a full moon, he looked down on the mountains and thought of the ranch he'd never own. Handcuffed to his seat, one of the pilots asked him how he liked the free ride. "I'd sure a hell of a lot rather be paying my own way," he said.

They landed on May 12, shortly after 11 a.m., the agents heavily armed. Two of them carried Thompson submachine guns and another was holding a shotgun. SACs Dewey of Louisville and Earl Connelley of Cincinnati formed the welcoming committee, rushing him off before the crowd of spectators got more than a glimpse of him.

In the interview, Connelley asked Robinson if he'd committed any "indiscretion" with Mrs. Stoll during their time in the Indianapolis apartment. Robinson smiled "in a rather sinister manner," implying that possibly he had. That was like him, of course, for he'd always regarded himself as a smooth operator. And because of his lifestyle, Mrs. Stoll's attractiveness—and the inflamed imaginations of the tabloid public—the rumors would persist.

During FBI interviews, Robinson said he learned on May 7 of Karpis's arrest, which made him, Robinson, America's "Public Enemy No. 1." It was not a superlative that gladdened him, for it meant scrutiny would be even more intense. The next morning he went to the Los Angeles Federal Building, intending to surrender. Approaching an official at one of the desks, Robinson said, "Well, I see by the papers that I am now Public Enemy No. 1, and I want to surrender."

"What did you say?" asked the startled employee.

"I said that I am now Public Enemy No. 1 and I want to know how to reach the Department of Justice and surrender."

The employee, perhaps thinking he was involved in some kind of prank he didn't understand, told Robinson to take the elevator to the sixth floor. He watched Robinson walk down the hall toward the elevators, and he thought no more about him until he saw Robinson's pictures in the newspapers. Reported the *Los Angeles Times*, "Serene and composed—under their usual orders of secrecy—the agents couldn't say if they had sent a strange visitor back to a Glendale bungalow." Which was, of course, exactly what some front desk official had done.

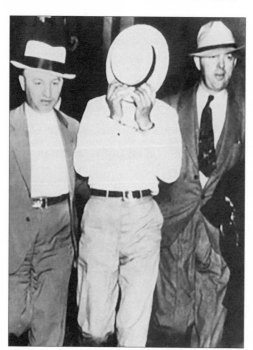

$ Karpis loses his number: he's off to The Rock.

On Wednesday, May 13, a wire service photograph of Robinson taken at the Louisville county jail hit the front page of newspapers from coast to coast. It was the first photograph taken of him since he started running from the authorities. He had a smallish mustache and looked somewhat like the English actor Robert Donat who starred in *The 39 Steps* and *Goodbye, Mr. Chips* (for which he won the Academy Award for Best Actor). Surely a Public Enemy No. 1, guarded by what seemed to be a brigade of agents, should look more menacing.

Robinson conferred with family attorneys Blaine Gabbard and Clem Huggins at the marshal's office before sentencing. His parents and his aunt, Mrs. Ernest Warner, also visited for about fifteen minutes, and agents heard family members trying to persuade him to plead guilty. Robinson's wife, speaking through her attorney, said only that she was glad "for the sake of her baby and mother- and father-in-law that Tom is living." Their child, Jimmy, then six-and-a-half years old, had been told his father was dead.

$ Mrs. Robinson Jr. and son Jimmy: those who were left behind.

Handcuffed to Agent Richard Smith, Robinson was brought quickly before Judge Elwood Hamilton and asked how he wanted to plead. He said only one word, "Guilty," and was sentenced to life. It was that simple. The public wasn't aware of how few federal criminal defendants went to trial, and that of those who do, most are found guilty. (Even in 2019, just two percent of them chose a trial.) Robinson's basic impetus was to avoid the death penalty, which might easily come with a court trial. Given his guilt—well documented by now—his guilty plea was likely the one thing that saved his life.

It was all a whirlwind for Robinson. In only a few days, he had been arrested, flown across the country, arraigned before a federal judge, pled guilty, and sentenced to life in prison. It was the tradeoff for his one year, six months, and twenty-five days where he had been splendidly at large with his $50,000 booty. Was it all worth it? He'd have endless time to consider the question. Yet the world had not seen the last of Thomas Henry Robinson Jr.

Implausible as it might seem, there was more to come.

RECEIVED _May 27 1936._

FROM _____WD-Kentucky Louisville._____

CRIME _____Kidnapping._____

MILITARY OR CIVIL _Civil._____

SENTENCE: _Life_ Yrs._____ Mos._____ Days

DATE OF SENTENCE_____May 13, 1936.____

BIRTHPLACE _Tennessee_____

RELIGION _____

EDUCATION _____

OCCUPATION _Law Clerk._____

MARRIED_____CHILDREN _____

RESIDENCE _____

HABITS_____

DESCRIPTION:

AGE_____29____ BIRTHDATE__May 5 1907._____

HEIGHT__6'1"____ WEIGHT____160_ BUILD_Medium_.

HAIR____Med.Ch._____ EYES_Lt.Hz.Lt.Blue.___

COMP___Medium_____ CHIN_Regular Cleft._____

MARKS AND SCARS:

None.

49074

I hereby authorize the Warden of the United States Penitentiary, Leavenworth, Kansas, or his authorized representative, to open all mail matter, and express or other packages which may be directed to my address, and to sign my name as endorsement on all checks, money orders, or bank drafts, for deposit to my credit in the Prisoners' Trust Fund as long as I am a prisoner in said institution.

Signature_____

FPI I&C—FLK—2-13-36—5000—6544-37

Robinson's Leavenworth intake card: welcome to the Big Leagues.

12 Last stop, hellcatraz

"Man has always been his own worst enemy, and I am no exception to the rule."

—Thomas Robinson Jr., Leavenworth, Kansas, 1937

On the train headed to the federal pen, the marshals kept Robinson in a compartment along with two FBI agents while two other agents slept. He was reading one of the newspapers, which had a story suggesting he should have used the insanity defense. He said—heard by the those around him—that he had used it once before on a local matter, and it likely wouldn't have worked if he used it with the federal charges.

He was allowed one last meal on the train and chose a breakfast of bacon and eggs, toast, and orange juice. He seemed to have kept a sense of humor, asking the waiter for juice from California oranges because it was something he had grown accustomed to while on the lam in the Golden State.

On Thursday, May 14—the day after Robinson's sentencing in Louisville—they arrived at Atlanta Union Station at 9:30 a.m. with G-Men and marshals surrounding him. Atlanta SAC Earl Conroy and five of his agents met them. The president himself might have had a smaller entourage. Conroy had made arrangements with Warden A. C. Aderhold, so the penitentiary would be ready to give Robinson its turndown service.

He smiled while walking through the station, dressed in light pants, a brown lumber jacket, and a gray felt hat. He enjoyed his celebrity status—after all, he'd seldom been out of the newspaper headlines for nearly two years—and he waved to spectators with his chain-cuffed hand. They exited to Alabama Street where three cars were waiting. Robinson was placed in the rear seat of car two, with Deputy Marshal Harold Hall and three other escorts. The trip to the prison took all of ten minutes and slightly before 10 a.m., Robinson stepped out of the vehicle, still smiling, moved up the steps, turned, and waved to those watching. He might have been a celebrity on a gangplank coming into a new country, which in a way he was.

While the heavy steel-gated entrance opened, his handcuffs and shackles were removed, and inmate number 49074 stepped into quarantine where the accomodations would be much more spartan than his previous ones. His mustache was shaved off, his hair cut short, and he was given a slightly oversized blue-gray prison uniform. The USP at Atlanta, a large white stone facility, housed nearly three thousand rough inmates, most of them spending their working hours tolling at either the prison farm or the cotton mill.

$

BREESE, WORKING THE ANGLES

In late May of 1936, Jean Breese sent Director Hoover a letter requesting a meeting. She was vague about why she wanted to meet with him and, of course, Hoover had no intention of seeing her. She talked, instead, to New York SAC Rhea Whitley, and to John Bugas from the Los Angeles office, who was asked by Hoover to be present. (Hoover accurately understood that Bugas was best equipped to interview Breese.)

Among other things, she told Bugas that she had never been a prostitute; she didn't think much of it as an occupation and, moreover, she could earn more by shoplifting. And she got to stay upright (physically if not morally). Bugas found her to be smart, cagey, and resourceful. In her unorthodox partnership with Robinson, Bugas thought, she might have been the guiding force. So much so that the agents came away from the interview without much useful information.

Her statement was riddled with inconsistencies and fabrications. Some of the old-time investigators would say, "Everybody lies." And Jean Breese was so deft at prevarication she even lied about her lies.

They did learn that after Breese had made the call to Bugas at the Los Angeles office and turned Robinson in, she hopped a bus to San Diego where she read about Robinson's capture in the next morning's paper. From there, she went by train to New Orleans, stayed with friends for a few days, then went on to Nashville where she contacted the Robinson family.

She and Robinson Sr. became immediate members of a mutual abhorrence society; Senior thought she was a crazy neurotic who couldn't be trusted, and she thought he was "a vicious, debased, degenerate individual" who stayed drunk for two-thirds of her

The G-men and the Heiress

visit. She didn't like Frances Robinson, either, although she'd been told by Junior that Frances helped plan the kidnapping, only to lose her nerve at the last minute and refuse to go with him. (If Frances *had* gone with her husband, Breese may never have met him so, theoretically at least, she should have felt some gratitude to the woman who, in effect, was resposible for her year-and-a-half vacation in the grand hotels of America.)

Breese did reveal a new kidnapping angle to the agents, even if it was nothing more than rumor: she said that Mrs. Stoll was a party to the kidnapping, and Robinson Jr. had told her. (An unimpeachable source if ever there was one.) Breese's reasoning was that if Mrs. Stoll did not assist in planning the seizure, she was still an accessory. Breese also knew—again from what Robinson told her—that he and Mrs. Stoll had been intimate.

Robinson, though, swayed back and forth, reporting that he either did or he did not have relations with Mrs. Stoll. As for Alice Stoll, she had spent six days with a clearly disturbed man in a one-bedroom apartment; what were people—including her own husband—going to think? And if people were going to believe what they wished to believe, why should she comment? As far as anyone knows, she never talked about the incident.

The only person Breese liked among the Robinsons was Mrs. Robinson Sr., whom she found gentle, with good character and a pleasing personality, the saint of the group, putting up with her noxious husband who carried on as if he were a martyr. She was the *real* martyr, even though they hadn't lived as man and wife for years, each inhabiting separate parts of the house. She would have divorced him years before but, alas, she was captive of the old-fashioned notion that those married should stay married (no matter the untenable psychological damage they might inflict upon one another).

Six months after Robinson went into the Atlanta penitentiary, his attorneys filed affidavits alleging that he was insane at the time he made his earlier guilty plea, and asked for a trial. The judge said that the crime required skill and insight, and Robinson

$ The USP at Atlanta—three thousand inmates, and counting.

had appeared sane when sentenced on May 14, 1936. The judge did, however, give the attorneys an additional two weeks to file further affidavits about Robinson's sanity, but apparently the attorneys thought better of their motion and abruptly abandoned their efforts. Robinson said the attorneys didn't represent him well and hadn't filed the required papers with the court.

His sojourn in Atlanta was brief. After twelve days, he was moved to Leavenworth, some twenty-five miles northwest of Kansas City. The country's oldest maximum security prison, it was called "the hot house" by author Pete Earley in his eponymous book because summer temperatures there might reach 115 degrees. "With its insular culture and attendant rituals, it is the kind of place where one inmate can stick a 17-inch knife in another man's back, and a lunchroom full of guards and fellow prisoners will barely look up," he wrote.

The first progress report on Robinson said he was reasonably cheerful, responsive, aware of his surroundings, and had made a proper adjustment. Which was saying quite a lot, considering Leavenworth's reputation. The next report, though, wasn't quite as bracing. This one found Robinson had an intrinsic absence of responsiveness to "social demands, truthfulness, decency, and consideration of others." He was, in a few words, plainly antisocial.

$

BUYING THE RANCH

At the end of June, 1936, he received his first visitor. Robinson wasn't sure how she had managed to be approved because she was not a relative, and she had a criminal record, as well (which would usually bar a person from visiting). She would have needed special permission, which she said was granted to her because she was working with the Department of Justice on cases in New York City.

He gave her his alias signature, "J. H. Kramer," which allowed her to superimpose it on a paper for written authorization at the American Storage Company in Los Angeles so she could retrieve the $7,500 he had stored in a filing cabinet. He also told her the code to the strongbox and slipped the written information to her with other legal documents relating to his Plymouth sedan that had been impounded back in Los Angeles County for overdue property taxes.

Breese was to take the money and buy a ranch—the driving fiction of Robinson's scattershot life. He did not know yet that she had turned him in, and the image of his ranch floated above him at night as though his cell had a twenty-first century streaming

The G-men and the Heiress

service. She said if she bought land in New Mexico, she would be closer to the prison and could visit him more often. He said she should take care of his parents, as well. She agreed, saying they could all live on the ranch together—she and Tom, Tom's mother, and that degenerate individual who stayed drunk for most of her Nashville visit.

By now, apparently, Robinson's overactive mind conjured scenarios that were more and more impossible. His life to date had been impossible, and even the impossible kidnapping of Alice Stoll—which should have been solved in an Evansville train station a few days after it happened—appeared now like a lurid Grade B film in which good fortune had favored the impossibly charmed Robinson at almost every turn.

During the visit, Breese said she was working on his behalf with the Department of Justice, which was, of course, patently untrue. (As usual, Breese was working solely for herself.) Robinson would be taken back to Louisville, she said, and re-sentenced to a term of twenty years instead of his current life sentence. He would be eligible for parole after just six years and released. She would have the ranch waiting when he got out. "We would be able to prop our feet up on the porch railing and forget all this trouble," she said.

Still blinded by Breese's witchery, he did not see that without her, he might actually have acquired his ranch. Or, as one good investigator said while reviewing the Robinson case long after the fact, "He should have stayed in New York, in those turkish baths."

He asked Breese how she thought he got caught, and she said he was, at some point, recognized by the FBI and followed back to their house. She said she was approaching the house and saw him being led away in handcuffs. That fall, in an obviously ghost-written series in the *Nashville Banner*, she said that after Alvin Karpis's capture—and Robinson's own elevation to Public Enemy No. 1—he was increasingly paranoid, seeing G-Men lurking everywhere. Once, she said, he thought their milkman was an agent—until she pointed out his milk wagon. "He was wilder than I had ever seen him," she said.

She wrote that the kindest thing she could do would be to turn him in. (It presaged the famous Vietnam quote of the late 1960s when after the battle of Ben Tre an army officer said, "We had to destroy the village in order to save it.") She told the Los Angeles agent, Bugas, "I am not selling Tom Robinson. I want nothing from the government."

What she *did* want, it seemed, was to walk away completely free from any fugitive-harboring charges, look sympathetic in the newspapers and to the public, and—most of all—the freedom to track down the remnants of the fortune that Robinson had mostly already spent on her. She did get that, and she received $10,000 for her story in the *Nashville Banner's* five-part series of newspaper articles, and she received other financial gain from presenting her story on stage, as advertised in *The Tennessean* on August 17, 1936.

Last stop, hellcatraz

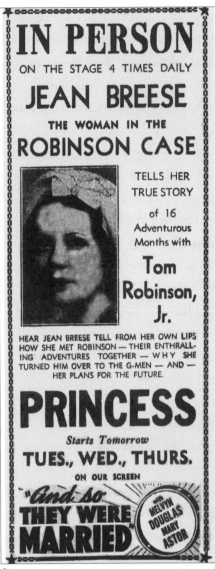

IN PERSON

ON THE STAGE 4 TIMES DAILY

JEAN BREESE

THE WOMAN IN THE

ROBINSON CASE

TELLS HER TRUE STORY

of 16 Adventurous Months with

Tom Robinson, Jr.

HEAR JEAN BREESE TELL FROM HER OWN LIPS HOW SHE MET ROBINSON — THEIR ENTHRALLING ADVENTURES TOGETHER — WHY SHE TURNED HIM OVER TO THE G-MEN — AND — HER PLANS FOR THE FUTURE.

PRINCESS

Starts Tomorrow

TUES., WED., THURS.

ON OUR SCREEN

"And So THEY WERE MARRIED"

with MELVYN DOUGLAS MARY ASTOR

$ Jean Breese on stage: her sixteen adventurous months.

Wisely, Robinson wasn't relying entirely on Breese to help him get out of prison (which was a good thing). He thought that by not putting up a fight when he was apprehended, as well as being on good behavior in prison (in spite of his antisocial tendencies) augered well for clemency at some point. His plans were to divorce his wife, Frances, and when he got out of prison, begin again with his present love, Jean Breese, "whose actions since my apprehension should convince everyone that she loved me dearly." He would explain that he wasn't a gangster, that he understood crime didn't pay (although, to date, his renumeration was quite good), that he wanted to teach a class in prison on how to get a job, and that he had no mental issues. (See Hare's Psycopathy checklist: "Do you lack realistic long-term goals?")

At some point, Robinson read Breese's five-part series and recognized that Breese wasn't as loyal as he had thought. Or perhaps she wasn't loyal at all. Neither Breese nor any of her family had been arrested; no one but him. And yet he sent her a general power of attorney to act on his behalf, as she saw fit. He seemed to be down with a glandular condition in which the organ of his devotion was significantly inflamed. "I loved her," he said, smiling and befogged as the knife slid between his ribs.

Breese, meanwhile, returned to Nashville. She wasn't finished with the Robinson family; she was after money Robinson had left his mother. Breese threatened Mrs. Robinson Sr. to get $3,700, which remained of the $4,000 her son had given her, saying she, Breese, would have her prosecuted. Thus Breese got her hands on the last of the ransom money, all in all, about $18,000 (some $350,000 in today's dollars). So much for the delusory dream of propping his feet up on the porch of their ranch.

The G-men and the Heiress

In March of 1937, Robinson was transferred again, this time to the San Francisco Bay and the dreaded penitentiary at Alcatraz known as "The Rock." He wasn't happy about the transfer, and neither was his mother, as they thought he had a deal with the FBI that he would stay where he was. He was transferred because of the length of time he had to serve and the type of crime he committed. The G-Men weren't going to make any arrangements with a kidnapper who had caused them so much consternation.

When he arrived at Alcatraz, just like at the other two prisons, he was given a mental examination by the resident psychiatrist, as he had at the other two prisons. Doctors at all three prisons agreed that he was not insane, had average intelligence, knew right from wrong, but was emotionally unstable. (Early on, Robinson had confided to record keeper Carl Sundstrom about his time at state mental hospitals in Tennessee, telling him faking insanity had been merely a ploy to stay out of the state prison for the robberies he'd committed.)

Robinson was assigned to the kitchen for five months in 1937, then again for seven months in 1938. He was forced to leave the kitchen during the first period because he couldn't get along with the other workers, giving off an air of superiority and wanting to be in charge. One of the other kitchen workers, Raymond Maple, saw Robinson walk

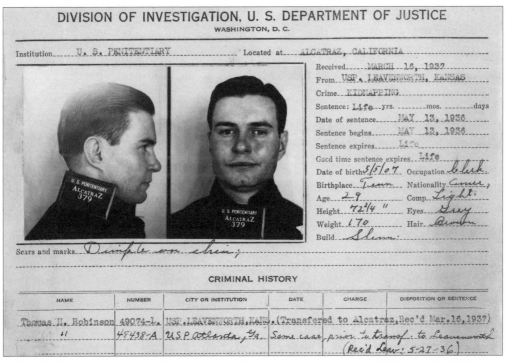

$ Robinson on tour: his intake card for Alcatraz, March 14, 1937.

into a corner or behind a door and talk out loud to himself whenever the deputy warden, doctors, or guards came near. When they left, he would act normal again.

In December of 1937, Robinson Sr. slipped on the sidewalk near his home, fracturing his skull. He hung on at Nashville General Hospital for ten days, finally succumbing at age 64. Robinson had upon numerous occasions regretted causing his parents much grief, and now he couldn't even attend his father's funeral.

Mostly he worked on his legal case, preparing all the documents in longhand then giving them to the associate warden, Edward Miller, who supervised the typing of numerous briefs and pleadings. There would be thousands of pages, all at considerable expense to the government.

In October of 1939, Robinson, with assistance, filed a writ of habeas corpus petition with the San Francisco federal court for his freedom, saying he had been deprived of sufficient legal counsel at his sentencing. There would be a delay in the decision until his mother and Fred Russell of the *Nashville Banner* could provide affidavits. (Russell had driven his parents from Nashville to Louisville for arraignment and sentencing. By the time they arrived, Robinson Sr. was intoxicated and in no condition to provide advice. Monte Ross of Nashville, the attorney hired to represent Junior, was unable to be in Louisville for the arraignment.) The court denied the new request, but this was just a minor roadblock.

Robinson would continue these efforts for years. Finally, in August of 1943, he won his fight for a trial, filing self-prepared legal documents with the court which were reviewed by San Francisco Federal Judge Michael J. Roche, who granted a writ of habeas corpus. Robinson's argument was that neither of his lawyers was next to him in the courtroom when he made his plea of guilty and that he received his death sentence at an abnormal hour of the day. The judge granted his request and ordered him to be taken back to Louisville within ninety days for trial.

It had taken seven years, with his mother sending him law books and asking people for financial support on his behalf. Now Robinson would get his day in court. He would, finally, face a judge and have a jury trial, which was a big gamble because with the Lindbergh Law, his life would be on the line.

His fate would now be in the hands of twelve jurors, and as every lawyer knows, facts to a jury are usually subservient to emotion. As the saying goes, a jury is twelve people who get to decide who has the best lawyer. Robinson had always been an uninhibited gambler. This time, however, he was betting everything.

In the terms of his dream life, he was betting the ranch.

The Rock

Early Native Americans didn't like the place, banishing troublemakers to the Island of the Pelicans ("Alcatraz" in Spanish). A rocky, twenty-two-acre island in the bay between San Francisco and Oakland, it was a military fortification and prison before the Department of Justice acquired it in 1933 when it became the place designated for troublemakers and dangerous inmates other prisons couldn't handle or didn't want (and fondly dubbed "Hellcatraz" by its inmates).

The first warden, James Johnston, known as "Old Saltwater" by the inmates, challenged the brutal approach of straitjackets and solitary confinement in darkness. Under him, inmates got better food, monthly movies, and a library with thousands of books. Alcatraz had less than three hundred prisoners, not quite one percent of the entire national inmate population. There were only a couple of dozen public enemies, the

$ Robinson's home away from home: the Alcatraz laundry.

most famous being inmate No. 85, Al Capone, although his company included Harvey John Bailey (the dean of American bank robbers), Arthur "Doc" Barker (the violent offspring of the infamous Ma Barker), and perhaps the most wicked of them all, Howard Dickerson, who set his house on fire and killed his family for the insurance money. While Alcatraz was not a country club, some of its tough-as-nails reputation came by way of the motion picture industry.

Over its almost thirty years, there were fourteen known attempts to escape, involving thirty-six inmates. Twenty-three were captured, six were killed during flight, two drowned, and five went missing and were presumed drowned. The water around the island runs cold (40-55 degrees F), the currents are strong (receding tides go toward the ocean rather than the city), and is inhabited by sharks.

It cost three times as much to run than other prisons, and saltwater slowly destroyed the pipes, leaking into the walls. Salt and wind wore the place down, causing crumbling. It became an escape risk as inmates could easily dig through the walls (the swim home was more difficult), and it closed in 1963, remaining perpetually in the public mind as the quintessential hardcase lockup.

LEAVING FEDERAL COURT are Mrs. Alice Speed
Stoll and her husband, Berry V. Stoll. Mrs. Stoll again
testified concerning her abduction in 1934 by Thomas H.
Robinson, Jr.

AP Photo.

Alice Stoll and husband at 1943
trial: laying the story to rest.

13

The trial: be careful what you wish for

"Well, Mom, they've given me the works."
—Thomas Robinson Jr.

At 9 a.m. on Monday, November 29, 1943, the trial of U.S. v. Thomas H. Robinson Jr. began in Louisville federal court with Judge Shackleford Miller presiding. Miller had taken the position vacated by Judge Elwood Hamilton, who had officiated over the trial of Robinson's wife and father in 1935, and thus Robinson would be tried in the same courtroom, which he regarded as a good omen.

The prosecutor was an assistant United States attorney, Eli Brown III, a Harvard Law School grad, and the defense counsel, selected by the judge, was Robert Hogan and J. Paul Keith. The unfortunate Hogan was a Bowling Green lawyer who didn't want the job as he had plenty to worry about with his law practice. At the trial's conclusion, Hogan estimated that Robinson's defense cost more than $100,000, which would be almost $1.5 million in today's dollars. (As an "officer of the court," however, Hogan was likely paid a pittance—court-appointed attorneys were often paid for an entire case what attorneys on retainer earned in a few hours. In addition, his co-counsel, Keith, had dropped out, leaving Hogan to carry the entire case. But his abiding presence throughout Robinson's legal travails demonstrated his fidelity to his client, who was both patently guilty and newly impoverished.)

The newspapers reported that potential jurors were asked only one question by the prosecution: can you recommend the death penalty? If the answer was "Yes," the juror was selected; if "No," they were excused. The defense had other questions (for instance, did the juror have any contact with the Speed family?), as well as routine questions about military experience and religious affiliation. Eleven jurors were chosen on the first

159

$ The Brown Hotel: where the jurors resided in style.

day, five of them with farming backgrounds. There was also a lumberman, a telephone company employee, a housewife, and a widow with a teenage son.

The jurors were taken to the downtown Brown Hotel, likely the highlight of many jurors' travel experience, as it had six hundred rooms and had been visited by both the famous and the near-famous (David Lloyd George, the former Prime Minister of the United Kingdom, was the first person to sign the guest register, and soprano Lily Pons brought along her pet lion which roamed around in her room). The place was also famous for the Hot Brown sandwich, an open-face turkey sandwich with bacon and a Mornay sauce, and afterward there were jurors, no doubt, whose sensibilities had been permanently altered. The bill to house the jurors was $1,581 (some $23,000 in today's dollars), and went to the U.S. marshal after the trial.

The final juror was sworn in on Wednesday, December 1, a farmer from Spencer County. The attorneys had vetted 103 candidates, and they were ready to go before noon. The prosecution had a list of over a hundred witnesses prepared to testify, and the opening statement was given by J. Dudley Inman, a University of Louisville Law School man who summarized Robinson's background, which due to arraignments, grand jury hearing, previous trial, and a thousand newspaper articles, could be recited by virtually everyone in Kentucky.

DAMSEL IN DISTRESS

Mrs. Stoll, now 37, was described as slim and graceful, wearing a brown wool dress and a small red velvet hat as she entered the jury box. Her testimony wasn't very different from her grand jury testimony in 1934, and again at the 1935 trial of Robinson Sr. and his daughter-in-law. It had been almost ten years since she had been kidnapped, and she was vague on minor details.

The G-men and the Heiress

On direct examination, she told of being ill with a bad cold on the day in question, resting in her upstairs bedroom. When the maid came to her room and said a man wanted to work on the master bedroom extension, she moved to the guest room. Half an hour later, the maid came in with the man holding a gun in her back.

"What are you here for?" she demanded.

"I am here to kidnap you," he said.

He was not dissuaded by Mrs. Stoll's protestation that her family wasn't wealthy, then she made the mistake of trying to grab the gun Robinson had left on the bed. He hit her with a pipe he was carrying, which caused a welt on her forehead and dazed her. She ended being tied up, her mouth taped, and lying in the back of Robinson's car, where she was covered with newspapers and a blanket. That was the beginning of her traumatic week-long ordeal during which she was never entirely sure whether she would remain alive.

After a two-hour drive, Robinson pulled into a dark residential garage located down an alley, and he told her they had arrived in Indianapolis. He asked her if she needed to be carried, and she replied that she could walk. They entered an apartment, which was in disarray with dirty dishes scattered about. She was dizzy and felt sick, her head wound still bleeding. At her request, he put mercurochrome on the wound but did nothing else to assist her.

She asked him to let her sleep on the couch in the living room, but he wouldn't allow it. Any time he left the apartment, she was tied up and locked in a tiny closet, sometimes for as long as three or four hours. When the ransom money didn't arrive when he thought it would, he was both furious and profane, as though she were personally responsible.

💲 The Indianapolis apartment where Alice Stoll's ordeal began.

The trial: be careful what you wish for

Within two days, Robinson had typed out one letter and dictated four more, which she wrote out for him by hand. Alice Stoll repeatedly told him to contact her family by telephone but he refused, telling her, "the phones were being watched." The letters were clumsily typed, half-capitalized, and lacked succinctness, all evidence that Robinson had not majored in English during his time at Vanderbilt. Alice seemed to have been trying to help him (at some point, after all, she probably wanted to go home). Her handwritten note was much more to the point.

Saturday,
October 13

Dear Mr. Intermediary:

This is Alice Stoll writing. We are sending my wedding ring on which is engraved my name if you look inside closely. I am well and being treated nicely. I have only a slight cut on my head.

If you have not already done so, please pay over the money to the one who this man tells you to.

Alice Stoll

P.S. The man I am referring to is the man who is sending this letter to you with instructions. Of course, you may have already paid it, in which event ignore this letter.

She told the jury that once she was released her head "was still thickly clotted with blood, and I was in a very weakened condition. I could hardly walk a block." And, too, her lips were raw from having the tape placed and removed so many times. She had previously read in the newspapers of a Reverend Clegg, whose wife she recognized as a cousin of her husband. The reverend lived in Indianapolis, and Mrs. Stoll asked Frances Robinson to take her there, and they went in a cab.

At the Clegg home, she looked out and saw a man on the front lawn, which frightened her. She ran to the back of the house, thinking that perhaps she had been followed. Robinson had said he had confederates; he might have been telling her the truth. Had she and Frances been followed to the Clegg house?

The prosecutor, Brown, asked Mrs. Stoll if she had been molested, and she said, "No, if he did, my husband would never stop until he had tracked him down and killed him." It

The G-men and the Heiress

was an obvious attempt by the prosecution to cast Robinson in the worst possible light (although Robinson was perfectly capable of doing that himself). Brown was already certain of what had happened. Before the trial, he'd had an hour-and-fifteen-minute conversation with her and came away convinced "beyond all shadow of a doubt that the allegations about intimacies at any time were untrue."

Mrs. Stoll was also feisty with the defense attorney, Hogan, as he repeatedly asked her the same questions. In her mind, she had resisted Robinson with all her ability, even though she had been wounded and remained in a state of fear. Hogan's line of questioning implied that she hadn't done enough for herself. He wanted to know why she hadn't called out to the milkman, and he quizzed her about the bathroom, asking her why she hadn't just locked the door behind her and gone out the bathroom window. His questioning obviated Mrs. Stoll's reality: her kidnapper spent much of his time sitting on the sofa holding a gun, and she spent a lot of her's either tied in a closet or onto the bedsprings.

$ The window in question: no transit in high heels.

At one point in the trial, Hogan introduced a partial replica of the bathroom—including the window—in the Indianapolis apartment, to show the jury that Mrs. Stoll *could* have escaped. To demonstrate, Hogan introduced Marjorie Kirchhubel, 5'3", 109 pounds, wearing pants, athletic shirt, and flat shoes. Prosecutor Brown objected, saying Mrs. Stoll had been wearing a kimono and high heels. Kirchhubel changed clothes and returned to step up on the toilet bowl, open the window, unhook the screen, and climb through—although hitting her head with a loud bang on the window frame. Thus Mrs. Stoll may have been able to escape, but probably not without more damage to her already injured cranium, whether from the window frame or getting pistol-whipped by Robinson. Hogan's valiant demonstration seemed to prove nothing but Mrs. Stoll's untenable position.

While Mrs. Stoll had looked elegant and fit when she took the stand, there was no way for any of the spectators to know if the ordeal had left her with any lasting effects, physically or mentally. Since 1936 she had been treated for minor ailments by doctors and in January of 1941 she began seeing Dr. Nora Pratner, a specialist in osteopathy, an alternative medicine involving manipulation of the muscle tissue and bones. The doctor seemed to think that the blow to the head she received during the kidnapping could have caused pressure to the spinal cord, which possibly caused impaired circulation issues to shoulder, neck, and head, and chronic right ear problems. Over one month, she had ten doctor visits with manipulation therapy, alleviating some of her issues but still requiring continued visits.

$

THE FORGETFUL MAID

The only other witness to the kidnapping was diminutive Ann Woolet, the former maid who, with her husband, Fowler, testified on Thursday, December 2. Robinson had wired Mrs. Stoll's wrists and he wired Woolet's as well, so tightly it cut into her wrists, then he shoved her to the floor, and wired her ankles together. After she heard his car leave, she managed to get her ankles unwired and tried the telephone, which had been disconnected. Badly shaken, she went into the bathroom to watch for the arrival of Mr. Stoll.

He arrived fifteen minutes later, and she heard him talking to the dog. When she called out, he ran up the stairs and asked her if she had cut her hand. He untied her wrists while she told him what had happened. Mrs. Stoll's mother, Mrs. Speed, described as "a take-charge woman," had Ann and Fowler Woolet come to the Speed residence on Lexington Road. Berry Stoll told the Woolets he wanted the cottage cleared for his wife's return.

Once at the Speed house, Mrs. Speed took them to the servant's quarters, a cold, bleak room containing only a bed and a dresser. Ann Woolet felt like she had been jailed. She was not happy, she didn't want to stay, and she wanted to see her mother. Mrs. Speed would not let them leave, however, saying, "There have been orders for you to stay here." The irony was that to all appearances, the Woolets had just been kidnapped, as well. (And to whom might *they* complain?)

The next day at 7 a.m., Mrs. Speed arranged for a cab to take them back to their living quarters at the Stoll cottage. Adding injury to insult, Berry Stoll told the Woolets their services would no longer be needed. The Stolls were going to close the cottage, he said, because "he just didn't ever want to see the place again."

Agnes Woolet, Fowler's mother, was at the residence on Sunday when the couple was preparing to leave. She asked Berry Stoll if he would provide a written statement that "these children (her son and daughter-in-law) were no longer under suspicion for

The G-men and the Heiress

the kidnapping." Berry said he would be glad to do it but never did. Ann Woolet wanted to see that Alice was okay, but Berry came down from upstairs and told her that Alice "couldn't see her, that she was resting and not feeling well." Berry gave Fowler some names to contact for a job in the oil fields at Owensboro, Kentucky, but none worked out and he was out of work for a year.

Robinson's destructive behavior, it seemed, had cast such a wide net that he managed to harm the lives of even those on the periphery of his activities.

Dr. Harry Frazier, who'd examined Mrs. Stoll the night she was released, testified for the prosecution that she looked fatigued and unhealthy. The cut on her head should have had stitches, he said, her appearance was unkempt (she had been unable to bathe during her week in captivity), and she had high blood pressue.

Hogan, working valiantly for his client, asked Dr. Frazier if a horse race could make a person's blood pressure rise, and the doctor said only if the person was a chronic gambler with a wad on the race.

Berry, during his testimony, said his wife's lips were "torn and bloody from adhesive tape, her head covered in blood. She was completely unnerved, completely shattered." All the blood on her bedspread had sent him out to look in the ditches on their property, thinking that at any moment he would find the body of his murdered wife.

The custodian of the North Meridian apartments in Indianapolis told the defense that the numerous opening and closing of the window blinds in the hideout apartment caused him no particular notice, and he provided a small moment of levity—although not for Hoover—when he said an FBI agent lived in one of the other nearby apartments.

ROBINSON THE ROGUE

On Friday, the trial went into its third day. Anna Webb, a Los Angeles real estate broker, said she'd met Robinson and Breese at the Los Angeles Biltmore Hotel. He was masquerading as an attorney from Highland Park, Illinois, and had what she thought were excellent references. She rented them a beach bungalow in Santa Monica, for $150 a month.

"He was so glib that he had answers to questions before you asked them," Webb said. "I think I'm above the average intelligence myself, and he was head and shoulders above me...I tell you, he was as smart as the mischief." Defense attorney Hogan asked her if she was attracted to the handsome Robinson, which made her laugh.

"Only to his capability," she said.

Body of evidence

They called him "Uncle Charlie," but Charles Appel was the father of the FBI Laboratory. For in 1932, he'd taken a borrowed microscope and a handful of supplies and moved into a break room of the Old Southern Railway Building. While Hoover used it for public relations purposes at first, the Division now had its own lab—no matter how humble—and it performed nearly a thousand examinations in its first year.

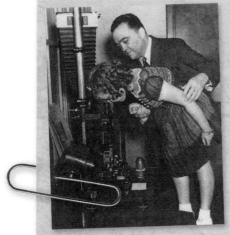

$ A closer look: Hoover shows Shirley Temple a lab microscope.

Appel's background was so diverse any one of his pursuits might have claimed him. He was an accomplished violinist, an engineer (he patented a device to protect the signatures on checks), a lawyer, and at the end of WWI he'd qualified as a pilot. By the 1920s, he was working for Hoover as a Special Agent; when discussions arose about the need for more scientific methods in their work, Appel persuaded Hoover to let him take a course in forensic evidence examination, and the agency's modern investigative path was set.

The 1930s was Appel's decade, for he not only coached the FBI ladies' softball team known as "Charlie's Chickens" (it played on the Ellipse near the White House), but he developed the lab, which presented crucial evidence in the Lindbergh kidnapping case. He and his men also examined thousands of Kansas City ballots cast in the 1934 elections, resulting in the indictments of nearly three hundred election judges, precinct captains, and clerks, and by 1940, the lab staff had forty-six people, most of them holding advanced degrees and a facility with varying scientific disciplines.

After leaving the FBI in 1949 (Hoover at first refused his resignation), he operated his own business in document examination, his work involving "some of the era's most famous and controversial people and events." Charlie's son, Edward, said his father had written a book on how to detect forgeries but left it unpublished even after his death because he thought it might be used by forgers as a primer.

Meticulous to the very end.

Henry Richardson, Robinson's former boss at the Stoll Oil service station in Louisville where Robinson worked in 1931, was asked by defense attorney Hogan if Robinson had a pleasing personality.

"Yes," Richardson said.

"He was attractive to the ladies, wasn't he?" Hogan asked.

"I don't know, mister," Richardson said. "I'm no lady."

The courtroom spectators liked Richardson's answer better than Hogan did.

The Federal Bureau of Investigation lab specialists played a big part in the investigation, and three of its experts provided testimony. There was a fingerprint specialist, an analytical chemist, and, finally, Special Agent Charles Appel, the twenty-year man who'd been a leading force behind the development of the FBI Technical Laboratory. Appel had compared the handwriting of the ransom notes in the Lindbergh kidnapping and identified it as being that of Bruno Hauptmann, who was convicted and executed. He compared the typed ransom note in the Stoll kidnapping with samples taken from the Corona portable typewriter Robinson left behind in the Indianapolis apartment and demonstrated their similarities.

KISS AND TICKLE?

On Monday, December 6, Robinson Jr. testified in his sharp Tennessee drawl how he had met Mrs. Stoll. She had testified that she never met him until kidnapped, but Robinson said she brought her car to the gas station where he worked, and they had flirted.

After a chance meeting near the Stoll refinery on River Road, she got into his car, and he drove to a deserted street leading to the Rose Island Ferry where they had sex. Afterward, he took her back to her car, and they planned to meet again.

A few days later, he met her in downtown Louisville and they drove out to the Beechwood Inn, registered as man and wife, and "engaged in sexual intercourse three or four times." They would return to this camp one more time, he said. In July, they went to the outskirts of Jefferson, Indiana, rented a log cabin, and "again had intercourse, I don't know how many times." He said he then left town and never saw her again until October of 1934.

Robinson's tale was perfect for the tabloid-readers, having all the scandalous elements of good girls gone wrong, or class warfare between the sheets (although in Robinson's telling, it would be the back seat of a Chrysler), as well as other detours into good old whiz-bang melodrama. While the truth of it could not be accurately known, most of the investigators—and others connected to the kidnapping—thought Robinson was an inveterate liar. In the kitchen of Robinson's mental house, the truth was an exotic, sel-

The trial: be careful what you wish for

$ Alice Stoll: Robinson's calumny against her seemed to be wishful thinking.

dom-used spice on a high shelf, something on the order of fennel pollen, say, or dried kaffir leaves. Only the tabloid-readers believed any of it.

At one point in the trial, four witnesses testified that one of the places where Robinson said he registered with Mrs. Stoll wasn't even in existence at the time of the reported assignation in 1931. One witness, Elmer Allen, who lived on the property, said there were no cabins, tourist homes, or any place for living quarters then.

Still, Robinson's calumny was infectious, for as late as 2011, a novel called *All That Money* took the basic details of the Stoll kidnapping, all readily recognized, including its major character—"Lucie Spode White"—and fictionalized them to the point of having White taking part in her own kidnapping. There was even a late moment of omniscient reflection by the writer, Steven Meyers, which was striking in its contemplation: "Lucie Spode White…a member of a community peculiarly webbed with calcified ancient connections, was burdened with social expectations and obligations. She met them all, always—never shirked. But early on, she established an absolute refusal to discuss her kidnapping. Quite naturally, especially at first, people were curious about her experience and frequently, with no intention of being rude, ventured to ask about it. But any such question instantly coated her in a kind of impenetrable shellac; she cut off eye contact and, if necessary, performed a sweeping pirouette that left her questioner tottering and exposed as at the edge of a cliff. Over time, fewer questions were posed to her."

$

JOHNNY SPENDTHRIFT

Robinson's ardent imagination did not stop with Alice Stoll, either. More testimony showed that he blamed C. C. Stoll as responsible for all his troubles. For one thing, C. C. had not rehired him. For another, he said, he had used C. C. as a reference on a hundred employment applications and was hired for none of them. "I then felt convinced that Mr. Stoll was preventing me from getting work," he said. "I felt inspired to do something about it."

The G-men and the Heiress

Mr. Stoll, in Robinson's mind, was a "powerful capitalist, and responsible for the Depression. ("This was akin to the famous remark by sportswriter Stanley Woodward after Army coach Red Blaik said his boys would have done better against Michigan if the center had given the ball a quarter turn before the snap. Said Woodward: "That's like blaming the Johnstown Flood on a leaky toilet in Altoona, Pennsylvania.")

In Robinson's thinking, *he* was the patriot here, the reincarnation of Patrick Henry, as he liked to remind people. Plotting something for C. C. wasn't revenge; it was a reckoning, a *political* act.

He went to the C. C. Stoll residence first but C. C. wasn't home, and he sought him next door at the house of his oldest son, George, but no one was home there, either. The next day, he decided on Berry Stoll (he had to look up Berry's address in the phone book). Alice, it seemed, was his third choice. One more missed opportunity by Robinson and he might have taken Berry's Great Dane, Hector (who, given his pacifistic temperament, would probably have gone gladly with him).

In one more of the many ironies in the case, the prosecution introduced one of C. C. Stoll's recommendation letters (from when he'd applied for a job with the Tennessee Valley Authority), in which Stoll wrote that Robinson was "earnest, a good worker, and ambitious to get along." Robinson had just denigrated—wholly inaccurately—the man who'd been his advocate.

The perpetual thin-ice skater, Robinson implied the kidnapping was a kind of adventure for Mrs. Stoll. They spent the time talking, reading the paper, and listening to the radio, and his control over her was so loose that, should she have wanted, she could simply have walked away. It was only after the deluge of news reports about the kidnapping that the incident turned into something much more serious.

The vestiges of Robinson's personal charm had always been a mixed blessing; sometimes the person most charmed was Robinson himself. He did not see, for instance, that the jury did not believe his version of Alice Stoll's behavior. The jurors were unconvinced, it seemed; they saw Robinson's account as a defamation. (In 1937, interviewed by agents at Leavenworth, he'd defended Mrs. Stoll's reputation. In another, called "Private Memorandum for Mr. J. Edgar Hoover," he'd discredited it.) Upon such moments, trials turn; Robinson had lost the jury.

His case wasn't helped when he described how he'd spent the ransom money. "That money," he said, "I threw it away, right and left." (The newspapers called him "Johnny Spendthrift.") Robinson hedged as to exact amounts, but the prosecution kept after him: there was the expensive Packard (bought with $100 bills), a second car, money to Breese's family, his family, money ferreted away in storage in California. And he'd crossed the country, coast to coast, three times, staying in the best hotels.

It was astute questioning on the prosecution's behalf because Robinson was talking to a jury composed of mostly farmers and laborers, the country was at war, and average annual wages were $1,200. Farmers likely made much less. To some of them, the numbers thrown around so unthinkingly by Robinson represented the earnings of a lifetime.

On Wednesday, December 8, his mother took the stand. Jessie Lois Preston Robinson, age 68, testified that her son was an ordinary boy who attended Sunday school and had his share of childhood illness. The early forced marriage, she said, caused a personality change and he became sullen, with a bad temperament, and he had come up with a foolish idea. It was a mother's plea for the son she loved, but it had little effect on the jury. They did not, of course, see the same little lost boy *she* saw.

There was no indication from Robinson, but somewhere inside himself he must have known his trial was not going as he had imagined. He'd pictured his vindication, a restoration to society. He'd make the jury understand he had not planned the kidnapping *alone*, that the victim was actually an *accomplice*.

Robinson's version of the events in his life, however, came from the 1930s when escapist fare topped the list of films. *That* was his milieu. But it was now a new, more complex decade. In keeping with it, Robinson's story—although he was the last to know—was 1940s film noir, made up of the genre's familiar elements—tough guys who weren't always tough enough, a convoluted story line, workaday greed, adultery, even the inevitable double-cross.

$ Thomas Robinson, the man of the hour: "Son...you might be convicted."

$

AVAILABLE FOR THE DRAFT

On Thursday, December 9, 1943, the tenth day of the trial, Dr. Leon Solomon and Dr. Thomas J. Crice—essentially hired guns for the defense—testified that Robinson was insane. When attorney Hogan asked Crice if Robinson knew right from wrong or had enough control over his mind not to commit the crime he was charged with, Crice said, "No."

Former Western State hospital director, Dr. Edmund Cocke, said Robinson had a psychopathic

The G-men and the Heiress

personality (anti-social personality disorder), which Cocke defined as "an individual ill-equipped to meet the demands of his environment." The doctor said Robinson was a danger to his community, needed additional medical help, and should never have been released.

Four other doctors, all well-known psychiatrists and authorized by the judge, had examined Robinson at the jail on October 11 before the trial got underway. They found him *not* insane but that he did have an anti-social personality. Defense Attorney Hogan then asked if Robinson was a psychopath, and Dr. William Gardner said, "He certainly doesn't fall within that classification." For the jurors, the testimony left them just about where they had been before all the psychiatric testimony. They must have felt as though they had just watched a big game, only to see it end in a tie.

A few nights before the verdict was rendered, Robinson had a conversation with U. S. Marshal Loomis Cranor and his chief deputy. Robinson, in keeping with his extravagent self-regard, thought he would be set free, and he asked Cranor if Cranor would help get him out of town quickly because he, Robinson, was afraid he would get rearrested for failure to register for the draft.

"Son," Cranor said, "if they free you, I will see that you get right to Nashville where you can register but, Tom, I've seen many juries and trials and you had better begin facing the fact that you might be convicted."

The prosecutor, Brown, gave such an emotional closing that while quoting Exodus 21:16, he moved himself to tears:

> *And he that stealeth a man, and selleth him, or if he be found in his hand, he shall surely be put to death.*

It also struck a nerve with the courtroom attendees as they, too, were reaching for their handkerchiefs. Brown had won the crowd, it seemed, and the jurors as well. Defense attorney Hogan, who'd had an uphill run throughout the proceedings, used two hours for his closing, then asked for an additional half hour.

He summed up Robinson's mental issues and suggested Robinson's testimony should be weighed with that in mind. As for his client's account of his relationship with Mrs. Stoll, Hogan said he wouldn't represent a client who could lie with such recklessness. Robinson said it was true, so Hogan was leaving it to the jurors to decide if it was. Unfortunately for Hogan—and Robinson—the jurors had already decided.

On Saturday, December 11, after twelve days and three night sessions, the jury received its instructions from the judge. After two and a half hours of deliberation, the jury returned and Judge Miller asked the foreman, William Lee Mattingly, if the jury had reached a result.

"We have your honor," Mattingly replied. "We find the defendant, Thomas H. Robinson Jr., guilty and recommend the death penalty."

After eight ballots, the jurors had arrived at a unanimous decision. Robinson, who had once received a 95 in his criminal law course in college, took the result calmly. Later, he told his mother, "Well, Mom, they've given me the works."

Robinson was returned to the Jefferson County Jail where he was welcomed by Deputy Jailer P. J. Noone and said, "I knew it was coming." His calm attitude was short-lived, and soon he threatened to kill Marshal Cranor, Judge Miller, and an unnamed reporter.

Even though the jury recommended death, the final decision was up to the judge; he could also hand down life in prison, or less. Appearing before the judge, pale and repentant (at least for the moment), his voice trembling, he made an emotional plea for his life. He had served time at three penitentiaries over seven years, he said, and he had an almost perfect disciplinary record. He wanted to be sent back to one where he might begin his life again.

"Don't give me a death sentence," he pleaded. (His attorney pleaded similarly, breaking into sobs and saying to the judge, "If you appreciate my services, don't kill my client.")

On Monday, December 13, however, Robinson was sentenced to die in the electric chair at the Kentucky State Penitentiary. The judge chastised Robinson by suggesting that if he hadn't fabricated having relations with Mrs. Stoll, the jury most likely wouldn't have recommended the maximum sentence. It was unpleasant for the jury to recommend death, even more so for the judge, although even some of the public thought the penalty was too harsh—no one had died, after all. But Robinson, as usual, had been his own worst enemy.

The judge praised Hogan for representing his client diligently and efficiently—as well as any attorney could have done in such a complicated, practically hopeless case. He had appointed Hogan because of his integrity and ability, and while Hogan hadn't wanted the job, he performed admirably. The proceedings had taken its toll on Hogan; overweight at the beginning of the trial, he was now much slimmer, visibly aged, and his pleasant demeanor was frayed. (There always seemed to be a price paid by Robinson's various associates—both the willing ones as well as the unwilling.)

As for Robinson himself, the fat lady hadn't sung just yet.

But you could hear her backstage, running through scales.

The G-men and the Heiress

A travesty for Mr. Gooch

There was only one person ever executed for a kidnapping in which the victim was unharmed, a supremely unlucky career criminal named Arthur James Gooch. He and his partner, Ambrose Nix, broke out of a Holdenville, Oklahoma, jail in 1934, then pulled a heist across the state line in Tyler, Texas. The next day, when two unsuspecting policemen approached their car, they jumped the officers, put them in the back of their own patrol car, and fled back across the border where they released the two men, chagrined but unharmed. There was no ransom attempt.

A month later, in a shootout with other officers, Nix was killed and Gooch captured. Suicide-by-cop would have been preferable to what happened to him next. Yes, Gooch had violated the Lindbergh Law, but as one writer pointed out, "his crime wasn't exactly the scenario that legislation's drafters had foremost in mind." And it displayed one of the precarious dimensions of the death penalty, which is the discretionary power of prosecutors and judges.

If poor Gooch had only limited his wandering to one state or the other, a small-town crime might have remained just that. But the state line—and the new Lindbergh Law—elevated Gooch's misdeed into a capital one, and it did so on what was basically a technicality.

The lawless 1930s had given rise to new tough-on-crime stances, and no one wanted to be seen as weak.

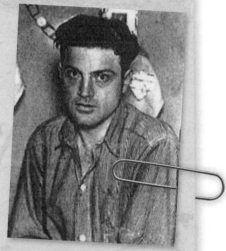

Gooch was sentenced to death, and the state of Oklahoma sent Gooch off to the gallows where a blundering executioner oversaw the fifteen minutes it took him to strangle. Gooch's last words: "It's kind of funny—dying. I think I know what it will be like. I'll be standing there, and all of a sudden everything will be black, then there'll be a light again. There's got to be a light again—there's got to be."

💲 Arthur Gooch: the unluckiest criminal of them all.

There probably wasn't, but his retrograde feat did earn him a spot in Wikipedia where he resides even today, sandwiched between two other Arthur Gooches, one an Australian football player and the other a retired British army officer.

The trial: be careful what you wish for

The Jefferson County Jail: unable to catch a break.

14 Dead man talking

"I just can't understand the boy…he seemed as though he didn't care."

—U.S. Marshal Cranor at the Kentucky State Penitentiary

As usual, nothing was predictable about Thomas Robinson. He had been held in the Jefferson County Jail since his trial, and in February of 1944 he was awaiting the result of his appeals as they worked their way through the system. Then the U.S. Marshal, Cranor, either had a tip about a possible jailbreak, or perhaps it was simply a premonition on Cranor's part—Robinson, after all, had already theatened to kill him. To be on the safe side, he placed a twenty-four-hour guard on Robinson.

On Sunday, February 13, around 6:30 p.m., in spite of Cranor's preemptive efforts, Robinson and three younger inmates made a break for it. Exercising in a barred first-floor corridor, they bent an iron bar to get into another corridor. From there, previously sawed bars—the blades had been smuggled in to them by a trusty—allowed them into a hallway where they climbed up the cell bars to the top floor of the jail. They surprised a guard and threatened him with iron supports they'd pulled off their bunks.

"Boys," said the guard, "it won't do you any good to kill me. I haven't got the keys (to the kitchen door that led outside) and you can't get out."

One of the inmates had wanted to kill the guard, but Robinson said they weren't going to kill anybody, especially as they had no way out of the building. The inmates climbed back down the way they'd come, but Robinson took the stairs, surprising the guard at the cellblock door, who asked him what he'd been doing.

"Getting some exercise," Robinson said.

The U.S. government was spending $547 a month to house Robinson (twice what annual wages were in 1944), plus $5.75 a day to each of the three guards who watched him around the clock. There was also a dollar for Robinson's overhead, so he was no bargain, and the authorities wanted a more secure environment for him, if not a cheaper one. So within days, attorney Hogan, Cranor, and two deputies loaded Robinson into a police van and transported him to the train station where he was shipped off to his newest residence.

Hogan told Robinson that his attempted escape was ill-advised and wouldn't help his appeals; Robinson promised to behave which, given Robinson, suggested he might remain on good behavior for a small and unspecified amount of time. He was hand-cuffed and shackled with leg irons where he wisecracked that he was carrying "enough iron to sink me."

The group arrived at the train station, surrounded by newsmen and photographers, and Robinson, in a jovial mood, suggested the guards should sit closer together to get in the photographs. The train arrived in Detroit around 8:30 the next morning, and from there he was off to his new home at the Federal Detention Farm at Milan, Michigan, where he would be designated inmate number 10249. He spent more time than anyone would have thought at Milan while his appeals worked through the process, temporarily staving off his execution, which was scheduled to take place at the Kentucky State Penitentiary.

In June of 1944, as Robinson languished in Michigan, Robinson's attorney, Hogan, appealed to the U.S. Sixth Circuit Court of Appeals in Cincinnati. Hogan argued be-fore the panel of three (with Judge Xen Hicks presiding) for an hour and forty minutes, explaining that capital punishment in the Lindbergh Law could not be invoked if the victim was released unharmed. United States Attorney Eli Brown argued half as long, his verbal efficiency resulting in Robinson's conviction being upheld.

Hogan then appealed to the U.S. Supreme Court on the grounds the Lindbergh Law was unconstitutional, but in December the court refused to review the conviction. In mid-January of 1945, the Supreme Court changed course and decided it *would* allow Robinson a rehearing. Limited to questions on the Lindbergh Law, the argument would again be based upon Hogan's logic that the death penalty could not be imposed if the kidnapped person had been released uninjured.

On March 5, the Supreme Court, in a vote of 7–2, upheld the death sentence. In the minority, Justices Wiley Rutledge and Frank Murphy considered the kidnapping statute murky and felt Robinson should be resentenced to a lower penalty. They both thought that "liberated" and "unharmed" in the statute was vague and that Congress should amend the law. The majority of justices, though, did not agree.

The G-men and the Heiress

$

A FLURRY OF LETTER-WRITING

Robinson didn't have a high opinion of Cranor, the Jeffersonville Marshal, and contended he had been set up by Cranor at the jail (although it's difficult to imagine exactly how Cranor inveigled Robinson into acquiring saw blades and overpowering a guard). Whatever Cranor may have thought about Robinson, he still dreaded the job of executing the man. He wanted no spectacle, the act done simply, procedures properly followed. Only three news agencies, Associated Press, United Press, and International News Service, were allowed to have a correspondent present, and there would be no interviews.

Robinson was understandably unhappy, as well. He wrote to his attorney, Hogan, and said, "If the Stolls, Speeds, Eli Brown, J. Dudley Inman, and certain G-Men had my fighting spirit they would be in uniform fighting Axis and not persecuting Americans such as I." (This, of course, from a man who had not yet registered for the draft and was sitting out the war at government expense.)

His letter-writing grew more prolific as the date of his execution neared. Hogan made some suggestions, the most significant being for Robinson to obtain recommendations halting the death penalty from the two Supreme Court Justices who had dissented in his case. Robinson sent letters to all nine justices, asking them to recommend clemency to the president.

He also sent off a fusillade of correspondence complaining about his negative coverage. There was, for instance, the "un-American" activity of Attorney General Francis Beverley Biddle and Director J. Edgar Hoover, who, Robinson said, had his hands all over the decision to deny Robinson's appeal (which, in this case, may actually have been true).

There was also *The Courier-Journal* and *The Louisville Times* that, Robinson felt, were out for his neck. They had printed articles titled "Without Bloodthirst" and "Robinson Simply Asked For It," and he wanted his mother to appeal to the American Newspapers Association, telling them the Louisville papers had prejudiced his case to such a point that a fair trial was impossible. Then he went straight to the horse's mouth, insisting that the owner/publisher Barry Bingham and editor Mark Foster Ethridge were good friends with the Stoll and Speed families, so what could one expect? He did, however, praise *The New York Times* for writing a story that told his side of things (disregarding the fact that *The Times* called him "insane"). He wanted his mother to promise she would carry on even if he were executed, continuing to hold accountable the "little Hitlers and hangmen," as he called them.

Dead man talking

At one point, he suggested that his funeral be held at his aunt's house, and he wanted a decent burial with flowers even if he *were* unable to smell them. It bothered him that his head would be shaved for the execution and that his body would be "burned black and eyeballs burst." (Robinson wasn't exaggerating: no less a reviewer than Supreme Court Justice William Brennan described one execution as the body "turning bright red as its temperature rises, and the prisoner's flesh swells and his skin stretches to the point of breaking. Sometimes the prisoner catches fire...")

When the time came, Robinson wrote, "I'll go like a man, with a smile, and I will walk, not have to be carried."

At the end of April, he sent his mother a letter suggesting she get an audience with President Truman, because Truman was a farmer, and Robinson wanted her to tell Truman of his gardening experience at Alcatraz and his interest in ranching. He said she was "the world's No. 1 mother," and that she had the admiration and respect of many federal prisoners and officials for her efforts on his behalf. She had much to be proud of, he said (in spite of the shame he had visited upon her).

Even with their shared agricultural leanings, Truman denied Robinson clemency. (It was likely Truman had other things on his mind; he had just been sworn in after Roosevelt's sudden death, he'd just learned about the atomic bomb, and Hitler had shot himself in his Berlin bunker.) Robinson, meanwhile, heard he'd been denied clemency on the radio, and the next day, he fulminated against everyone: President Truman, prison officials, his defense attorney, *The Courier-Journal,* Kentucky politicians, and G-Men. He was particularly unhappy with publisher William Randolph Hearst whose newspaper chain printed a story of Robinson as a cross-dresser. Another article had appeared titled "He Talked Himself into the Electric Chair," the first one a lie, he said, and the second one had harmed his chances of clemency.

$

ROBINSON'S MOTION, CHAIRED

For his execution, Robinson had been brought from Milan to the Kentucky State Penitentiary at Eddyville by his *bête noire*, U.S. Marshal Cranor. Robinson put on his best face and told attorney Hogan he didn't want to die a hypocrite by embracing religion in the final days. He wasn't a believer in heaven and thought hell was on earth. His creed was "eat, drink and be merry," his guiding philosophy being apparently hedonism (especially when using someone else's money). He also took another shot at the FBI, saying, "A national secret police system suggests a Gestapo carrying out the dictates of native fascists."

The G-men and the Heiress

Old Sparky

On June 9, 1945, before leaving the Kentucky State Penitentiary for Leavenworth, Thomas Robinson was still reveling in his near-death experience when he asked the warden if he could sit in the thick oak electric chair that had been reserved for him. The warden, with a gallows humor all his own, granted the request and Robinson sat down, placed his arms on the armrest, and flashed a big smile.

"It isn't so bad after all," he said.

He smiled because, once again, good fortune had unexpectedly fallen upon him, and he had just narrowly avoided becoming the one hundred and thirty-fifth prisoner executed in the chair since 1911.

The Kentucky penitentiary was merely one more residence befitting his life as a fugitive spent largely in the historic hostelries of America. The Kentucky penitentiary had been built in the late 1880s

💲 Eddyville place of honor: "abandon hope, all ye who sit here."

by Italian stonemasons on a hill overlooking the Cumberland River (and called, not without reason, "the Castle on the Cumberland").

The prison was already a quarter of a century old before the chair was added in 1911 and a convict named James Buckner, who'd had the poor judgment to kill a police officer a few weeks earlier by stabbing him nineteen times, received first honors. (Buckner claimed self-defense.) Old Sparky's historic moment, however, came in 1928 when seven men were electrocuted, one after the other, setting an unenviable national mark. (And unlucky, at least for the immediate company: the date was Friday, July 13.)

(A sentimental Eddyville favorite was the execution of Ballard Ratcliffe in 1930 for murder and robbery; he'd killed a man with a hammer while the man was bent in prayer over his wife's grave.)

In 1975, the *Murray Ledger* reported that Old Sparky, at age 64, needed an overhaul before being used again. The warden said the chair, last used in 1962, "is not even hooked up for electricity." It needed new straps and new wiring, he said, and it reminded observers of the old joke by an inmate as he approached the chair: "Are you sure that thing is safe?"

Somehow, Robinson's continual harange of officialdom actually worked in his favor, for on June 6, 1945, at the eleventh hour—less than a day and a half before his scheduled execution—Robinson's sentence was commuted from death in the electric chair to life in prison, with no parole. It came upon the recommendation of Attorney General Biddle who, no doubt, had been inundated by letters from Robinson's long-suffering mother. (The "no parole" clause was added because officials still thought Robinson was a menace to society and should be confined for protection of the community. Yet "no parole" didn't necessarily mean none at all, as there was still the concept of time off for good behavior.)

Warden Dewey Ward said Robinson, when told of his commutation, said nothing; he was "cool as a cucumber."

Cranor said Robinson acted like he "was on a picnic...I just can't understand the boy...he seemed as though he didn't care."

The next day, June 7, attorney Hogan, still dutifully on the job, requested a sanity hearing (although by now, he might have felt as though he should be requesting one for himself). He, along with prosecutor Brown, appeared before Judge Shackleford to determine whether Robinson would end up back at Alcatraz or an insane asylum in Illinois. By this time, being insane seemed like a viable option because the Michigan authorities had told Robinson that if he went back to Alcatraz, he'd be assigned to the laundry. He'd worked in the laundry before, which meant being isolated again. "I'd just as soon die in the chair as dying by degrees at Alcatraz," he said.

The prosecutor had three doctors give evidence, and they agreed Robinson was "in excellent control of his reasoning powers; he was emotionally stable; his judgment was unimpaired...a perfectly sane person." Hogan used Dr. Leon Solomon, who said he'd found Robinson "in sweet possession of all his faculties." This was not what Hogan wanted to hear; he wanted his client in an asylum, which he—and Robinson—regarded as a better alternative than the Alcatraz laundry. But for whatever reason, Dr. Solomon had gone off the psychiatric reservation.

Once at the USP at Leavenworth, though, Robinson was out of the frying pan (quite literally) and into the fire: he did not receive the proper welcome of an alumnus, and he wrote his mother who in turn wrote the acting director of the Bureau of Prisons, A. H. Conner. She said that her son had been "stripped stark naked every day and was made to parade in the walk before other inmates, and while he was out of his cell, the guards tore his bed up and scattered his clothes all over the floor. When asked why this was done, the guards stated they just wanted to worry him..."

The G-men and the Heiress

💲 Alcatraz: the touring criminal's last resort.

Conner passed this information along to the Leavenworth warden, Walter Hunter, who said that Robinson arrived at Leavenworth under maximum custody and had been placed in a segregation unit for a short period pending removal to Alcatraz. Policy dictated inmates in segregation got strip-searched once a day and their cells examined for contraband. Warden Hunter denied that disturbing things happened to Robinson, although his implication was that a penitentiary was not necessarily a Sunday school, rather a place where the word "disturbing" possibly took on new meanings.

On July 2, he arrived for his second tour of Alcatraz where he was now a seasoned hand. He occupied his time by filling the justice system with complaints. He was unhappy with his mother because she'd dropped her complaints of the Bureau of Prisons. "What kind of a man do you want me to be, honey?" he asked her. "A nincompoop, a jellyfish, a Casper milquetoast?"

On and on he went, saying that if he sat in prison and did nothing, he would deteriorate both mentally and physically. He had to fight, or he would never read a newspaper, hear a radio program, smoke a cigar, or enjoy a chocolate bar. He wasn't going to lie down like a yellow dog; he was going to continue fighting the Department of Justice.

Hoovering

With any keen overview of the decade, there's no difficulty in understanding why the old boy was so incensed by Thomas Robinson: it was essentially an issue of timing. Hoover had just begun his meteoric ascent into power and acclaim, both for himself and his institution. In 1933, it has been pointed out, he was little known. A year later, he was a household name. It was pure coincidence that the Alice Stoll kidnapping occurred in 1934, but it thrust a bumbling layabout and minor criminal into national prominence just as Hoover was making himself into America's criminal avenger, the man who could keep America safe.

Robinson did not help this picture, making off with a small fortune in bills that proved to be untraceable and eluding Hoover's best agents for upwards of two years. Robinson didn't stop Hoover's rise, but he put a dent in it. Small wonder that even after Robinson's imprisonment, Hoover watched his every move. Hoover had big fish to fry, and Robinson was a minnow that nipped at his public esteem.

This esteem, of course, is what drove Hoover, and he became not just a public hero but, in Nicholas von Hoffman's felicitous phrase, "the national mythic principle of goodness in combat with evil." There was no one like him, Hoffman said, "in power, fame, and longevity in office." What Hoover intuitively understood was that real power was the ability to implant yourself in "the popular imagination," which he did, using the pulp magazines of the era to help create the image of a gallant public servant overseeing a lionhearted force of men who were able to vanquish every public threat.

His FBI, said Hoffman, was not to be a national police force but to be "the unifying symbol of stability, family, flag, and fair play." That it wasn't—at least not always—was overcome by Hoover's indomitable image. He was a prime example of the great line from *The Man Who Shot Liberty Valence*: "When the legend becomes fact, print the legend." Hoover made a powerful institution, but first of all—and for better or worse—he made *himself*.

$ Portrait of the G-Man on his way up.

The G-men and the Heiress

BACK HOME AT THE ROCK

The FBI, of course, knew everything Robinson was up to. Once he was back at Alcatraz, agents inquired about copying Robinson's communications, but it was 1945 and the world had not yet received the miracle of electronic communications in which megabytes of words *and* pictures might flow unimpeded into every mailbox. It was not practical for the prison to mail Robinson's correspondence to the San Francisco FBI office for copying, and the prison had no instrument for copying, so the FBI loaned Alcatraz a portable photostat machine—approved ultimately by Director Hoover, who seemed personally vested in keeping an eye on Robinson.

So Robinson kept up a voluminous correspondence, giving the portable photostat machine a good workout, and occasionally he was allowed to see a movie. He was particularly fond of the musical, *Diamond Horseshoe,* which starred Betty Grable, and he described her (if politically incorrectly) by writing "she could soak her socks in my coffee." He may have seen something of himself in the plot, in which a med student who really wants to be a crooner gets himself involved with a showgirl with an ulterior motive.

In the spring of 1946, he wrote his mother that he was staying in shape by playing handball, and he and a teammate had won sixteen games straight, losing only four out of twenty-seven. The food in the joint was good, but he was staying lean as a racehorse and had dropped a considerable amount of weight since being confined, now topping the scales at a svelte 157 pounds.

His major exercise was still his correspondence, though, and he petitioned the U.S. attorney general, Thomas Clark, asking credit for time he'd already served. The petition was signed by several hundred citizens of Nashville, including attorneys, two senators, and several members of Congress, but the Justice Department and the FBI opposed it, primarily because it would have made Robinson eligible for parole in 1951. According to the U.S. Parole Board, the president's commutation made him eligible for parole in fifteen years—June 5, 1960.

On June 13, the attorney general asked Hoover his opinion on Robinson's petition. "I wish to state I am strenuously opposed to giving any favorable consideration to this request on the part of Robinson," Hoover wrote. He said Robinson had used a handgun during the crime, hit Mrs. Stoll in the head, tried to escape from the county jail, and disparaged Mrs. Stoll's reputation at trial. He'd been previously arrested for assaulting and robbing two women, committed to a mental institution, and, according to Hoover, was a pervert with syphilis. Surely, Hoover indicated, he'd *earned* Alcatraz. (In Hoover's heart

Dead man talking

of hearts, he thought Robinson had earned Old Sparky at Eddyville, but the Director was a circumspect man, and for the moment, he'd just work to make sure Robinson's parole was somewhere off in the very distant future.)

In August of 1948, Robinson went before the Alcatraz Classification Committee and requested a transfer to the USP at Atlanta, so he could be closer to his aging mother in Nashville. He received an excellent performance report from the associate warden about his laundry room duties. (He'd obviously resigned himself.) He was described as friendly and got along with his fellow workers (although he was not especially popular with the general prison population). He kept his bed made, his cell—and his nose—clean, and his appearance neat. The committee recommended a transfer to Atlanta, but it was turned down.

The 1950s arrived, and Robinson was still behind bars, sending and receiving letters from his mother. He had missed the advent of credit cards, diet soda, roll-on deodorant, and color television. In addition to his kitchen duties, Robinson worked in the garden, hospital, library, and as an orderly. Any additional waking hour was put to use honing his legal knowledge, most of it gained in his extended journey through the country's prison system.

He had, by this time, spent nine years at Alcatraz where he was described as a model prisoner, no mean feat, as he shared company with other former Public Enemies No. 1 such as Alvin "Creepy" Karpis. Robinson got a mention in Karpis's memoir, *On the Rock: Twenty-Five Years in Alcatraz*, and it seemed appropriate they were prison pals for they had much in common: neither liked work, both had begun with theft, then gone on to graduate work in kidnapping. They were, in other words, sociopaths-of-a-feather, and the biggest difference was that Karpis had murdered a law enforcement officer and should have gotten the electric chair, while Robinson hadn't killed anyone and barely managed to dodge it.

$

THE TIME OF HIS LIFE

Robinson's model prisoner status finally helped his move to Atlanta in 1954, and after a tranquil five years, Robinson was transferred from Atlanta to the Federal Correctional Institution at Tallahassee, Florida, in 1959. There, he was assigned recreational duties, which included the care of two tennis courts and supervising the players. The work was a walk-off for a man who had never obeyed the rules. He had permission to go outside the gate to retrieve tennis balls hit over the fence, and because of his performance

The G-men and the Heiress

SEP 10 1962

September 5, 1962

Mr. John F. Kennedy, President of the U.S.
White House
Washington, D.C.

This letter is being written in the hope that consideration may be
given Tom Robinson who , I feel, along with hundreds of others, has
more than paid his debt to society for the unfortunate folly of his
earlier years.

As the enclosed clippings and editorials will attest, this man has
spent approximately 25 years for a crime that many have served much
less for a murder charge. It is felt by many that undue pressure has
been brought to bear preventing this man from being released to be
given an even chance to become a useful citizen.

It is indeed unfortunate that in this Great Country of Ours one man
would be "Forgotten and it is with the desire that something may
be done for Tom Robinson that this is being brought to your attention.

Very truly yours,

Myrna Caruthers

Myrna Caruthers
Kingston Springs, Tennessee

💲 A Tennessean implores President Kennedy on Robinson's behalf.

he received a $10-a-month award that lasted for a year and a half, and he helped build two new courts.

In June of 1960, Robinson asked to be released to take care of his 84-year-old mother and elderly aunt, who lived together on $90 a month, and the parole board began reviewing his case. Mrs. Robinson Sr. provided a letter to the board requesting her son's discharge, and one former district attorney, as well as Berry Stoll, opposed it. A Tallahassee judge passed the buck to the higher-ups at Washington, DC.

In early January of 1961, though, Robinson was once again denied parole, most likely because he lied when he had testified in 1943, and because he continued to draw attention to himself with his legal efforts and in the press. Some thought Robinson should never see the light of day, and Director Hoover was likely at the top of the list.

Dead man talking

Jack of many trades

Of all the good men who'd been FBI agents, none ended up with a resumé like John ("Jack") Bugas. The son of Austrian immigrants, he grew up in Wyoming where he was a star athlete and paid for law school by working as a forest ranger. In 1934, he became

one of Hoover's men smack in the middle of the agency's most swashbuckling decade. Described as "adept at the art of fisticuffs while wearing a suit," he was quickly promoted and in 1938 became head of the FBI's Detroit office.

The geography, along with the timing, proved crucial because of the automobile industry and the agency's watch over wartime sabotage. Bugas was at the front of the FBI's

💲 John Bugas: the agents' agent (seen here with Walter Reuther).

notable cases (including the gunpoint arrest of Tom Robinson when he was Public Enemy No. 1); he also broke up two Nazi spy rings, and he was so well-liked he was known as "the agents' agent-in-charge."

In 1944, he went to work for the Ford Motor Company and Henry Ford II to weed out the gangster element in the plants. His aptitude soon came to legendary prominence; sent by Ford to fire the entrenched ex-boxer Harry Bennett, head of Ford's security ("cold and ruthless," one story called him), Bennett pulled a gun and so did Bugas. "I'll put one right through your heart, Harry," he said, and Bennett took him at his word. One newspaper called Bennett's security department as "the largest private quasi-military organization in the world."

Bugas rose even faster in the company, remaining Henry Ford II's right-hand man through the company going public in 1956. He came close to being named FBI director by Richard Nixon, but took on other directorships in other companies before returning home to Wyoming where he owned twenty thousand acres in the Sunlight Basin. There, his ranch was used as the film setting for the Marlboro Man cigarette ads. If they'd given the Marlboro Man a shoulder holster, John Bugas could have been the guy.

In December of 1961, Robinson was interviewed, at his request, by the chairman of the parole board, who recommended his release in March of 1962, saying there was no reason to keep him in prison. Fred Wilkinson, the warden during Robinson's time in Atlanta, wrote a letter on his behalf. Robinson and Wilkinson had played tennis, and perhaps the warden was predisposed to Robinson because Robinson never beat him. (On such small moments, empires turn.)

During the interview, Robinson supplied information about possible jobs, if and when he was released. In an unexpected turn, Robinson had written former agent John Bugas, who had arrested him in Los Angeles in 1936. Bugas had left the FBI and was now vice president of the Ford Motor Company, and he sent Robinson an application indicating a job might be waiting at a Ford glass facility in Nashville.

Robinson had spent almost twenty-five years behind bars for the kidnapping of Alice Speed Stoll. He had tried everything to free himself. He had pressed his aging mother to fight for him, contacted politicians, filed court petitions, communicated with three presidents, and even resorted to good behavior, all to no avail.

Undaunted, he would have more antics up his sleeve during the rest of the 1960s. Just when he should have settled in and completed his time in some leisurely fashion, his behavior would become even more bizarre.

Robinson arrested in 1965 at Nashville after his second escape.

15 Robinson takes a hike

"He's not a vicious criminal, he's a nice guy."
—St. Elizabeth psychiatrist, about Robinson

As 1962 rolled around, Robinson had spent the previous twenty-six years incarcerated, and some thought that was enough for the crime he committed back in 1934. He had recently submitted yet one more petition for the commutation of his sentence, but the pardon attorney at the Department of Justice turned it down. The attorney, said Robinson, was arguing legal issues better suited for the court, and he suggested Robinson resubmit the pardon request explaining his positive adjustment to prison life.

But, Robinson wondered, where was his reward for all his "positive adjustment?" In the past decade alone, Robinson had seen two of his writs dismissed (one by the Supreme Court), and four motions denied, including two to set aside his original conviction and another for amnesty. If Robinson had ever applied himself to the workaday world as he did to his judicial paperwork, he would have been a corporate executive wearing a tailor-made suit.

The Federal Correctional Facility at Tallahassee, Florida, wasn't exactly a retirement colony with shuffleboard courts, but neither was it Alcatraz (once described as "the great garbage can of San Francisco Bay, into which every federal prison dumped its most rotten apples"). Robinson was a trusty, allowed to work outside the prison, and the warden, Walter Jacquot, considered him "model." Therefore Jacquot was perplexed when in late July his model prisoner fled; he thought Robinson's escape was brought about by concern for his mother.

Jessie Robinson was 87 and looked even older. She had been at the Sunny View Nursing Home in Nashville for about a year, recovering from a broken hip, and still needed help to walk. She had been in financial straits for years, and because her husband had been a Mason, she received a small amount of help from the Widows and Orphans Fund of the Masonic Grand Lodge of Tennessee. She hadn't seen her son since sometime in the 1950s, at the Atlanta Penitentiary.

She was surprised—and perhaps a bit apprehensive—when reporters from a Nashville newspaper showed up, and she asked them, "Do you have any news about Tom?"

"No," they said, not telling her about the escape.

"I've been expecting him home for twenty-eight years," she said timidly. "And I'm still waiting."

She told the reporters that when she went to bed at night, her mind wandered back in time. "I can still hear him whistling up the back stairs as he did when he was a boy," she said.

The story appeared in the *Nashville Tennessean* under the headline, "Aged Mother Waits, Hopes," where she was described not inaccurately as one "whose life has been spun of hope and sacrifice."

$ Another walk-off: the Federal Correctional Institution in Tallahassee.

The G-men and the Heiress

ON THE RUN AGAIN

Robinson had simply walked away from the Tallahassee institution. ("I was under no restrictions and was allowed to go into town, so one day I just didn't come back," he said afterward.)

He had $100 in cash and caught a bus to Atlanta where he purchased a .38 caliber handgun for $15. He was, indeed, headed for Nashville to visit his mother but he knew agents were watching her, so he went to Chicago, where he previously lived and which was familiar to him.

Law enforcement had civilian planes searching for Robinson with the head of the Jacksonville FBI office (which covered Tallahassee), SAC Donald Brown, leading the search, and—no matter that Robinson was in Chicago—calls about Robinson sightings flooded in to the authorities.

Robinson escaped on July 21, a Saturday, and was a free man until the following Saturday when, out of money and growing desperate, he held up the Berliant Prescription Pharmacy, which netted him only $14. A shop employee followed Robinson out of the establishment, waved down a Chicago Police Department patrol car that happened to be passing by, and Robinson was apprehended without incident. (For once in his otherwise charmed life, his timing had betrayed him.)

He told Detective Russell Miller that he was an escaped federal prisoner, that he'd run out of money, and seemed astounded by prices (the price of a Reuben sandwich had more than doubled since the last time he'd bought one, and everything else seemed to have doubled, as well). "Prices on the outside today are ridiculous," he said. "Food, bus rides, hotel rooms, everything was more expensive. I guess I'm doomed to end my days behind walls."

He said he'd come close to finding a job but "the prices just caught up with me." Being free had been exhilarating, though. "I felt ten feet tall walking down Michigan Avenue in Chicago," he said.

The Cook County Felony Court dismissed the case at the request of the state attorney's office, which turned Robinson over to his federal keepers. Robinson's ill-fated venture outside did result in one positive, if for only one old lady at the Sunny View Nursing Home in Nashville. For Robinson was taken to the Davidson County Jail in Nashville where he was met by two prison officers from Atlanta, and after he showered and put on fresh clothes, they took him to see his mother.

"Is this a joke?" she asked when Robinson walked in. Then she wanted to know about the men with him. Robinson said he'd been given "special permission" to see her, and in an unusually generous gesture, none of the officers—nor the reporters—told her he'd just escaped and held up a Chicago pharmacy.

The visit lasted all of forty-five minutes because she quickly tired, but he was taken back the next day where he was reunited with his son, James, who by this time was married and brought along his wife, Robinson's new daughter-in-law. His aunt, Mrs. Warner, who lived nearby, arrived by ambulance, and it was quite a reunion for her; because of their poor health, they hadn't seen one another in years. The papers and records do not clearly say, but this may have been the first time Robinson saw his son since he was a baby.

Both the *Nashville Tennessean* and the *Nashville Banner* showed up and while they couldn't photograph Robinson's mother because of her health, they hung around and took photographs when the group was leaving. Robinson was cooperative throughout the process, appreciative of the visits with his mother, and he apologized to the Bureau of Prisons officers for his escape.

He was taken back to the USP at Atlanta where he forfeited 444 days of Extra Good Time he had earned, and he settled back into prison life where, by all accounts, he was once again well-behaved. Surely, though, his keepers were by now watchful in the face of Robinson's studied tranquility. (Recall, if you will, the Hare Psychopathy checklist, with its twenty items ranging from "need for stimulation" to "poor behavioral controls." Robinson was an IED—Improvised Emotional Device—who might go off at any time.)

$

RUN FOR YOUR LIFE

He remained at Atlanta for the next two years, then was transferred to Texas where, approaching 60, Robinson demonstrated that he was still Robinson. In July of 1965, he walked away from a minimum-security facility, the Federal Correctional Institution at Seagoville, a suburb of Dallas, a facility for minimum-security male offenders that had been an internment camp during WWII (it boasted at the time a German-language newspaper and held some fifty Japanese language teachers, all on a footprint that resembled a college campus, that is, if a college campus were administered by a warden).

Once again, Robinson was assigned outside work (the fresh air seemed to stimulate him), and while dressed as an umpire calling softball games, he walked off again. This escape was even more perplexing than the previous one, for the parole board had met

The G-men and the Heiress

the month before and its decision was pending. Perhaps Robinson had been denied so many times, the process had become a foregone conclusion, and he kept doing it merely to hone his evolving legal skills.

He headed back to Nashville and, somewhere along the way, telephoned a friend in Arkansas, told him he was getting released (which in a way, he was), and persuaded him to wire a $100 money order. (Robinson might have remembered how far a C-note took him last time but perhaps all the fresh air left him too excited.)

After hitch-hiking to Arkansas, he bought a .32 caliber revolver from a West Memphis surplus store, then caught a bus to Nashville. On Wednesday, July 14, eight

$ Thomas Robinson in 1964, still on camera.

days after his escape, he attempted to rob the downtown branch of the Third National Bank of Nashville. There, even older and with graying hair, he was recognized by a former Vanderbilt University man, Walter Jones, the bank's vice-president.

Robinson tried to bluff Jones by telling him to follow orders "because his wife was in custody." Jones was angered by that, and he grabbed Robinson and pinned him down (which upon reflection, Jones said was a foolish move on his part). Robinson hit Jones over the head with the weapon, it fell to the floor, and accidentally went off. Or, depending upon which newspaper one believed, Robinson shot at Jones, barely missing him. ("That poor dumb cluck," Jones said later.)

Tom Sawyers, a teller, ran to Jones's aid, struggled with Robinson, and got the gun, telling Robinson, "You move, and I will have killed my first man."

"You got me," Robinson prudently replied.

When police sergeant Ed Herdon arrived, six bank employees were hovering around a slightly injured Robinson, who was on the floor as docile as a new Easter lamb. Jones was treated for the pistol whip injuries, first by bank employees, then by a doctor at the scene. At the station, Robinson admitted the attempted bank robbery but said he wanted an attorney. "If I had known Jones was there, I never would have gone inside," he said, thinking perhaps how poorly the incident reflected upon a former Vandy man.

He later told both police and the newspapers that due to the illness of his mother and elderly aunt, and the frustration over being brushed off by the parole board, he'd lost his temper and the escape was just a reaction to that. He did not attempt to rationalize the armed holdup; it had come out of the ether. It appeared to be simply one more example of Robinson's lifelong predilection for remaining the villain protagonist of his own story.

The U.S. District Court judge in Nashville was so confounded by Robinson's ambiguous behavior, he sent him off to the St. Elizabeth Hospital in Washington, DC, for a mental evaluation. St. Elizabeth was the first federally operated psychiatric hospital, and Robinson's name was added to its list of the infamous, i.e., the attempted assassins of presidents Andrew Jackson and Ronald Reagan, as well as the man who killed President James Garfield.

In October of 1965, St. Elizabeth advised the court Robinson was competent to understand the charges against him. The psychiatrist who had been examining him for the past six weeks found it difficult to reconcile the man and his past.

"He's not a vicious criminal, he's a nice guy," the doctor said, and in an interview by the *Washington Post's* news service, he said Robinson appeared to be one of those chronic inmates who had become so conditioned to incarceration that they had lost all familiarity with the outside world. "Freedom can be a terrifying experience," he said, "and they'll do anything, even break the law, in order to return to the security of their cells." The doctor called this condition "flight into custody."

Said the *Post* article, tellingly, "There is still the possibility that Robinson might eventually win parole and his freedom, if he can stand it."

On November 3, Robinson pled guilty to escape and bank robbery before U.S. District Court Judge William Miller and was sentenced to fourteen years in prison for bank robbery and five years for an escape to run concurrently with his life sentence. Parole was left to the discretion of the parole board.

Perhaps it was nothing more than what Robinson had told his mother in a letter when he was in jail in Michigan, expecting his own execution: "I don't ever expect to see freedom again. My life has already been lived. I'm through, washed up. The only thing I have left is plenty of fight. I loathe and despise the forces responsible for my predicament, and I'm going to harass, embarrass, and fight them till I die." (See, once more, the Hare Psychopathic checklist: "exaggeratedly high opinion of self.")

The G-men and the Heiress

HOME, SWEET HOME

At the end of 1965, the holidays looming, Robinson was back where it all began, at the Atlanta Penitentiary, which surely by now had a wing named for him. After a quiet two years, he was back in the news in 1967, contesting his aunt's will. She had left her small estate (stocks and bonds) in a trust for him, then after his escape attempt in Texas, she had the will rewritten, making Robinson's son, James, the sole beneficiary. Robinson wanted the original will restored because he needed to show the parole board that upon his release he would have some means of support (even if it *did* come at the expense of the son to whose welfare he'd contributed nothing but disgrace).

Robinson's son was unusually charitable. "After all," James said, "he's been in prison for thirty years. I don't feel harshly toward him and sympathize with the way he feels." He didn't contest his father's actions, which weren't successful anyway, and the young man remained his great-aunt's beneficiary.

Undeterred, Robinson was back in court, filing a twenty-eight-page motion with the Sixth U.S. Circuit Court of Appeals in Cincinnati to vacate his sentence. In it, he argued that the courts were guilty of double jeopardy, that is, trying him twice for the same offense, that the kidnapping act itself was unlawful, that he'd received un-usual punishment, and been refused due process and a fair trial. The court overruled his appeal.

He was assigned as an orderly, ending up in E cellblock where he was given a food service assignment. He was being represented by Atlanta attorney Thomas Gresham, who described him as a friendly, likable fellow, and intelligent (although some of his legal ideas struck Gresham as "hare-brained"). With Gresham's assistance, the U.S. District Court in Atlanta restored some of Robinson's prison good time forfeited after the Texas escape. Gresham also went out on a limb and contacted *Atlanta Constitution* publisher Ralph Emerson McGill who, in turn, contacted a Georgia friend in the White House about Robinson's case, although ultimately nothing came of it.

In the fall of 1970, after serving thirty-four years in half a dozen jails and prisons, Thomas Henry Robinson Jr. was released on parole from the USP at Atlanta. He had been a substantial drag on the system for over three decades, singlehandedly responsi-ble for thousands of man hours by federal agents, local law enforcement people, prison officials, doctors, lawyers, and various others. He had been chased for eighteen months (requiring some twenty-five thousand man hours by Hoover's men), responsible for three trials, room and board at half a dozen jails and prisons, hours of psychiatric review, even

Robinson takes a hike

$ Robinson in 1970 after half a life behind bars.

the cost of an airplane used to locate him after one of his escape attempts. The cost was easily well in excess of a million dollars.

Robinson's greatest earning period was 1934 to 1936, and prorated over his lost time came to some $1,400 a year. He, himself, said crime didn't pay. But how many among us had a two-year spree like his, in which he lavished away the equivalent of

The G-men and the Heiress

nearly a million dollars? It wasn't that crime didn't pay; it was merely that it didn't pay *long*.

He remarried his previous wife, Frances, found work as a clerk, and by all existing accounts he seemed to have finally become a model citizen, not just in his various lockups, but on the *outside*. He had outlasted the opinion by the St. Elizabeth psychiatrist who said his life seemed to be "a flight into custody." He'd outlived other things as well: the Packard Motor Car Company stopped making Robinson's favorite car; his arch-nemesis, Hoover, was dead; Old Sparky at the Kentucky Penitentiary was retired; Alcatraz closed and began to offer cruises ("Experience the beauty, history, and infamy of Alcatraz Island!"); and the federal kidnapping law was no longer a capital offense (if the victim was left unharmed).

The *Jackson Sun* in Jackson, Tennessee, ran a feature on him when he was in his 70s, reporting that Robinson visited the post office nearly every day, picking up his mail and studying the wanted posters. It seemed as if he were looking for something—or someone—familiar. He never saw anyone he knew, though, for all his old prison pals—Doc Barker, Alvin Karpis, the mild-mannered Machine Gun Kelly—were long since departed. Perhaps it was nothing more than nostalgia for the time when he, too, had been a public enemy, his picture on all the posters, a man to be reckoned with.

Perhaps he was simply looking for himself, a man he'd never found.

Robinson takes a hike

(Concurrent Sentence)

Name	ROBINSON, Thomas Henry Jr.	No.	A-48438-A
Alias			5-12-69

Crime Kidnap & Bank Robbery & Escape fm Fed. Cust.

District N/Ga. - W/Ky   Race W   Age 62

Sentence: Life-14 - 5 yrs. Concur.   Fine and Costs: $

Date	12-13-43	Committed Fine	Not Committed
Sentence begins	6-6-45	Rate per mo. g.t.	
Committed to Fed. Inst.	6-8-45	Total g.t. possible	
Elig. for parole	5-10-51	Extra g.t.	
Expires w/g.t.		G.T. forfeited or withheld	
Expires (extra-part) g.t.		G.T. restored	
Expires full term	Life	Date of release	
Full term less 180 days		Method of release	
Residence	Nashville, Tenn.	FBI NO. 842 779	

PAROLE
10-15-70

Name ROBINSON, Thomas Henry Jr.   No. A-48438-A

Robinson's get-out-of-jail card, at long last.

Epilogue

16

"I'd love to go back to Alcatraz."—Thomas Robinson Jr.

When Thomas Robinson finally got out of prison in 1970, from the USP at Atlanta, he had missed the tumultuous upheaval of the 1960s, the Civil Rights movement, the Vietnam war protests, political assassinations, the moon landing, the baby boomers' generation gap with their parents, and perhaps this: the emotional bond of raising his son and the companionship of a mate.

Mrs. Stoll, when reached by a *Nashville Banner* newspaper reporter, had no comment. Fred Russell of the *Nashville Banner*, a sportswriter who later became the paper's vice-president, was listed on Robinson's Parole Progress Report as his advisor. He and Robinson had corresponded during his incarceration. Robinson registered with the local police, keeping them up to date on his whereabouts. It appeared that the time of his many aliases was finally over, and he would henceforth be easily found. He and his wife lived on his clerking job, some money left to her, and—ultimately—social security. He had the outline of a memoir and was considering a ghostwriter and publication, but no manuscript has come to light.

There were many acts in the Robinson saga; it was hard to keep them all straight, but the play was over. There was one more small stint in the public eye, which came in 1980 when he was interviewed for an article that recounted his boisterous year and a half on the run, saying, "He stayed in the uptown hotels, drank in the swank spots, drove a big Packard, and donned the best clothes."

Frances had kept some of his old clothes, which he liked to wear, and he was still trim even after years of prison food. On vacations, they traveled. He liked to visit old haunts. (There was no mention of what Frances thought, as she hadn't been along.)

"I'd love to go back to Alcatraz," he told the reporter, "that's one of the things I must do. It would be just a kind of satisfaction to thumb my nose at it."

He said he didn't regret his two escapes, and he seemed philosophical, that it was all fate. "It's just like they say," he said, "Kismet, fate, you can't quarrel with the old lady."

Frances died in April of 1985, a full decade before Robinson. Their son, James, died in 1993, a year before his father. All are buried at the Sears Cemetery in Pegram, Tennessee, a tiny rural town not far from Nashville.

Alice Helen Speed Stoll was a reserved, private person and never talked about the kidnapping, even when family members tried to pry it out of her. Shortly after the event, she did, however, write down her remembrances of the incident, revealed only to a small cadre of family members. She spent her time gardening and she and her sister, Virginia, owned Cave Spring Farm in Jessamine County, Kentucky, still held today by the family. They raised thoroughbreds, selling the foals as yearlings, rather than training them to race.

The Speed Museum was founded by her stepgrandmother, Hattie Bishop Speed, and named after her grandfather James Breckinridge Speed. Mrs. Stoll was vice-president and a member of the museum's board of governors for thirty years and an avid

$ Alice Stoll at 88, as debonair as ever.

The G-men and the Heiress

collector of Eighteenth Century French art. During her life, she donated nearly twenty paintings to the museum.

Even though she would have preferred to have forgotten about the kidnapping, it never completely went away. The newspapers mentioned the event on every fifth increment anniversary, during Robinson's trial, appeals, escapes, and upon his death. As might have been expected, the kidnapping was referenced upon her death on March 26, 1996, at age 90, but what really must have caught everyone's eye was her worth —$159 million. (Her burial site in the Cave Hill Cemetery is marked with a simple, flat marker, containing only her name and dates.)

She never had children but was generous to relatives and others, leaving a sizable sum to six nieces and nephews. A cousin was the recipient of the five hundred-acre Waverly Farm in Woodford County, Kentucky, and an additional million dollars. The gardener, Michael Oliver, of the Stoll estate, was given $1 million, and so was the caretaker, Loxley Watler of the farm.

A significant portion of her estate, $50 million or so, including her residence—the big house at 5721 Stoll Hill Road and The Cottage at 5720 Stoll Hill Road—and estimated to be worth $3.5 million at the time, were donated to the Speed Museum. In 1998, the museum sold the property for $2.75 million.

Berry Vincent Stoll, at age 88, preceded Alice Stoll in death on January 30, 1983, at Pease Bay, Grand Cayman, their second home. He was known as "an operator," selling sand from the beach to those interested. There was no obituary for Berry in either Louisville newspaper. Mrs. Stoll had become even more reclusive by this time and didn't want any publicity. Berry left everything to his wife, although the will didn't disclose a dollar amount.

Jean H. Breese performed a dog and pony show in 1936 in Nashville about her time with Robinson, then seemed to vanish. She turned up in Los Angeles in 1942, her engagement announced in the *Los Angeles Times*. The newspaper listed her age as 41 and her fiance as Curt Hasspacher, 53, a printer. They were married on April 4, 1944, and true to form, she lied on the marriage license which said she had never been married. Not much is known about Jean after this, other than at some point she left Hasspacher. She moved in and out of the lives of her kinfolk, disappearing for years and not surprisingly was considered the black sheep of the family. At some point, she moved back to New York where she lived with her sister Ethel and later with a friend before entering a nursing home at Port Jefferson, New York. She died there in September of 1977.

All the players are long gone, the Stoll cottage where the crime took place was sold in 1998, and the house expanded, the older part becoming the north part of the new one. Harrod's Post Office and Grocery, where the press hunkered down during the six days while Mrs. Stoll was held, was torn down in 2018. The apartment building in Indianapolis where she was held is now a parking lot. The Starks Building, where the Louisville FBI office reopened in 1935, is still in place, but the FBI moved out four years later. The U.S. Post Office, Courthouse, and Custom House, where the Robinson family trials took place, is now the Gene Snyder United States Courthouse, and two more courtrooms have been added. The Brown Hotel, where the jury was sequestered in 1943 during Robinson Jr.'s trial, is still operating and opulent, although its heyday of 1,200 guests attending a nightly dinner-dance is long past. The USP at Alcatraz, where Robinson served most of his sentence, hasn't been a prison for over fifty-five years but is open to the public for tours. The voluminous Stoll FBI kidnapping file is available at the National Archives at College Park, Maryland; otherwise, the retelling of the story would be incomplete. The FBI file is a little worse for wear, which is not surprising, alas, as both the paper and the story are over eighty-five years old.

The G-men and the Heiress

SAME FOR MRS STOLL

EXCEPT AMOUNT → $50,000 (FIFTY)

AMOUNT OF RANSOM: ~~$30,000(thirty thousand dollars)~~.

~~$15~~,000 to be in $10.00 bills, and ~~$15~~,000 to be in $20.00 bills.

Put this money in as small a paste-board box as possible; pack and wrap it carefully so that it will be accepted by the Railway Express Agency; declare the value of package at $10.00; do not state what it really contains.

Address it carefully and plainly; then send it by RAILWAY EXPRESS ONLY, to the INTERMEDIARY WHO STOLL AND ONE OF OUR MEMBERS AGREE ON BEFORE HE IS TAKEN FROM THE HOUSE.

THIS INTERMEDIARY'S NAME WILL BE FILLED IN AT THE BOTTOM OF THIS PAGE BY STOLL. It will have to be one of several business men living in Nashville, Tennessee, who we know to be a friend of Stoll, and who we are prepared to watch in order to see if you try to set a trap for us. We will allow Stoll to choose one of these men.

THIS INTERMEDIARY MUST HAVE ABSOLUTE FREEDOM FROM POLICE. HE MUST NOT EVEN BE QUESTIONED BY ANYONE. YOU MUST NOT CORRESPOND WITH HIM. IF HE IS PUT WISE, THE DEAL IS OFF, AND WE WILL CARRY OUT OUR THREAT AS TO STOLL. We must have a clear opportunity to contact the intermediary. We cannot do that with police surrounding the house. If they do, you can take our word that we will know of this fact in advance, and then we will make no effort to collect the money,but will then do what we have said we would about Stoll.

STARTING THE DAY AFTER THE KIDNAPING, WE GIVE YOU 5 (five) DAYS(not including a Sunday) TO GET THE MONEY INTO THE HANDS OF THE INTERMED- IARY. THIS MEANS THAT IT MUST BE SENT ON THE FOURTH DAY IN ORDER TO ARRIVE ON THE FIFTH. Do this sooner, if possible, as the sooner Stoll is returned, the easier it will be on him.

THEN, JUST AS SOON AS WE GET THE MONEY INTO OUR HANDS, STOLL WILL BE RELEASED UNHARMED. To this we give you our word.

We will call Express Agency in Nashville and see when your package arr- ives. (We will call from a pay station far from where we hold Stoll).

Do not take the serial numbers of the money.IF YOU MAKE ANY PUBLICITY OF THIS CASE AFTER STOLL IS RETURNED, OR TRY TO CATCH US IN ANY WAY AFTERWARDS, WE WILL SHOOT DOWN YOUR FAMILY FROM OUR CAR WITH A 30-30 RIFLE.

Do not waste our time or yours trying to reduce the ransom. You can get $30,000 or else------.

THERE CAN BE NO OTHER NEGOTIATIONS. WE DO NOT HAVE TIME TO BARGAIN. IF YOU DELAY AND STALL FOR TIME, WE HAVE TOLD YOU OUR POSITION, AND WHAT MUST HAPPEN TO STOLL. We have no other alternative if we do not receive the money. THIS JOB IS SO ARRANGED THAT NO ONE OUTSIDE THE STOLL FAMILY WILL KNOW WHAT HAS HAPPENED AT THE START. It is for you to keep it that way.

Explain Stoll's absence as illness or say he is out of town.

IF THIS IS GIVEN TO POLICE OR PRESS, NOTHING CAN SAVE STOLL.

NAME OF INTERMEDIARY (~~to be filled in by Stoll~~)

Mr. *T. H. ROBINSON*

Street *1716 ASHWOOD AVE*

Town   NASHVILLE, TENNESSEE

WE ASSURE YOU THAT PACKAGE OF MONEY WILL NOT GET INTO WRONG HANDS, SO DO NOT TRY TO CONTACT THIS MAN, AS IT MAY UPSET PLAN OF PAY-OFF.

$ The original note: "Burn his body; scatter his ashes..."

Agent bios

The loose trilogy of books that began with *The G-Man and the Diamond King*, a 1935 story of the murder of Cincinnati FBI Special Agent Nelson B. Klein, was followed by two other cases, Klein assisted in investigating. A 1929 Washington, DC, murder case, *The G-Men and the Nurse*, and now *The G-Men and the Heiress*, highlight agents that were pioneers of the organization. The 1930s was the time of the gangster and outlaw and the G-Men, for the most part, were ill-equipped to handle the onslaught. It was fortuitous that in 1924 a young J. Edgar Hoover was named director, leading the way with his administrative and organizational skills.

The FBI played catch-up, using new laws, authority to carry weapons, enhanced training, and the power to make arrests. Hoover had the foresight to order the formation of a training academy to provide agents with the application and practice of the legal statutes. Last, by combining the nation's fingerprint cards in one repository, the FBI Identification Divison was born, as was the Laboratory Division, with crime now being fought scientifically.

Hoover formed the organization with the help of headquarters' personnel and SACs in the field. But for the most part, it was the 1930s brick (street) agents who made the cases, receiving little, if only occasional, recognition from the press. In many instances, agents that investigated the Stoll kidnapping went by first and middle initials, making it difficult to find records. Also, since this story began in the 1930s and dragged on into the 1970s, there are plenty of files at the National Archives at College Park (12,000), San Bruno (3,000), Atlanta (2,100), Kansas City, and Chicago.

An exhaustive search of FBI Files, www.Newspapers.com, www.findagrave.com, www.ancestry.com, city directories, *The Grapevine*, and www.historicalgmen.square-space.com, helped determine full names, biographical information, and nuances about the agents.

The complete stories of agents Hilary William Costello, Lyman Morris Chipman, Crawford H. Carson, William Troup Morton, and Monti Clair Spear, to name just a few, have yet to be told. There is little information; they, for the most part, were invisible, which is just how Hoover wanted it. In Hoover's FBI film, after all, he and the organization were to be the only significant stars. Information obtained about the agents raised a dilemma of where the data should get placed in the manuscript. What follows is a list of those who investigated the Stoll case, which by no means is all-inclusive:

Appel Jr., Charles A., came from healthy stock as his grandfather was a Civil War cavalry hero, and his father was with the IRS and owned a plumbing company. He was born in 1895, raised in Washington, DC, graduating from McKinley Technical High School. In 1924 appointed an agent with the FBI, while in Detroit was involved with a successful police corruption and prostitution case. The defense would claim he drank alcohol and used prostitutes to entrap pimps and the police. His life threatened by the mob, he got a transfer to Dallas, investigating bankruptcy fraud cases. Then it was on to headquarters where he helped start the FBI Laboratory in the early 1930s. Later he had plenty of experience in the analysis of document examination, handwriting, hand-lettering, typewriting, and printing, testifying in state, federal and Military courts, Court of Claims, and before Congress. A document expert examines not only handwriting but the paper and how it's made, the composition and age of the inks and dyes used in documents, and ways documents may get altered. He retired from the FBI in 1949 and started his own company in document examination, testifying as an expert witness. He died in Washington, DC, at age 86.

Barber, Almon P., was assigned to the Stoll case and assisted in the felony car stop of the vehicle containing Mrs. Stoll. He was born in 1902 and served as a Cleveland police officer before entry into the FBI (1934–1944). On October 12, 1937, he was on scene with other agents and police in Bangor, Maine, when two members (Alfred James Brady and Clarence Lee Shaffer, Jr.) of the Al Brady gang were cornered and killed. The group was prolific car thieves, bank robbers, jewel thieves, and murderers. Of the 45 rounds fired that day by agents, it got reported that 43 hit their mark. A third member, James Dalhover, was captured that day, and later executed for the murder of Indiana State Police Trooper, Paul Vincent Minneman.

Bellino, Carmine S., was in the Chicago office when he was assigned to assist with the Stoll case. He served with the FBI from 1934-1945. Later, he was a Congressional investigator for 30 years, helping to bring down teamster leaders James Hoffa and David Beck. He was named an assistant to President John F. Kennedy and was the chief investigator for the Senate Watergate committee. He died in 1989, at age 84.

Bennett, Lorenzo Thompson, was assigned to the Chicago office when he was sent to Indianapolis to assist with the Stoll case. He was born in 1912. After the FBI, he practiced law and then became an Associate Judge in Kalamazoo, Michigan, in the 1950s. He died in 2004.

Billings, Thomas Elton, was assigned to the Los Angeles office when he participated in the arrest of kidnapper Thomas H. Robinson Jr. He was born in 1905 and, after serving in the FBI, was appointed in 1959 by Governor Edmund G. Brown to head the California state agency, which regulated private detectives. He died in 1985.

Black, Earle Manuel, was assigned to Detroit when he was ordered to Indianapolis to assist with the Stoll case. He was born in 1898 in South Carolina and served two years with the Army during WWI. He joined the FBI, and in 1932 was serving in Washington, DC. After leaving the organization, he practiced law. He died in 1984.

Boardman, Leland "Lee" V., was assigned to the Chicago office when sent to Indianapolis to assist with the Stoll kidnapping case. He served in the FBI from 1934-59, heading up offices in Milwaukee, Cleveland, Kansas City, Seattle, Philadelphia, and New York City, then named Assistant Director heading the Investigative Division, retiring as SAC of the Washington Field Office. Born in Hot Springs, Arkansas, in 1911, his family moved to Minnesota, later obtaining a B. A. and LLB from the University of Minnesota. He died on May 8, 1987, of complications from Parkinson's disease.

Brown, Donald Kenneth, was born in Arizona, and after graduating from Arizona State Teachers College he joined the FBI in 1935 as a clerk in the Phoenix office. He became a Special Agent three years later and would lead eleven FBI offices during his 33-year career. Brown retired as SAC of the Jacksonville office in 1968 to become Chief of the Jacksonville Police Department. When the police and sheriff's departments merged, he became Undersheriff. Brown was the grandnephew of Brigham Young, founder of Salt Lake City. He died in 1975 of a heart attack during a round of golf.

Bugas, John S., was a graduate of the University of Wyoming and joined the FBI in 1935 after practicing law. He resigned as SAC of Detroit in 1944 to take a position as Vice President of Industrial Relations for Ford Motor Company. Just a year later, he was instrumental in ousting Harry Bennett from the company. Bennett had become the might behind the company as the elder Henry Ford I had succeeded power. Bugas described entering Bennett's office and walking the long-distance and standing before his desk. "Bennett then jumped up and screamed you're behind all this, you sonofabitch." Then he opened the desk drawer and pulled out a .45 revolver, slamming the weapon on the desk. Bugas had a .38 revolver inside his jacket and was ready. Bennett, still cursing Bugas, finally ran out of steam and sat back in his chair. Bugas told him he only had himself to blame; then he turned his back and took the long walk out of the office. It allowed Henry Ford II to take charge of the company; they became good friends. Bugas retired from the Ford company in 1968. Bugas died in 1982 at age 74.

Agent bios

Burrus, Robert P., was assigned to the Washington, DC, office when he covered a lead to determine whether Thomas H. Robinson Jr, had applied for a US passport. He served in the US Army from 1917-1919 as an officer with the Quarter Master Corp. In 1924 he joined the FBI serving fourteen years when his employment got terminated due to poor health; he died in 1941.

Carson, Crawford H., was assigned to Nashville during the Stoll case and was involved in the interview of Thomas H. Robinson Sr. He was born in Farmville, VA, and began his career in the FBI in the 1930s. He headed the Miami, Los Angeles, and San Francisco offices in the 1950s. On July 29, 1959, he died at Mills Hospital at San Francisco, age 51, while still with the FBI.

Chaffetz, Maxwell, was assigned to the Chicago office when attached to the Stoll case. He was born in 1909 and served 17 years with the FBI. He was a new agent assigned to the Chicago Squad that killed John Dillinger, checking the fingerprints of the body at the morgue to verify it was, in fact, Dillinger. He took retirement at age 57, managing a company that manufactured pretzels at Reading, PA, which later became part of the food division of the Borden Company. He died in 1986 in Florida.

Chipman, Lyman Morris, was assigned to Little Rock when sent to assist with the Stoll investigation. He was born in Utah in 1898 and obtained his law degree from George Washington University. Employed from 1924-1928 with the adjudication service of the Veterans Bureau, then joined the BOI. He served as SAC in Des Moines in the late 1930s. His brother-in-law was Samuel P. Cowley, killed in a gunfight with Baby Face Nelson. Chipman retired after 37 years of government service from the Louisville FBI office. He died on Christmas day 1986.

Clegg, Hugh H., upon his second retirement on June 30, 1969, received The First Federal Foundation Award from the University of Mississippi for outstanding achievement and distinguished service on behalf of Mississippi. He was with the University as an Assistant to the Chancellor and Director of Development. Born on July 17, 1898, in Mathison, MS, raised in Anguilla, MS. In 1920 he graduated from Millsaps College, Jackson, MS, with a bachelor's degree in Arts and then attended George Washington Law School. On August 12, 1926, he was appointed a Special Agent with the FBI working in New Orleans. He planned to serve for two and a half years, resign, then return to Mississippi and practice law. He became a supervisor and would receive low marks in the area of office work (keeping cases administratively pure) and executive ability, which would turn out to be prophetic during his long career. Later he would head offices in Atlanta, Washington, and Chicago. He

The G-men and the Heiress

would have an up and down relationship with Hoover, praised one moment then criticized the next. Hoover would be critical of him on some occasions for providing Agents under his charge with excellent evaluations when the most recent inspection of the office rated them unsatisfactory in specific areas. Later he was promoted to Inspector; then, in 1932, he was appointed to Assistant Director.

On April 22, 1934, it was Clegg, not SAC Purvis, who was the ranking FBI official at the ill-fated shootout at the Little Bohemia Lodge, in Manitowish Waters, WI to capture John Dillinger. Having a Master's degree in education, he was selected in 1935 to head the FBI Academy, leading both Training and Inspection. In 1940-41 he traveled to England to study Wartime Intelligence under the British Intelligence Service. He died on December 12, 1979.

Connelley, Earl John, had his eye on the ball and his nose to the grindstone, according to fellow SAC Thomas H. Tracy, who authored an article about Connelley for *The Grapevine*, the former FBI agents association magazine. In his opinion, Connelley "never flaunted his knowledge, and a job well done was more important to him than a promotion." He was born January 31, 1892, in Cincinnati and raised in Columbus, Ohio. In 1917 during WWI, he joined the Army and served as a private in the Signal Corps. At the end of the war, he had risen to the rank of first lieutenant. In 1919 Connelley studied law and accounting at Pace & Pace in New York City. He joined the BOI in January 1920, and his first official assignment was Cincinnati. In 1927 he was appointed SAC in St. Louis and subsequently served in the same capacity in Seattle (1928), Chicago (1928-30), New York (1930-32), and Cincinnati (1932-36). Throughout his thirty-year career, Connelley got involved as a SAC and Inspector (promoted June 10, 1936, and based in Cincinnati) in many of the most prominent Bureau cases, especially those of the gangster era. Connelley essentially replaced Inspector Samuel P. Cowley in Chicago in late 1934, after Cowley had been killed. In addition to the significant Kidnapping cases (Bremer, Weyerhaeuser & Hamm), he led the raid in Chicago, capturing Arthur "Doc" Barker. Subsequently, he took his men to Florida to get the Barker-Karpis Gang and found Ma Barker and her son Fred. This 1935 arrest attempt led to a gunfight whereby both Barkers got killed.

During WWII, he worked out of the New York office and oversaw the investigation of the Nazi saboteurs who landed in the US via submarine. He also played a lead role in the Alger Hiss investigation, a US State Department and U. N. official who got accused of being a Soviet GRU spy convicted of perjury in 1950. On June 24, 1940, he was promoted by Director Hoover as "Assistant Director of Major Investi-

Agent bios

gations in the Field," and retired in 1954. He died at Holmes Hospital in Cincinnati on July 20, 1957, and is buried at Gate of Heaven Cemetery, Montgomery, OH.

Conroy, Edward Eugene, was SAC of Little Rock when he sent two agents to assist with the Stoll investigation. By 1936, SAC Conroy was assigned to Atlanta, he and five agents met Robinson Jr. and his security at the Atlanta train station before Robinson entered the USP at Atlanta. He was born in 1895 and served with the Army during World War I, rising to the rank of captain. He saw action at Verdun and Belleau Wood, where he was wounded, receiving the Croix de Guerre, Silver Cross with cluster and the Purple Heart. A graduate of Cornell University, he entered the BOI in 1922. He would lead eleven FBI Field Offices over a 24-year career. Retiring in 1946, he died ten years later.

Costello, Hilary William, was one of the agents along with US Marshals that transported Thomas H. Robinson Jr. via train from Louisville to the USP at Atlanta. He was born in 1910 and was with the FBI from 1934-1946. He left to practice law in Washington, DC, and died in Catonsville, Maryland, in 1991.

Cowley, Samuel Parkinson, in 1934, was sent to the Chicago office to coordinate efforts to capture John Dillinger, and while there got promoted to Inspector. The office would be looking for Public Enemy Number One, Baby Face Nelson, and along with John Paul Chase, was observed first by other agents. Inspector Cowley and Agent Herman Hollis proceeded to the location. On November 27, 1934, at Barrington, Il, a gun battle ensued, with Nelson and Chase whereby both agents were mortally wounded and later declared dead at the hospital. Gillis didn't survive, and his body would be found the next day with nine bullet wounds he received during the shootout. Cowley born on July 23, 1899, in Franklin, Idaho, graduated from Utah State Agricultural College and later obtained a law degree from George Washington University. He entered the FBI on March 11, 1929, and served in offices in Los Angeles, Detroit, Washington, DC, Butte and Salt Lake City. He was later assigned to Headquarters in October 1932 then appointed as senior administrative assistant to Harold Nathan.

His body lay in state in the rotunda of the Utah State Capitol before his funeral. After his death, his wife, Lavon Chipman (August 10, 1902-October 30, 1999) became a clerical employee with the FBI in 1936, serving in Los Angles and Washington, DC, until 1948 when she resigned.

Daley, James E., was assigned to the Chicago office when sent to assist on the Stoll case in Indianapolis. He began his career with the FBI in 1934, served as SAC in Los Angeles, and died in 1985.

The G-men and the Heiress

Dewey, Orville Culbertson, during WWII, served as a Lieutenant Commander with the US Navy and then with the reserves. He was born on July 11, 1903, in Wheeling, WV, and attended local schools. In 1922, he joined the BOI as a clerk, a year later, the position was renamed to Special Employee. He was appointed a Special Agent on February 16, 1925, and served in nine offices.

In March of 1931, he was suspended via telegram by Director Hoover for two weeks for the loss of two manuals (Rules & Regulations, Instructions). He responded to Hoover via a letter dated March 12, regretting his negligence, accepting the punishment, and requested that he be allowed to continue to work on investigations that he had an interest in, even without pay. Hoover responded in kind via a letter stating, "given the excellent spirit with which you accepted the disciplinary action I have issued orders terminating your suspension," which was effective March 16.

He was SAC of the Des Moines office, and in July of 1933 in Perry, Iowa, he questioned Marvin "Buck" Barrow. Barrow was the leader, and along with his brother Clyde Barrow and others formed the Barrow gang. Dewey asked Barrow at King's Daughters Hospital about the Kansas City Massacre as Barrow lay dying with head, back, and other bullet wounds. Barrow could not remember about the massacre, and Dewey made statements to the press to the effect that the Barrow gang did it.

Dewey was also assigned to Chicago and worked on the John Dillinger case and Bremer and Robles kidnappings, which both took place in 1934.

In 1935 he opened and led the Louisville office, and in September 1936, he filed an Official Injury Report. It seems that in July and August of the same year, Dewey attended five firearms training sessions held at the Rifle Range at the Marine Barracks at Quantico, VA. As a result of the firing of high-powered rifles, he had constant ringing in the ears and slight deafness. He listed Agent Frank Baughman as one of the witnesses.

On May 16, 1939, Dewey resigned as SAC of the Chicago office to take a position as Chief Investigator with the Sears Roebuck Company of Chicago, Il. In his resignation letter, he typed the following: "It goes without saying that at heart I will always be a Special Agent and that I take with me the spirit of the Bureau. I regret to leave the association of so many friends in the service, but I want you to know that I shall always be willing and ready at any time to be of service to you and the FBI." He was a prolific letter writer to Hoover submitting over fifteen suggestions to better the outfit. Sometime later, he was employed with the CIA and left after eighteen years. Dewey died on May 20, 1967.

Agent bios

DiLillo, Dante F., was assigned to the Pittsburgh office when he was deployed to Indianapolis to assist with the Stoll case. While in Indianapolis, it seems New York SAC Francis X. Fay had a new kidnapping in New York City and needed an Italian speaking agent to transcribe the wiretaps, which were all in Italian. DiLillo was ordered to New York and immediately left by airplane. Born in 1893, he began his career with the FBI in 1919. He investigated significant cases out of the Chicago office in the 1930s as well as the Lindbergh kidnapping. He later became a field supervisor retiring out of the Pittsburgh office in 1951. He died on September 29, 1980.

Donaldson, Edwin R., before becoming a Special Agent with the FBI, was with the National Bureau of Standards as a research chemist and a micro-analyst/chemist with the Metropolitan Police Department in the District of Columbia, as well as the Coroner's Office. He testified in 1943 that on October 16-17, 1934, he analyzed the pink bedspread from the Stoll home with the initials A. H. S. (Alice Helen Speed) and determined that the stains found were human.

Douglas, Hal Cooper, was assigned to Nashville and conducted a background investigation of Thomas H. Robinson Jr., testifying before the grand jury about Robinson's history. He was born in 1906 at Bentonville, AK, and graduated from the University of Arkansas with a law degree. After the FBI, he served four years of active duty during WWII in Naval Intelligence, rising to Lt. Commander. After the war, he was Secretary-Treasurer of the *Northwest Arkansas Times*, then the publisher; he died in 1988.

Falkner, Murry Charles "Jack," had two famous brothers, William Cuthbert Faulkner and John Wesley Thompson Faulkner III, who were novelists. William's most famous work is *The Sound and the Fury*, written in 1929. There were four brothers; all were pilots, with Dean the youngest dying in a plane crash at 28. After retiring from the FBI with over 30 years in 1965, Murry took up the family mantle of writing and, in 1967, published *The Falkners of Mississippi: A Memoir*. Falkner was born in Ripley, MS, on June 26, 1899. He joined the Marines during WWI and served as a private with the American Expeditionary Forces in France, where he was wounded and received the French Brigade Citation and the Purple Heart. Falkner obtained a law degree from the University of Mississippi in 1922 then practicing in Oxford, MS. In 1924 he moved to Washington, DC, and secured a position with the IRS, a year later he joined the BOI. He left the BOI after three years but returned in 1934.

During his career, he was assigned to assist with the Dillinger investigation and was at the raid on April 2, 1934, at Little Bohemia Lodge, Manitowish Waters, WI.

The G-men and the Heiress

Dillinger and Baby Face Nelson and other gang members were at the lodge, snow was on the ground, even though it was April when agents arrived the dogs began barking, thus warning people inside. Agents approached the Inn at around 8 pm, and three citizens came out, Murry and the others identified themselves as agents, then the lights inside went out. "That was all the gang on the second floor needed. They began blazing away at us from the upper windows with everything—submachine guns, rifles, pistols, everything." The gang jumped out the windows into snowdrifts and got away.

He used an FBI bonus to take flying lessons at the Albuquerque Airport and obtained his pilot's license in 1936 while assigned to the El Paso office. Most of his official FBI flying duties were in the West Texas and New Mexico areas. During WWII, he served in Algiers as an officer in the Army Counter-intelligence Corps; after the war, it was back to the FBI. He died on December 24, 1975.

Farland, Albert Edward, was assigned to the Kansas City office when Thomas H. Robinson Jr., while housed at the USP at Leavenworth, sent a letter in 1936 to the Kansas City SAC. Farland testified at Robinson's trial in 1943, identifying the message whereby Robinson was inquiring about his abandoned Plymouth vehicle left in Los Angeles when arrested in 1936. He was born on March 29, 1878, in Palmer, MA serving in the US Army, 6th Infantry, during the Spanish American War in the Philippines. In 1901 after Army service, he spent two years with the Manila Police Department and another thirteen years with their Secret Service handling German and East Indian investigations. Farland began his employment with the BOI on August 10, 1917, as a Special Employee at the Houston office, later San Antonio, when his headquarters got changed to the Dallas office in November 1918. He then transferred to the Atlanta office, and in June 1920, his title was changed to Special Agent with no increase in pay as he had already received an increase from $5 to $7 a day in May. While in Atlanta in 1922, he was involved in an investigation of the Ku Klux Klan. On October 23, 1924, Farland reported for duty at the Omaha Office, and a month later was sent to Butte, MT. Omaha SAC B. G. Hancock sent a letter to Director Hoover dated December 2, 1924, suggesting that it would be better to have Farland assigned to a more significant city. While in Omaha, he received all matters dealing with the Police Department developing a closer relationship. In January 1925, he was transferred again, to El Paso. In February 1925, Farland received a Letter of Commendation from Director Hoover, who indicated that both the Omaha and Butte SACs had given him glowing remarks related to his performance. Hoover stated, "The spirit which you have evidenced during the last few months has been a source of pleasure to me, and I am gratified to know that you have served as a good soldier." While at this office in November 1925 he came under internal inquiry, for allegedly making derogatory remarks in public about the Director, Agents, and indulging in the use of intoxicating liquors while having parties at his apartment. He reportedly called a new agent a "night school lawyer," having no brains and referred to Agents in El Paso as "Sapp heads." The FBI did not provide his full personnel file, so the outcome is not known.

Fish, B. H., was one of the first Indianapolis agents on the scene of the Stoll kidnapping at the residence. Contact with the FBI, FOIPA Section reflected that they had no record or file on Fish.

Fitzsimmons, Bernard Francis, was assigned to the Nashville office and was filling in for the SAC when the Stoll case broke. He would get involved in surveillance in the case and have Thomas H. Robinson Sr. come to him and SAC Rorer for advice on what to do about the delivery of the ransom money. Fitzsimmons would obtain the only copy of Robinson Jr.'s fingerprints from the police, then forwarded to Louisville with copies made and then sent to the Division Laboratory in Washington for comparison. He was born in Denver, CO, on September 1, 1901, graduated from Catholic University with a law degree and joined the FBI in 1930. He lived in Miami in 1935 and resigned in 1940 and took a position as chief investigator and assistant security director with Douglas Aircraft Company, then became director. Fitzsimmons developed standardized security procedures for all Douglas plants, then copied within the industry. He died on April 13, 1958.

Fletcher, Chapmon, was assigned to the St. Louis office when sent to assist with the Stoll case. He was born in Richmond, VA, in 1895. Appointed to several FBI offices, he later served as SAC at Phoenix, Little Rock, and Sioux Falls. He died in 1957, age 62.

Hall, Oscar George, was assigned to Detroit when he was ordered to Indianapolis to assist with the Stoll case. Born in Wisconsin in 1900, he went by his middle name, George. His first official assignment was Columbus, Ohio, in 1929, when the office closed, he got transferred to the Lexington, Kentucky Resident Agency which was part of the newer Cincinnati Division. He died in 1964.

Hanson, John Harold, was the SAC in Birmingham when he sent two agents to Nashville to assist with the Stoll case. He was a native of Minnesota and joined the FBI in 1930. He would be appointed SAC of the Los Angeles office in 1935 and resign three years later to become Director of plant protection for Lockheed Aircraft. In 1947 he became chief investigator for Gov. Earl Warren's Commission on Organized Crime. He died in Los Angeles in 1978, at age 74.

Harris, Howard D., was assigned to Cincinnati during the Stoll investigation, searching a train in Ohio looking for Robinson as well as involved in surveillance, and filling in for SAC Connelley, who was in Louisville supervising the case. He spent nine years with the FBI leaving in 1939 to take a personnel position with the Kroger Grocery and Bakery Company in Cincinnati. Harris regretted leaving informing Director Hoover that it was for the good of his family. He retired from Kroger in 1964 and died ten years later.

Hirsh, Bennett M., was assigned to the Chicago office when sent to assist in the Stoll case. He began his career with the FBI as a fingerprint classifier in 1928 and played on the Bureau's first basketball team that won the government league championship. Becoming a Special Agent in 1933, spending 26 years before retiring, then became a private investigator out of Jacksonville, FL. He died in 1987, at age 79.

Hollis, Herman Edward "Eddie," along with SAC Purvis, would drive Mrs. Stoll home upon her release. He was more than proficient in the use of the Thompson sub-machine gun and other weapons. He was one of the three Agents who fired upon and killed John Dillinger. Born in Iowa in 1903, he obtained his law degree from Georgetown University in 1927 the same year he joined the FBI. On November 27, 1934, at Barrington, IL, a gun battle ensued between Hollis and Inspector Samuel P. Cowley with Baby Face Nelson and John Paul Chase, whereby both agents were mortally wounded and later declared dead at the hospital. Nelson didn't survive, and his body would be found the next day with nine bullet wounds he received during the shootout.

Hopton, Winfred Earl "Bud," served with the FBI from 1934-1955. In September 1979, *Time* magazine printed a story whereby an East Liverpool, Ohio police officer, said he had shot Pretty Boy Floyd. He also said SAC Purvis had ordered Agent Herman Hollis to execute Floyd. Hopton sent a letter to *Time*, advising them that the article was a complete falsehood. Hopton was on scene that day, and agents killed Floyd, and Hollis, who he knew personally, was not even there that day. Upon retirement from the FBI, Hopton became Director of the Tennessee Bureau of Investigation held until 1971. He died of natural causes in 1998 at the age of 93.

Hurley, Francis "Frank" Eugene, while assigned to Indianapolis obtained from the Louisville Police Department, Fingerprint Examiner, Lt. John I. Messmer items received from the Stoll home on the day of the kidnapping. He was born in 1889 and served with the FBI from 1922-1941. During WWII, he held a position with the Security Department of the US Air Force. He died in 1950.

Hurt, Clarence O., was one of the gunslingers that Assistant Director Harold "Pop" Nathan recruited for the Chicago "Flying Squad" to rid the country of the gangsters of the 1930s. He had been a patrolman, city jailer, detective, sergeant, and Assistant Chief of Police in Oklahoma City, then Detective Lieutenant in 1930 before beginning his career with the Division in 1934. Hurt had the stuff that makes legends as his Chief said Hurt killed six men. Born on March 14, 1897, in Springfield, IL, he moved with his family and attended schools in Hollister and Frederick, Oklahoma, where he attended business College in 1917. Hurt along, with Agents Charles Winstead and Herman Hollis, were credited with shooting John Dillinger, with reports that Dillinger died in his arms. He was involved in most of the significant investigations of the 1930s; "Pretty Boy Floyd," "Machine Gun" Kelly, Bonnie and Clyde, Matt Kimes, and the Barker gang. He retired from the FBI in 1955 and went into ranching, and in 1958 he was elected Sheriff of Pittsburgh County, Oklahoma, then reelected. He served as a consultant on the 1973 film *Dillinger* starring Warren Oates and Ben Johnson who, at 6'2," was an unusual choice to play Melvin Purvis, known as "Little Mel," who stood at 5'4." He died on November 4, 1975.

Jenkins, Joseph Oscar, was one of the first agents that responded to the Stoll estate on the day of the kidnapping. He was born on December 23, 1892, beginning his federal career with the IRS, then became an investigator with the US Navy during WWI. While with the FBI, Jenkins specialized in bank fraud investigations, retiring in 1948. He died in Dallas, Texas, in 1976.

Johnson, Edwin N., covered leads looking for fugitive Thomas H. Robinson Jr. He was in the FBI from 1935-1937. In 1953 he was a Liquidation Analyst with the Federal Deposit Insurance Corp. in Washington, DC.

Johnson, Joseph S., covered leads looking for fugitive Thomas H. Robinson Jr. He was born in North Dakota and was a veteran of WWI, serving with the FBI (1929-1950). He was a member of the squad that brought down the Brady Gang. After retiring, he became a teacher at the University of Louisville Law School for nine years. He died in 1970, at age 74.

Keith, John Milton, as an Inspector, was assigned to the Stoll case coordinating wiretap monitoring in Nashville. He was born in Texas in 1885, beginning with the FBI in 1918. Keith helped set up the FBI Firearms Program and headed four offices leaving in 1936. He became chief investigator for the Philco Radio and Television

Corporation at Philadelphia, PA. He had a nervous breakdown in 1937 and committed suicide at home in bed with a handgun in 1938.

Kenney, John H., was assigned to the Omaha office when he investigated a possible sighting of kidnapper Thomas H. Robinson Jr. dressed as a woman. He was with the FBI from 1934-1937, then practiced law in Delavan, Wisconsin.

Kerr, Stuart Robert, was at Louisville police headquarters when the ransom letter was copied, and the original turned over to him, forwarded to the FBI Laboratory. Kerr was born in 1904. In the 1940s, after FBI service, he joined the Department of Commerce Office of the Secretary as a Foreign Service Officer. He died in 1978.

Klein, Nelson Bernard, was assigned to the Cincinnati office and helped investigate the abandonment of Thomas H. Robinson Jr's car at Springfield, OH, also conducting Robinson family interviews in Ohio. He joined the FBI in 1926 and would pay the ultimate price, killed in a shootout with car thief George W. Barrett at West College Corner, Indiana, on August 16, 1935, leaving a wife and three children. Klein's name is read yearly at FBI offices throughout the country during Police Week. Klein remembered, nationally, was all but forgotten locally until retired Agent Timothy P. Tracy found Klein's gravesite in disrepair in 2009. The Society of Former Agents restored his grave at Evergreen Cemetery in Southgate, KY, in 2009; in 2013, a memorial plaque in his honor got added to the lobby of the Cincinnati FBI office. In 2017, an Indiana State Historical Marker was placed not far from where the shooting took place. See *The G-Man and the Diamond King* by this author detailing the shootout.

Knowles, John Philip, by 1943, had been with the FBI, Identification Division, Single Fingerprint Section for seventeen years. He was a graduate of George Washington University with a degree in mathematics and from Benjamin Franklin University with a Bachelor of Commercial Science degree and previously employed with the War Department as a fingerprint expert. Born in Vail, Iowa, on July 12, 1897, and served with the US Navy during WWI. Knowles retired from the FBI as a Fingerprint Specialist and died of cancer on September 21, 1979, and is buried at Arlington National Cemetery. In a letter dated March 29, 2018, the FBI advised they could provide no record for Knowles.

Kremer, Martin J., of the Louisville office, was one of the agents that met Thomas H. Robinson Jr. at the Louisville Airport, arriving from Los Angeles via plane in 1936. He served with the FBI from 1934-1937. Later he was a District Claims Representative with the Equitable Life Assurance Society of the US.

Laughlin, Robert H., of the Louisville office, was one of the agents that met Thomas H. Robinson Jr. at the Louisville Airport when he arrived from Los Angeles via plane in 1936. He served with the FBI from 1934-1945 and died of complications from lung cancer surgery in December 1973.

Lawler, John Edward, was assigned to the Los Angeles office in 1936, participating in the arrest of Thomas H. Robinson Jr. He was born in Mobile, AL, and began his career with the FBI in 1935. He would rise to the rank of SAC Richmond, where he resigned in 1950 and became affiliated with an insurance company. On December 31, 1983, Lawler was found bludgeoned to death at his home in Richmond. Four youths got convicted of either murder or robbery.

Lawrence, Robert Edwin, was assigned to Little Rock when sent to assist with the Stoll investigation. He served in both World Wars, then with the FBI from 1934-35. His July 1934 FBI training class was the first to be issued revolvers. He was neither an attorney nor an accountant and believed his hiring was due to his his proficiency with firearms and his almost ten years in law enforcement with the city of Palo Alto, CA. He had served as an enlisted man on a destroyer during WWI, with the Navy being his first love. A reserve officer in Intelligence from 1928, then in 1935, accepted an appointment with the Navy. In 1943 he left Naval Intelligence and took charge as C. O. of three bases in the Southwest Pacific. In 1945, he was promoted to captain, then served in Washington, DC. He retired as Director of Security of the Pacific Gas & Electric Company at San Francisco, in 1965.

Leckie, Arthur Bernard, was assigned to Los Angeles, providing security of Thomas H. Robinson Jr. when transported from Los Angeles via plane to Louisville after his arrest in 1936. He was born in Alabama and joined the FBI in 1935, leaving after five years. During WWII, he served as a Lieutenant in the US Navy then became a Private Investigator investigating communism with the Congressional Un-American Activities Committee testifying at the hearings. He died from complications of diabetes in Los Angeles in 1962, at age 57.

Lemaire, Arnold J., of the Louisville office, was one of the agents that met Thomas H. Robinson Jr. at the Louisville Airport when he arrived from Los Angeles via plane in 1936. He was born in Indiana, trained as an accountant, and graduated from the Old Jefferson Law School, Louisville, KY, in 1929. He served with the FBI from 1934-1942 and left to practice law. He died of a heart attack in 1967.

Lorry, Wilfred R., served with the FBI from 1934-1944. He was assigned to the Chicago office when ordered to Indianapolis to assist with the Stoll case. He graduated

The G-men and the Heiress

from the University of Pennsylvania with an undergraduate and law degree. He resigned from the FBI, to practice law, dying in 1981, at age 76.

Loughran, Harry Arthur, was assigned to the St. Louis office when sent to assist with the Stoll case. He was born in Minnesota in 1902 and graduated with a bachelor's and master's degrees in English, Philosophy, and Psychology from St. Thomas College. He obtained his law degree in 1928 from Georgetown University. He served with the FBI from 1934-1941. He then became an Executive with the Association of Casualty and Security Executives of NY, leaving to become the Security Manager of Brewster Aeronautical Corporation in New York. He died in 1977.

Madala, John "Johnny" L., while an agent in the Kansas City office in 1937, took a 111-page signed sworn statement from Thomas H. Robinson Jr., while housed at the USP at Leavenworth. Madala identified the body of Baby Face Nelson through fingerprints at the morgue. He also helped investigate the Bremer (1934) Kidnapping investigation perpetrated by the Barker Gang. He was at the six-hour shootout where it was reported agents fired 3,500 rounds in the house where Ma and Fred of the Barker Gang were killed at Ocklawaha, FL. He was one of the agents at the Biograph Theater when John Dillinger was shot and killed on July 22, 1934. Born in Hungary on May 6, 1909, Madala grew up on the south side of Chicago and graduated from Fenger Academy High School then attended Illinois University. In 1930, he began his fifteen years with the FBI as a file clerk and was appointed a special agent then Assistant SAC in the Miami office. He left the FBI in 1946 to become a racetrack security director. He died in 1983, of an apparent heart attack at Miami International Hospital.

Maynor, Horace Gordon, was assigned to the St. Louis office when sent to assist with the Stoll case helping perform a felony car stop containing Mrs. Stoll. He was born in 1883 and was a southern Illinois farmer and a schoolteacher before joining the FBI. Later he would be the prosecuting attorney for Pope County, IL. He died in 1966.

McKean, Clarence Dodge "Mac," was head of the Boston office during the Stoll case and sent an agent with stenography skills to assist. He was born in 1886 in New Hampshire and graduated from Manchester High School. In 1904, he went to work for his father in the clothing business. He obtained an appointment as a clerk at the House of Representatives, Post Office, Washington, DC, and later graduated from Georgetown University in 1916. He began his career with the BOI in 1917 in Boston. McKean would rise to the level of SAC serving in Pittsburgh, Detroit, Oklahoma, and lastly, Boston, retiring in 1937. He was the first to head the FBI's Fingerprint

Section in Washington, DC. Upon retirement, he became manager of the Massachusetts Claims Investigation, looking into claims against insurance companies and public utilities.

McKee Jr., Samuel Kerr, was on-site April 22, 1934, at the disastrous raid at Little Bohemia Lodge, Manitowish Waters, involving the Dillinger gang. He was at Ocklawaha, FL, where Ma and Arthur Barker got killed. On October 22, 1934, SAC Purvis, McKee, and Agents W. E. "Bud" Hopton, D. E. Hall, and four officers of the East Liverpool Police Department were looking for Charles Authur "Pretty Boy" Floyd. They were in two vehicles approximately two miles south of Clarkson, OH, when they spotted a car containing two women, a man dressed in farm clothes and a man in a navy blue suit, with no hat. Upon approaching the vehicle, they determined the man in the suit to be Floyd, who exited the car and began to run in a zig-zag pattern. The agents and police left their cars and called upon Floyd to halt, which he ignored. McKee and Hopton had Thompson submachine guns, Purvis and Hall had revolvers, and the police had two revolvers, two shotguns, and a rifle between them. Floyd, while running, pointed his two Model 11, US Army .45 caliber automatic pistols at the followers, at which point they fired upon him. It was McKee, not SAC Purvis, who attempted to question Floyd about the Kansas City Massacre as he lay dying, as Purvis had gone to get an ambulance. Floyd was asked if he was involved in the massacre, and he answered, "To Hell with Union Station," McKee persisted and advised him he was dying, and he stated, "I know I'm through." McKee asked again did you, and Adam Richetti and Verne Miller do the shooting at Union Station, he answered: "I ain't telling you nothing, you____." Floyd became semi-conscious, which ended the questioning. McKee gave a sworn statement of facts to a stenographer on the same day for the inquest. The autopsy determined that death was by two shots from .45 caliber ammunition.

McKee was a graduate of the University of Richmond Law School and served with the FBI from March 31, 1930, until February 28, 1953. He was named SAC, Washington Field Office (1941-1943), and Newark (1943-1953). Upon retirement from the FBI, he obtained employment with McGregor-Doniger, Inc. as Personnel Director. He later became Director of the Investigative Division of the Wackenhut Corporation, Miami, FL, in the fall of 1960. McKee died on September 28, 1986.

McKee, Harry Hilton, was assigned to the Los Angeles office in 1936 when he participated in the arrest of Thomas H. Robinson Jr. He obtained his law degree from the University of Alabama in 1930. He joined the FBI in 1933, and after 25 years, he left as Senior Resident Agent at Tucson, AZ. Later gaining a position as chief deputy to the Pima County Recorder for a year, then becoming Chief Zoning Inspector. He died in 1981 at age 75.

Merritt, Edward Kellogg, was assigned to the Los Angeles office in 1936 when he participated in the arrest of Thomas H. Robinson Jr. He served in the Army Signal Corps as a pilot during WWI. After leaving the FBI, again, joining the Army, rising to the rank of Colonel. He died of a heart attack at age 59 in 1958.

Metcalfe, James J., was assigned to the Chicago office when attached to the Stoll kidnapping case. He was born in Berlin, Germany, and joined the FBI in 1931. He was a member of the Chicago Squad that tracked down John Dillinger—leaving the Bureau in 1935 to become a well-known author of poems, "portraits" that appeared daily in more than 150 newspapers. He died in 1960 at age 53.

Meyerson, Murray B., was assigned to the Los Angeles office in 1936. He was the first agent to talk with Jean Breese, then meet with her obtaining information on the location of fugitive Thomas H. Robinson Jr. He also participated in the arrest of Robinson. Meyerson joined the FBI in 1929 after serving as a bank officer with expertise in accounting. Upon retiring in 1950, he and his wife operated the Fireside Restaurant in Escondido, CA; he died in 1970.

Miller, William Eric, was assigned to the Kansas City office when he was ordered to Indianapolis to assist with the Stoll kidnapping investigation. He was born in Missouri and received a law degree from the University of Missouri. He began his career with the FBI in 1924, appointed during Director Hoover's housecleaning of political hacks. In a 34-year career, Miller served in ten offices, with 22 years in Phoenix. Upon leaving, he spent five years as Chief of Security for Motorola Corp. He died in 1994, age 96.

Morton, William Troup, was born August 13, 1907, and while with the FBI, he lived in Memphis and later was in Augusta, GA. During the Stoll investigation, he participated in interviews of Thomas H. Robinson Sr. Morton served in the US Navy during WWII (October 2, 1941, to December 28, 1945) and rose to the rank of Commander. He was married to Marguerite Wilson and died on October 17, 1992, in Augusta, GA.

Nathan, Harold B. "Pop," was issued badge number 2, and as expected, Director Hoover carried badge 1. As Hoover's right-hand man, he got involved in just about every major case. After compiling a list of fewer than twelve agents that were capable of handling severe gangster apprehensions, Hoover assigned Nathan with hiring the so-called "gunslingers" from southern law enforcement agencies to rid the nation of the ruthless public enemies in the early 1930s. Born September 22, 1880, in New York City, he got educated in public schools. In 1900 he graduated from City College of New York with a Bachelor of Arts Degree. He served with the Department of the Navy (1903 to 1910) and with the Immigration Service (1910 to 1917). In 1917 he began as a special agent with the Bureau of Investigation at a salary of $5.00 per day. He spent his early career in Norfolk, Charleston, and Baltimore and, in 1921, was appointed SAC, Baltimore, and later Pittsburgh. On May 1, 1925, he was named by Director Hoover as Assistant Director of Investigations, the first person to hold that position.

In 1941 he was sent to San Diego as SAC, supervising fifteen agents at the onset of WWII. The director visited the San Diego office, and Nathan was introducing him to agents in the squad area. Nathan stopped at the desk of an agent and said to Hoover, you will remember him "he is the one who shot a hole in the ceiling while dry-firing his revolver." Hoover recalled that someone at headquarters wanted to transfer him to the Sioux Falls office before Nathan put an end to it. Nathan joked that SAC Hanni at Sioux Falls was a young SAC while Nathan was old, and if the bullet hit Nathan, it would be okay, but if he shot Hanni, it would be awful. Subsequently, becoming the Assistant Director of the Identification, Training, Laboratory & Administrative Divisions. In 1944 he was named SAC of the Richmond office, retiring in 1945 after 28 years of service moving to San Francisco, where he resided with his wife, Sue Angel. He was an active member of the San Francisco Society of Former Agents and regularly visited the local FBI office and Headquarters, where he was known as "the grand old man of the FBI." Nathan lived by himself at the Canterbury Hotel until he died of a stroke on July 9, 1963.

Nemitz, Donald F., was with the Louisville FBI and took photographs in 1943 of the Stoll residence.

O'Hair, James R., was assigned to Cincinnati during the Stoll case conducting subject Thomas H. Robinson Jr.'s family interviews in Ohio. He spent ten years with the FBI and later became president of the Commerical Banking & Trust Company at Parkersburg, WV.

Paulson, Glenn A., was assigned to the Chicago office when ordered to participate in the Stoll kidnapping investigation. He served during WWI as an officer in the US Army Signal Corps. Paulson had a vital role in the Duquesne Spy Case, which resulted in the arrest of a Nazi spy ring. After spending 36 years with the FBI he retired in 1962. He died in 1981 at age 87.

The G-men and the Heiress

Peterson, Rueben Ervin, was assigned to St. Louis when he was designated to conduct surveillance of Mrs. Robinson Jr. when she traveled by train to deliver the ransom money to Indianapolis. He was born in 1902 and received a law degree from the University of Minnesota. After eleven years with the FBI, he joined the CIA at their headquarters in Washington, DC. He died in Falls Church, VA, of a heart attack in 1953, age 51.

Peterson, Virgil W., was assigned to Chicago when he got detailed to the Stoll case and helped perform a felony car stop containing Mrs. Stoll. He served with the FBI from 1930-1942, then became Executive Director of the Chicago Crime Commission, he died in 1989.

Pickard, Carey Owen, during the Stoll case, was assigned to listen to wiretaps of the Robinson family. He joined the FBI in 1930 after graduation from Mercer University Law School. A native of Georgia, he was on leave visiting family and friends, playing a round of golf when ordered to fly back to his assigned office of Nashville.

Pickering, Samuel F., was born in 1892 and was one of the first members of the FBI Technical Laboratory. He was a Document Examiner specializing in chemical analysis and handwriting review. In March of 1935, he testified at the trial of John Paul Chase for the murder of FBI, Inspector Samuel P. Cowley. Chase had used a Winchester repeating rifle that day, shattering the bandit's vehicle firing from the inside out, according to Pickering's testimony. He died in 1953 in Tokyo, Japan, and is buried in Cleveland, OH.

Purvis II, Melvin Horace, received plenty of fan mail at the height of his popularity in the 1930s. The *Literary Digest* conducted a poll in 1934 of the ten most famous people in America, and Purvis came in second to President Franklin D. Roosevelt. He was a lawyer by education but chose to join the Bureau of Investigation on February 4, 1927, because he thought it would be exciting. He got more than he ever could have imagined as he was involved in some of the most significant FBI investigations, bank robberies, kidnappings, and manhunts of the 1930s. Unfortunately, some of these cases gained substantial media attention giving him a higher profile than his boss, J. Edgar Hoover. Thus, Hoover would later relegate Purvis to lesser matters, breaking his spirit, and as a result, he resigned from the FBI on August 5, 1935, after 8 ½ years.

He was born on October 24, 1903, in Timmonsville, SC, and graduated from the University of South Carolina Law School in 1925 and then practiced law. He got promoted to SAC, leading offices in Cincinnati, Washington, DC, Oklahoma City, Birmingham, and in 1932 was named to lead the Chicago office. He directed a squad to get Dillinger and led one of the raid teams on April 22, 1934, a disastrous encounter with the Dillinger gang at Little Bohemia Lodge, Manitowish Waters, WI, 50 miles north of Rhinelander, WI airport. Most believe Purvis was in charge that day while Inspector Hugh Clegg, was the highest-ranking official. Also present were Inspector William A. Rorer, and St. Paul SAC Werner Hanni, who arrived with his agents after the event was over. Purvis chartered two airplanes in Chicago, which carried eleven agents, four more had previously left for the location via automobile. They had planned to make the raid at 4:00 am the next morning but received updated information that the gang was planning on leaving after dinner. They rented five automobiles to drive the 50 miles; one broke down because of bad roads, and agents had to ride on the running boards. It was dark when they arrived, the dogs started barking, which they had no prior knowledge of warning the outlaws. Agents formed a partial outer perimeter around the Bohemia Inn; they had no local law enforcement with them who knew the location. Three men then exited the Inn and entered a vehicle and started to leave, Agents gave commands for them to halt, but they had been drinking or were drunk and had the radio up so loud they didn't hear. Agents opened up with their Tommy Guns as they were on edge as Dillinger had escaped in the past. Those inside the Inn opened up with their weapons from the second floor. Unfortunately, one individual in the vehicle was killed, who turned out to be a Civilian Conservation Corp employee. The gangsters fled, and a short time later, at a nearby location, Agent Carter Baum ran into Baby Face Nelson and was killed. While it was the worst thing to happen in Clegg's career, Purvis, who was devasted by Baum's death, took most of the heat with the press.

Purvis supervised the crew that killed John Dillinger on July 22, 1934, outside the Biograph Theatre in Chicago while signaling his men by lighting his cigar, as Dillinger left the movie house. He led efforts to capture "Public Enemy Number One," Charles Arthur "Pretty Boy" Floyd, who was shot and killed on October 22, 1934, in a cornfield behind a house in East Liverpool, Ohio, while being pursued by local law enforcement and Division agents. Purvis being a stand-up guy when telling about both incidents, would say he never fired a shot.

After leaving the FBI, Purvis practiced law and promoted some products such as Gillette razors and Dodge automobiles. In 1941 he was activated for service with the US Army as an intelligence officer during World War II in Africa and Italy. He served a year as deputy director of the War Crimes Office, assisting with compiling evidence against Nazi leaders during the Nuremberg trials in 1946, and was discharged as

The G-men and the Heiress

a Colonel. He then practiced law in Florence, SC, and owned a radio station and participated in running a TV station. Purvis tried obtaining other positions with the federal government, but Director Hoover blocked his efforts. He was ill most of 1956 in and out of four hospitals, but finally on the mend. In September 1959, he accepted a position in Washington, DC, to serve as counsel for a Senate committee to survey the Federal Court System to promote economy and efficiency. On February 29, 1960, he was found by his wife with a single gunshot wound to his jaw, with the coroner designating the cause of death as "unknown" and others calling it a suicide.

Reinecke, Herold Herman, had the burden of being the SAC of Indianapolis, which covered Kentucky when the Stoll kidnapping broke. He was born on August 16, 1900, in Elkader, IA. He obtained employment with the *Des Moines Register-Tribune* before earning a law degree from the State University of Iowa in 1923, then practiced law for two years. In June 1925, Reinecke married Myra Hess in Omaha, NE, and joined the FBI the same year.

In 1934, he was in the Chicago office and was heavily involved in the search for John Dillinger and his gang. Reinecke was present on April 22, 1934, at the botched raid of the Dillinger gang at Little Bohemia Lodge, Manitowish Waters, WI. He reportedly earned the ire of Dillinger when he got accused of browbeating his girlfriend, Mary Evelyn "Billie" Frechette. Frechette testified at her harboring trial of Dillinger that Reinecke struck her during interrogation. Reinecke denied the allegation testifying that he did place his hand under her chin to raise her head so she would look at him during questioning. Frechette was convicted of the charge and got two years at the Federal Correctional Institution at Milan, MI.

Reinecke got promoted to SAC Indianapolis in 1934 and then spent a short time in 1936 as SAC Detroit, then back to Indianapolis in 1937. In the 1930s, he held a commission in the United States Naval Reserve. On September 16, 1939, he resigned to take an executive position as Director of Company Protective Service at Montgomery-Ward & Co., of Chicago, IL. Reinecke died at Sarasota Memorial Hospital in Florida on May 6, 1985.

Reynolds, James David, testified in 1943 to obtaining samples on October 16, 1934, from an L. C. Smith-Corona portable typewriter found at the Indianapolis apartment where Mrs. Stoll was held. He told of copying the entire ransom note using the instrument. He also inspected the typewriter ribbon, and on the red half, he found the same phrase in red that was on the ransom note. Reynolds testified that the red part stated, "starting the day after the kidnapping, we will give you five days." He was born in Kentucky in 1907 and became an FBI agent in 1933. He headed the Louisville FBI office from 1938-1940. He left the FBI to become director of plant protection with the Reynolds Metals Company (no family connection) at Louisville. One of his reasons was to maintain a permanent residence. Reynolds died in 1999.

Rhodes, Marion B. "Dusty," was assigned to Chicago when attached to the Stoll case. In the FBI for 25 years leaving in 1951, taking a position as Managing Director of the Kansas City Crime Commission. He died in 1957, age 59.

Rorer, William Asbury "Ash," was born on May 1, 1898, and grew up in Lynchburg, Virginia. He served in the US Army during WWI then attended Randolph-Macon College, the University of Virginia, and earned a Law degree from National University in 1921. Rorer joined the BOI in 1929 and spent eight years in thirteen different offices. He assisted with the Lindbergh (1932), Bremer (1934), Stoll (1934) Kidnapping investigations. In 1933 while SAC of Birmingham, he and his team of agents captured George "Machine Gun" Kelly Barnes at Memphis, TN. J. Davis Rorer, his son, claims his father told him many times of the story of Kelly, stating, "Don't Shoot G-Man!" He resigned from the FBI in 1937 and took an executive position with Colonial Dairies, Inc. of Albany, GA, of which he was an investor, also heading the Georgia Draft Board during WWII. Rorer died at age 69, on May 20, 1967, after a stroke.

Ross, Robert T., was assigned to the Chicago office when sent to assist with the Stoll investigation. He was born in 1902 in Detroit and earned a degree from Wayne State University. He was with the FBI from 1934-1944. In 1943 he was assigned to the Detroit office as Assistant SAC. After leaving the Bureau, he took a position with the Ford Motor Co. retiring in 1967. He was one of the founding members of the United Foundation and Director of the Ameican Red Cross. He died in 1992.

Russell, Absalom Crosem "AC," while assigned to Cincinnati, helped investigate Thomas H. Robinson Jr's abandoned car at Springfield, OH. He was a native of Jackson, Kentucky, graduating from Berea College and Yale University Law School. He served with the FBI for five years, then practiced law. In 1938 he accepted a teaching position with the University of Louisville (U of L), serving as Dean of the Law School from 1946-57. In 1948 Russell was tasked with revising the Kentucky Criminal and Civil Codes. He retired as a professor in 1972, with a bronze bust placed at the U of L in his honor. Russell died in 1992, age 90.

Shivers, Robert Larrimore, was assigned to the St. Louis office when sent to assist with the Stoll case. He enlisted in 1918 during WWI and was discharged a year and

The G-men and the Heiress

a half later as a sergeant. Shivers joined the FBI in 1920, selected by Hoover in 1938, to head the Honolulu office. In April of 1942, he led a raid along with Army and Navy Intelligence Investigators, members of the newly formed Espionage Section of the Honolulu Police Department, and others to round up illegal alien Japanese. Despite these raids, he rejected rounding up all Japanese. In 1943, he transferred to the mainland, then retiring due to poor health. In 1944 he was appointed US Collector of Customs in Honolulu. He died in 1950.

Sisk, Thomas H., was brought in to assist the Stoll case from his assignment in New York City as he had led the Lindbergh kidnapping squad. He got plenty of press while assigned to the Lindbergh case described as "slight in stature and unimpressive in looks, quiet and soft-spoken." Like others, he thought there were more conspirators involved with the Lindbergh case other than Bruno Hauptmann. Sisk made the telephone call to Director Hoover advising agents had intercepted the vehicle driving Mrs. Stoll to Louisville. He was born in Oakland, CA, and attended the University of Oregon. He served in several FBI offices. In 1940, he was the Resident Agent in Charge at Houston, TX. By 1942 he had left the Bureau and was employed with the Hughes Aircraft Company. He died in 1992.

Small, Hugh F., served with the FBI from 1934-1955. He graduated from St. John's College in Minnesota and Marquette University School of Law. In 1960, the car he was driving collided with an auto transport truck, killing him instantly. Small was 55.

Smith, Richard E., of the Louisville office, was one of the agents that met Thomas H. Robinson Jr. at the Louisville Airport when he arrived from Los Angeles after his arrest. He was born and raised in Minnesota and received his law degree from the University of South Dakota. Smith served with the FBI from 1932-1941, serving in Miami from 1938-1940. After leaving, he was the director of two Aviation companies. Smith took a leadership role with the Society of Former FBI Agents and the American Society of Industrial Security. He died in 1975.

Socey, Louis David, was assigned to Detroit when he was ordered to Indianapolis to assist with the Stoll case. Born in 1905 in Pennsylvania, he joined the BOI in 1927 as a fingerprint classifier and became an agent in 1930. After serving in several field offices, he became Assistant in Charge of the Identification Bureau. Socey moved over to the United States Secret Service in 1935 and ran offices in Charlotte and Nashville, retiring in 1959. He died in 1989.

Spear, Monti Clair, was assigned to the Kansas City office when he was deployed to Indianapolis to help with the Stoll investigation. A graduate of the University of Kansas, with a law degree, he served with the FBI from 1930-1942. He left to practice law. He died in 1990, at age 85.

Stapleton, Theodore Newton, was SAC at Charlotte when he sent three agents to assist with the Stoll case. He was born in Colquitt, GA, and obtained his law degree from Mercer University. He spent seven years with the FBI. In 1938 he joined Du-Pont Corp as an Attorney in their legal department. He died in 1992.

Strain, George Lee, of the Louisville office, identified photographs he took of the Stoll house testifying at the 1943 trial of Robinson Jr. He was born July 13, 1916, in La Junta, CO, and attended public school. He obtained a degree from the University of Colorado in 1938, where he was a Phi Gamma Delta and a clarinetist in the Men's Marching Band. Strain received his law degree from George Washington University then it was on to the FBI. He served in offices in Detroit, Buffalo, Louisville, New York City, and Washington, D.C. After his FBI service, he returned to La Junta, where he practiced law, became a prosecutor, and then an Otero County judge. He died on January 20, 2010, at Pueblo, CO.

Tamm, Edward Allen, was born on April 21, 1906, in St. Paul, MN, and was an accounting major at Mt. Saint Charles College and later at the University of Montana. Although under the agent age requirement, he entered the BOI in 1930, with a high-test score and as a graduate of Georgetown University Law School. In March 1931, he got promoted to supervisor in Division 2, and six months later moved to Division 4. In the same year, he was first Acting SAC in the New York Office and then the Pittsburgh Office, which was made permanent in January 1934, and five months later, he was back at headquarters as a Supervisor. In 1935 he was named Inspector, and in August 1937, he became Assistant Director. He would serve as assistant to the director from 1941 to 1948. He resigned from the FBI and was named to the United States District Court in 1948 and later to the appeals court by President Lyndon B. Johnson in 1965. In a noted 1977 case, Judge Tamm set aside a Federal Communications Commission ruling that seven words, referring to such things as sexual activities and portions of the female anatomy, could not be used by radio stations. He wrote that the FCC order carried the agency into the "forbidden realm of censorship." He died on September 22, 1985, of cancer, at age 79.

Thornton, Joseph E., was assigned to the St. Louis office during the Stoll case and was involved in following Mrs. Robinson Jr. while on a train to deliver the ransom money to Indianapolis. He was born in Nebraska and served with the FBI from 1934

The G-men and the Heiress

until 1961, ultimately leading nine offices. He had two brothers, Parnell and Tom, who were FBI agents. He died in 1984, age 78.

Tillman, Fredrick G., in February 1935, was assigned to Charlotte, and while in Washington, DC, for training, got advised to report to Nashville on the Stoll case. He flew from DC, leaving at 2:00 pm EST arriving in Nashville at 4:50 pm CST, obtaining lodging at the Noel Hotel. Tillman would be on wiretaps in Nashville as well as help to transport Thomas H. Robinson Jr. to the USP at Atlanta in 1936. In December 1935, Agent Tillman would get word from FBI higher-ups that he would not receive his scheduled raise. During surveillance in North Dakota, the subject gave him the slip, which now cost him $300. He was a native of Montana born in 1907, served as a deputy sheriff in Idaho Falls, entering the FBI in 1934. During World War II, assigned to the Philippines, then Chief of the FBI's Tokyo office. In 1945 he was involved in the capture of "Tokyo Rose." Tillman retired in 1960 and died in 1995.

Treadwell, George Hardy, was assigned to Nashville during the Stoll case and was involved in covering leads searching for Thomas H. Robinson Jr. He was with the US Navy during WWI, then obtained a law degree from the University of Georgia. He served with the FBI from 1933-1964 and died in 1988.

Van Eps, James Dawson, of the Indianapolis office identified photographs he took of the Indianapolis hideout apartment testifying at the 1943 trial of Robinson Jr. He was born on February 18, 1906, in Schenectady, NY, and was a 1928 graduate of Union College with a Bachelor of Arts degree in English literature and a member of Kappa Alpha. He was involved in the investigation of JFK's assassination and David Ferrie in the 1960s. He died on January 29, 1997, at Schenectady, NY. In a letter dated March 29, 2018, the FBI advised they could provide no record for Van Eps.

Vetterli, Reed Ernest, was SAC of the St. Louis office when he sent four of his agents to assist in the Stoll case. A native of Salt Lake City, Utah, born August 20, 1903, attending local schools graduating from East High School. He moved to Washington, DC, and while employed by the Reconstruction Finance Corporation and other federal agencies, he obtained a law degree from George Washington University. He began his career with the BOI in 1929 and later headed offices in Kansas City, Atlanta, New Orleans, San Francisco, St. Louis, and New York. He was wounded during the Kansas City Massacre in 1933. During his career, he headed the kidnapping investigations of Mary McElroy (1933) and Charles F. Mattson (1936). He resigned in 1940 and became the police chief of the Salt Lake City Police Department, a position he held for five years. He was a member of the International

Association of Chiefs of Police and a member of the Society of Former Agents. He died on June 16, 1949.

Voshell, Robert E., was assigned to Los Angeles in 1936 and on the arrest team that captured Thomas H. Robinson Jr. After FBI employment, he moved into the Private Investigation business. In March of 1940, he testified in court that for eighteen days, he listened to conversations at the suite of the speaker of the California State Assembly. The purpose was to determine if lobbyists were trying to influence the speaker.

West Sr., William Joseph, while assigned to Louisville, covered leads looking for fugitive Thomas H. Robinson Jr. He joined the BOI in 1917 and served most of his career in Boston or New York after stints in Louisville and Detroit. He was born May 7, 1885, in Boston and was a graduate of Northeastern University. Before the FBI, he was employed for five years by the Navy then ten years as an Inspector with the Immigration and Naturalization Service. He retired after thirty-seven years as Assistant SAC in Boston. He married Lenore F. McCarthy on July 28, 1913, and had sons William Jr. who served as Captain with the Navy during WWII and Kenneth, who was an agent with the FBI. He died on April 19, 1954.

Whitely, Rhea, joined the FBI in 1928 and would serve as head of the New York office for three years, resigning in 1940. He was commissioned in the United States Navy serving in the Office of Naval Intelligence, leaving in 1946 with the rank of Commander. At the time of his death in 1968, he was an attorney in Delray Beach, FL.

Whitten, Charles Alvin, was assigned to the Charlotte office when sent to assist in Nashville with the Stoll case involved with surveillance of Thomas H. Robinson Sr. He was born in 1893 and served in WWI. He was with the FBI from 1927-1948 in a half dozen offices. In retirement, Whitten spent time as a farmer and lawyer at Eatonton, GA. He died in 1971.

Wynn, Earl James, was the first Indianapolis Division of Investigation agent to become aware of the Stoll kidnapping. It just so happened he was in Louisville staying at the Tyler Hotel. Wynn was provided the details about the incident at 5:45 pm CST by Lt. Roy F. Parsons of the Louisville Police Department. A native of Indianapolis, he was born in 1902, attended local schools, and was a graduate of Butler University and Indiana University School of Law. He joined the BOI in 1931 and served in Cleveland. Later he was SAC of Indianapolis retiring in 1944 then practiced law. Wynn was involved in some of the high profile investigations of the era involved in the search for John Dillinger. While assigned to the Cleveland office, he was detailed to interview Clayton Hall at Youngstown, OH, a cohort of Alvin Karpis. Wynn died at age 55 in 1957.

The G-men and the Heiress

References

Introduction

1. Gerdes, Louise I., Ed. *The 1930s*, (San Diego: Greenhaven Press Inc. 2000) 30-31,161.
2. Helmer, William J. *The Complete Public Enemy Almanac*, (Nashville: Cumberland House Publishing, Inc. 2007), 15.
3. Sutton, Willie & Edward Linn, *Where the Money Was: The Memoirs of a Bank Robber* (New York: The New Viking Press 1976), 159,161.
4. *United States of America vs. Thomas H. Robinson Jr.*, District Court Western District of Kentucky at Louisville, Transcript filed February 12, 1944, 1065.
5. "WWI," *The Life History of the United States, Vol 11: 1933-1945* (New York: Time-Life Books 1964) 7,8,10.

Chapter 1 Caught (kid)napping!

1. Connelley, E. J., Division of Investigation, Summary Report, October 27, 1934, 11,14,15,16,18, 46,47,58,107,108; FBI file 7-1128 serial 564.
2. "Mrs. Stoll Under Guard Since Child," *Hartford Courant*, October 17, 1934, 22.
3. *United States of America vs. Thomas H. Robinson Jr.*, District Court Western District of Kentucky at Louisville, Transcript filed February 12, 1944, 489.
4. "Where the Blow of the Kidnapper Fell, *The Courier-Journal* [Louisville, Kentucky] October 11, 1934, 17.
5. Wynn, Earl J., FBI Summary Report, November 28, 1943, 2,37,101-103,102f; FBI file 7-1128 serial 3828.

Chapter 2 Mad as a hatter?

1. Connelley, E. J., Division of Investigation Summary Report, October 27, 1934, 91; FBI file 7-1128 serial 564.
2. Douglas, H. C., United States Bureau of Investigation Summary Report, November 3, 1934, 2; FBI file 7-1128 serial 651.
3. Jackson, Gordon, FBI Summary Report, November 11, 1943, 2; FBI file 7-1128 serial 3795.
4. Madala, John, L., FBI, Kansas City, Missouri, "Statement of Thomas Henry Robinson Jr." Leavenworth, Kansas, February 23, 1937, 3, 7, 15, 23, 29, 30; FBI file 7-1128 no serial number.
5. McCarthy, Joseph P., Division of Investigation Summary Report, October 20, 1934, 6; FBI file 7-1138 serial 305.
6. "Memorandum for The Director," FBI, November 27, 1943, 2; FBI file 7-1128 serial 3825.
7. Neal, Tom E., FBI Summary Report, October 25, 1943, 2; FBI file 7-66 no serial number.
8. Reinecke, H. H., FBI Summary Report, May 08, 1935, 12; FBI file 7-1128 serial 1762.
9. "Robinson, Stoll Kidnapper, Caught: Is on Way From California," *The Courier-Journal* [Louisville, Kentucky] May 12, 1936, 8.
10. Rorer, W. A., United States Bureau of Investigation Summary Report, October 24, 1934, 6; FBI file 7-1128 serial 541.
11. Rorer, W. A., United States Bureau of Investigation Summary Report, October 24, 1934, 10; FBI file 7-1128 serial 591.
12. Transcript of Interview of Sue Anne Tubbs Baucom, FBI, Nashville, TN, November 5, 1943, 21, FBI file 7-1128 serial 3788 (with transcript attached).
13. *United States of America vs. Thomas H. Robinson Jr.*, District Court Western District of Kentucky at Louisville, Transcript filed February 12, 1944, 1064,1100.
14. "Wealthy Kentucky Beauty Kidnapped in Bedroom," *Valley Morning Star* [Harlingen, Texas] October 26, 1958, 8.

15. Wynn, Earl J., FBI Summary Report, November 28, 1934, 160, 307; FBI file 7-1128 serial 3828.
16. "Youth Blames Dual Personality For Gem Thefts," *The Nashville Tennessean*, June 7, 1929, 1.

Chapter 3 Louisville debutante

1. "Church Wedding Miss Alice Speed and Mr. Berry Vincent Stoll Married Saturday," *The Courier-Journal* [Louisville, Kentucky] June 12, 1927, 30.
2. Connelley, E. J., Division of Investigation Summary Report, October 27, 1934, 103; FBI file 7-1128 serial 564.
3. "Death Takes James B. Speed," *The Courier-Journal* [Louisville, Kentucky] July 8, 1912, 1.
4. "George Stoll's Selection as Layman of 1953 Spotlights an Amazing But Modest Family," *The Courier-Journal* [Louisville, Kentucky] January 25, 1953, 39.
5. "J.B. Speed's granddaughter leaves museum $50 million," *The Courier-Journal* [Louisville, Kentucky] April 09, 1996, 1.
6. "Lincoln Statute J.B. Speed's Gift," *Messenger-Inquirer* [Owensboro, Kentucky] October 11, 1934, 1.
7. "Little Hope For J.B. Speed," *The Courier-Journal* [Louisville, Kentucky], March 1, 1911, 1.
8. "Oil Tow and River Barges to be Sold," *The Courier-Journal* [Louisville, Kentucky], May 14, 1921, 4.
9. "Sale of Stoll Oil Holdings to Sinclair Oil Announced," *The Courier-Journal* [Louisville, Kentucky], February 1, 1952, 41.
10. "Stoll South's Oldest Independent Oil Company," *The Courier-Journal* [Louisville, Kentucky], June 17, 1924, 33.
11. "Stoll-Speed," *New York Times*, June 12, 1927, 25.
12. "Tribute to Lincoln By State and Nation," *The Courier-Journal* [Louisville, Kentucky], November 9, 1911, 1.
13. www.Ancestry.com
14. Yater, George H., *Two Hundred Years at the Falls of the Ohio: A History of Louisville and Jefferson County* (Louisville: The Heritage Corporation 1979), 194-195.

Chapter 4 The kidnapping racket

1. Alix, Ernest Kahlar, *Ransom Kidnapping in America, 1874-1974; The Creation of a Capital Crime* (Carbondale: Southern Illinois University Press 1978), 78,123.
2. Bolmar Jr., Horace L., "The Lindbergh Law," *Law and Contemporary Problems*, Vol. 1, No. 4, October 1934, 435.
3. Borne, Ronald F., *Troutmouth: The Two Careers of Hugh Clegg* (Jackson: University Press of Mississipi 2015), 74.
4. "Crime of Kidnapping Becoming More Common," *Bernardsville News* March 17, 1932, 11.
5. Cushman, Barry, "Headline Kidnappings and the Origins of the Lindbergh Law," 55 St. Louis U. L. J. 1293 (2010-2011), 1295.
6. "Death Penalty for Kidnappers," *The Kerrville Times*, January 22, 1931, 4.
7. "History and Early Association of the Karpis-Barker Gang, Prior to the Abduction of Mr. Bremer," FBI Memorandum, November 19, 1936, 1,3,59,68; FBI file 7-576 no serial number.
8. "Kansas City Agent Insuring Patrons Against Abduction," *The News Journal* [Wilmington, Delaware], May 30, 1930, 13.
9. Ernst, Robert R., *Robbin' Banks & Killin' Cops: The Life and Crimes of Lawrence Devol and His Association With Alvin Karpis and the Barker-Karpis Gang* (Frederick: Publish America, March 2009).
10. "Kidnapping Ancient Bible Reveals," *Republican & Herald* [Pottsville, Pennsylvania], March 9, 1932, 7.
11. "Lloyds is Writing Kidnap Insurance," *The New York Times*, August 5, 1933, 3.
12. Hoover, J. Edgar, FBI Letter, March 5, 1936, 1; FBI file 7-1128 serial 2611.
13. https://shsmo.org/historicmissourians/name/r/reed/

The G-men and the Heiress

14. *Manual of Instructions-1936*, Federal Bureau of Investigation/Department of Justice, Section 20: Kidnapping Investigations, 1-2.
15. "Texas Has Death Penalty for Kidnapping," *The Canyon News*, April 2, 1931, 19.
16. "279 Kidnapped in 28 States Survey for 1931 Discloses," *New York Times*, January 27, 1932, 44.
17. Wack, Larry, www.historicalgmen.squarespace.com
18. www.archives.fbi.gov/archives/news/stories/2003/september/hamm
19. www.deathpenaltyinfo.org/methods-execution
20. www.findagrave.com
21. Zierold, Norman, *Little Charley Ross* (Boston: Little, Brown and Company 1967), 11,122,128, 194,223,229,236.
22. Zorn, Robert, *Cemetery John, The Undiscovered Mastermind of the Lindbergh Kidnapping* (The Overlook Press, New York 2013) 15, 151.

Chapter 5 Manhunt: wanted by the Division of Investigation

1. "Bliss Morton Was Early Agent Of FBI," *The Indianapolis News*, October 26, 1978, 44.
2. "Bliss Morton, Pioneer FBI Agent, Dies At 94," *The Indianapolis Star*, October 26, 1978, 69.
3. Connelley, E. J., Division of Investigation Summary Report, October 27, 1934, 4-5,7,11,86; FBI file 7-1128 serial 564.
4. "Fear For Life Of Kidnaped Woman; $50,000 Demanded," *The Decatur Daily Review*, October 11, 1934, 1.
5. Hoover, J. Edgar, Director, Division of Investigation "Memorandum for Mr. J.W. Gardner, General Agent, and Chief Clerk," September 26, 1933, 1, FBI file 66-2710 serial 210.
6. Hoover, J. Edgar, Division of Investigation Memorandum, October 11, 1934, 1; FBI file 7-1128 serial 55.
7. Hoover, John Edgar, Division of Investigation Memorandum, October 11, 1934, 2-3 FBI file 7-1128 serial 87.
8. Hunt, Brian, "The Kidnap Racket: E.J. Connelley and the Weyerhaeuser Kidnapping," *The Grapevine*, June 2015, 32-34.
9. "Morton's FBI Story," *The Indianapolis Star*, April 6, 1975, 212.
10. "No Laws Against Wire Tapping, But Phone Man Knows," *The Oshkosh Northwestern*, October 22, 1934, 16.
11. "Pierpont In Chair; Dies for Murder," *The Indianapolis Star*, October 17, 1934, 1.
12. "Stoll Kidnap Car Traced To Lake Louisvilla Road; $50,000 Ransom Prepared," *The Herald-Post* [Louisville, Kentucky], October 11, 1934, 2-3.
13. Purvis, Alston, *The Vendetta* (New York: Public Affairs, 2005), 344.
14. Quinn, T. D., Division of Investigation Memorandum, October 13, 1934, 1; FBI file 7-1128-serial 181.
15. Reinecke, H. H., Division of Investigation Summary Report, October 18, 1934, 2,4; FBI file 7-1128 serial 91.
16. Reinecke, H. H., Federal Bureau of Investigation Summary Report, May 8, 1935, 16; FBI file 7-1128 serial 1762.
17. Reinecke, H. H., Division of Investigation Memorandum, October 10, 1934, 1; FBI file 7-1128 serial 2.
18. Tamm, Edward A., Division of Investigation "Memorandum For the Director," October 13, 1934, 1; FBI file 7-1128 serial 79.
19. Tamm, Edward A., Division of Investigation "Memorandum for the Director," October 15, 1934, 1; FBI file 7-1128 serial 193.
20. Tamm, Edward A., Division of Investigation Memorandum, October 11, 1934, 1; FBI file 7-1128 serial 6.

21. Tamm, Edward A., Division of Investigation Memorandum, October 11, 1934, 2-3; FBI file 7-1128 serial 8.

22. Tamm, Edward A., Division of Investigation Memorandum, October 11, 1934, 1; FBI file 7-1128 serial 63.

23. Tamm, Edward A., Division of Investigation Memorandum, October 12, 1934, 1; FBI file 7-1128 serial 9.

24. Tamm, Edward A., Division of Investigation Memorandum, October 12, 1934, 7; FBI file 7-1128 serial 133.

25. Tamm, Edward, A., Division of Investigation "Memorandum For The Director," October 22, 1934, 1; FBI file 7-1128 serial 501.

26. Tamm, Edward, A., Division of Investigation Memorandum, October 14, 1934, 1; FBI file 7-1128 serial 60.

27. Tamm, Edward, A., Division of Investigation Memorandum, October 14, 1934, 1-2; FBI file 7-1128 serial 76.

28. "Urlic Bell, 68, New York Executive And Former Writer C. J., Dies," *The Courier-Journal* [Louisville, Kentucky], January 18, 1960, 13.

29. Wack, Larry, www.historicalgmen.squarespace.com

30. Weiner, Tim, *Enemies: A History of the FBI*, (New York: Random House 2012) 76-77.

31. "Wire Tapping by U.S. Agents Gets Official O. K. In "Specific Cases," *Rutland Daily Herald*, February 22, 1931, 1.

32. "Wire-tapping Thumbed Down," *The Pittsburgh Press*, January 1, 1930, 7.

33. www.findagrave.com

Chapter 6 Kidnapper makes contact

1. Connelley, E. J., Division of Investigation Summary Report, October 23, 1934, 63,83,85-88; FBI file 7-1128 serial 564.

2. Hoover, John Edgar, Division of Investigation Memorandum, October 15, 1934, 1-2; FBI file 7-1128 serial 81.

3. Hoover, J Edgar, Division of Investigation "Memorandum for Edward A. Tamm," October 16, 1934, 1; FBI file 7-1128 serial 88.

4. Hoover, J Edgar, Division of Investigation "Memorandum for Edward A. Tamm," October 16, 1934, 1; FBI file 7-1128 serial 124.

5. Hoover, J Edgar, Division of Investigation "Memorandum for Edward A. Tamm," October 16, 1934, 1; FBI file 7-1128 serial 127.

6. "Kidnapping Contact Indicated By Actions of Stoll Family," *The Herald-Post* [Louisville, Kentucky] October 16, 1934, 1.

7. "Mrs. Stoll Tells Own Story of Kidnapper from Witness Stand at Robinsons' Trial; Identified Photo of Fugitive as Abductor," *The Cincinnati Enquirer*, October 8, 1935, 2.

8. Pickard, O. C., Division of Investigation Summary Report, October 23, 1934, 2; FBI file 7-1128 serial 456.

9. Pickering, S. F., Division of Investigation Laboratory Report, October 15, 1934, 1; FBI file 7-1128 serial 61.

10. Purvis, Melvin, H., Western Union Telegram to Director, Division of Investigation, October 17, 1934, 1; FBI file 7-1128 no serial number.

11. Reinecke, H. H., Division of Investigation Summary Report, October 18, 1934, 2; FBI File 7-1128 serial 91.

12. Rorer, W. A., Bureau of Investigation Summary Report, October 24, 1934, 2; FBI file 7-1128 serial 541.

13. Rorer, W. A., Bureau of Investigation Summary Report, October 24, 1934, 10,17-19,591; FBI file 7-1128 serial 591.

14. Tamm, Edward A., Division of Investigation Memorandum, October 15, 1934, Pg. 1, FBI file 7-1128 serial 147.

15. *United States of America vs. Thomas H. Robinson Jr.*, District Court Western District of Kentucky at Louisville, Transcript filed February 12, 1944, Mrs. Stoll Testimony, 87, 513,514,516.

16. Wynn, Earl, J., FBI Summary Report, November 28, 1943, 50,68,73-75,79,85,87; FBI file 7-1128 serial 3828.

Chapter 7 Stockholm Syndrome, anyone?

1. Becket, Henry S. A., *The Dictionary of Espionage*, (New York: Dell Publishing Company Inc. 1986), 64.

2. Carson, C. H., Division of Investigation Memorandum, October 20, 1934, 5; FBI file 7-1128 serial 284.

3. Connelley, E. J., Western Union Telegram to Director J. E. Hoover, October 17, 1934, 1; FBI file 7-1128 serial 260.

4. Connelley, E. J., Division of Investigation Letter to Director, October 28, 1934, 1; FBI file 7-1128 serial 223.

5. Connelley, E. J., Division of Investigation Memorandum, October 23, 1934, 1; FBI file 7-1128 serial 467.

6. Connelley, E. J., Division of Investigation Memorandum, October 23, 1934, 44A,44-46,49-51,71,74,85,90; FBI file 7-1128 serial 564.

7. Falkner, Murry C., *The Falkner's of Mississippi* (Baton Rouge: Louisiana State University Press 1967) 91,100.

8. Hoover, John Edgar, Division of Investigation Memorandum, October 16, 1934, 1-2; FBI file 7-1128 serial 125.

9. Hoover, John Edgar, Division of Investigation Memorandum, October 16, 1934, 1; FBI file 7-1128 serial 225.

10. Hoover, John Edgar, Division of Investigation, "Memorandum to Attorney General," October 17, 1934, 2 FBI F\file 7-1128 serial 187.

11. Hoover, John Edgar, Division of Investigation Memorandum to Mr. Tamm, October 18, 1934, 1; FBI file 7-1128 serial 259.

12. "Kidnapper's Automobile Found in Springfield," *Springfield Daily News*, October 18, 1934, 1,3.

13. Madala, John, L., FBI, "Statement of Thomas Henry Robinson Jr," Leavenworth, Kansas, February 23, 1937, 27-28,33; FBI file 7-1128 no serial number.

14. McIntire, K. R., FBI "Memorandum for The Director," October 10, 1935, 1; FBI file 7-1128 serial 2106.

15. "Opens Home," *The Courier-Journal* [Louisville, Kentucky], November 27, 1914, 3.

16. Peterson, V. W., Division of Investigation Summary Report, October 18, 1934, 2; FBI file 7-1128 serial 231.

17. Purvis, Alton, *The Vendetta* (New York: Public Affairs, 2005) 236,241.

18. Purvis, Melvin H., Division of Investigation, "Letter to Director," October 17, 1934, 1; file 7-1128 serial 173-174.

19. Purvis, Melvin, Western Union Telegram to Director, DOJ, October 17, 1934, 1,2,4; FBI file 7-1128 serial 187.

20. "Quiet Lawyer Led Lindy Hunt," *The Des Moines Register*, September 24, 1934, 2.

21. Reinecke, Herold, H., Division of Investigation, Western Union Telegram to Director, October 18, 1934, 1; FBI file 7-1128 serial 252.

22. "Robinson, Jr. Abandons Auto In Springfield, Ohio," *Star Tribune* [Minneapolis, Minnesota], October 19, 1934, 1.

23. "Robinson's Car Abandoned in Ohio City; Fugitive Flees," *The Herald-Post* [Louisville, Kentucky], October 18, 1934, 1,3.

24. "Russell will stay close to his Students," *The Courier-Journal* [Louisville, Kentucky], June 11, 1972, G-2.

25. Tamm, Edward A., Division of Investigation "Memorandum for the Director," October 15, 1934, 2; FBI file 7-1128 serial 105.

26. Tamm, Edward A., Division of Investigation "Memorandum for the Director," October 16, 1934, 2-3; FBI file 7-1128 serial 432.

27. Tamm, Edward, A., Division of Investigation Memorandum, October 17, 1934, 1; FBI file 7-1128 serial 221.

28. Tamm, Edward, A., Division of Investigation Memorandum, October 18, 1934, 1; FBI file 7-1128 serial 397.

29. "Trigger Finger On Pen," *Press and Sun-Bulletin* [Binghamton, New York] July 30, 1965, 6.

30. *United States of America vs. Thomas H. Robinson Jr.*, District Court Western District of Kentucky at Louisville, Transcript filed February 12, 1944, 492-493,1102.

31. "U.S. To Ask Death Penalty for Kidnapper of Mrs. Stoll," *The Herald-Post* [Louisville, Kentucky] October 17, 1934, 2.

32. Wack, Larry, www.historicalgmen.squarespace.com

33. www.findagrave.com

34. Wynn, Earl, J., FBI Summary Report, November 28, 1943, 53,77,113,203-204,301; FBI file 7-1128 serial 3828.

Chapter 8 Time for a grand jury

1. "Digested History of the FBI," Federal Bureau of Investigation, United States Department of Justice, Washington, D.C. Memorandum October 15, 1938, 14.

2. Purvis, Alston, *The Vendetta* (New York: Public Affairs 2005) 202.

3. Hoover, John Edgar, Division of Investigation "Memorandum for the Attorney General," February 27, 1935, 1; FBI file 7-1128 serial 1365.

4. Hoover, John Edgar, Division of Investigation Letter, October 23, 1934, 1; No file number or serial number.

5. Hoover, John Edgar, Division of Investigation Memorandum, October 20, 1934, 1; FBI file 7-1128 serial 383.

6. Hoover, John, Edgar, Division of Investigation Memorandum, October 20, 1934, 1; FBI file 7-1128 serial 383.

7. Kenney, J. H., United States Bureau of Investigation Summary Report, January 4, 1935, 2; FBI file 7-1128 serial 1190.

8. Rorer, W. A., Division of Investigation Memorandum, March 26, 1935, 1-2; FBI file 7-1128 serial 1456.

9. Rorer, W. A., United States Bureau of Investigation Summary Report, October 24, 1934, 33; FBI file 7-1128 serial 541.

10. Rorer, W. A., United States Bureau of Investigation Summary Report, October 29, 1934, 27; FBI file 7-1128 serial 591.

11. Tamm, E. A., Division of Investigation Memorandum, December 24, 1934, 1; FBI file 7-1128 serial 1138.

12. Tamm, E. A., FBI Memorandum, March 7, 1935, 1; FBI file 7-1128 serial 1405

13. Tamm, Edward A., Division of Investigation "Memorandum for the Director," October 18, 1934, 1; FBI file 7-1128 serial 359.

14. "Thomas Connor, Last of Dillinger Detail, 91," *The New York Times*, April 21, 1997, B10.

15. "Thomas J. Conner Obituary," *The Grapevine*, September 1997, 24.

16. "Tom Connor Saw Plenty of Action While at Chicago Office of FBI," *The Grapevine*, September 1978, 32.

The G-men and the Heiress

Chapter 9 Wanted public enemy

1. Clarens, Carlos, *Crime Movies: From Griffith to Godfather and Beyond* (New York: W. W. Norton & Company Inc. 1980), 57.
2. "Here's What Happens at Harlem Famous, Ubangi Club," *Afro-American*, February 8, 1936.
3. "List 28 as Public Enemies," *Chicago Daily Tribune*, April 24, 1930, 1.
4. Madala, John, L., FBI, "Statement of Thomas Henry Robinson Jr," Leavenworth, Kansas, February 23, 1937, 37-40,45,47,52-53,57,62-64; FBI file 7-1128 no serial number.
5. United States Census-1910, New York City, New York Births 1846-1909.
6. Whitley, Rhea., FBI Summary Report to Director, Interview of Jean Breese by SA John S. Bugas, LA Office at New York City, June 6, 1936, 4-5,9-10; FBI file 7-1128 serial 3013X.

Chapter 10 Jekyll or Hyde, on trial in absentia

1. "And Here Seats Defense Squad For Robinson," *The Herald-Post* [Louisville, Kentucky) October 11, 1935, 1.
2. "Collapses on Witness Stand," *Moberly Monitor-Index*, October 10, 1935, 12.
3. Dewey, O. C., FBI Teletype, October 9, 1935, 1; FBI file 7-1128 serial 2094.
4. "Digested History of the FBI," Federal Bureau of Investigation, United States Department of Justice Memorandum, Washington, D.C., October 15, 1938, 14.
5. "Federal Agents Deny Hammering Bremer Suspect," *Chicago Tribune*, May 9, 1935, 10.
6. "Federal Agents to Open City Office," *The Courier-Journal* [Louisville, Kentucky], June 19, 1935, 1.
7. "Federal Jury to Get Robinsons' Case Today, *The Courier-Journal* [Louisville, Kentucky], October 12, 1935, 4.
8. "G-Men Heard In Stoll Case; Tell of Making Arrest," *The Courier-Journal* [Louisville, Kentucky], October 9, 1935, 2.
9. "G-Men Refused his Aid, Elder Robinson Says," *The Nashville Tennessean*, October 11, 1935, 1,22.
10. "Imposing Apartment Building to Be Built on North Meridian Street,' *Indianapolis Star*, December 14, 1919, 4.
11. "John Madala; Racetrack Security Expert," *Chicago Tribune*, August 25, 1983, 34.
12. "Jury Is Locked Up In The Stoll Case," *The New York Times*, October 13, 1935, 26.
13. "Madala On Mend From Gun Attack," *The Grapevine* March 1959, 9.
14. "Members of Jury," *The Indianapolis Star*, October 8, 1935, 3.
15. Purvis, Alton, *The Vendetta,* (New York: Public Affairs, 2005), 293.
16. "Report Robinson Jury Deadlocked," *The Messenger-Enquirer* [Owensboro, Kentucky], October 13, 1935, 2.
17. Smith, W. A., U.S. Department of Justice Letter to Director, May 15, 1935, 1; FBI file 7-
18. 11128 serial 1645.
19. Smith, W. A., U.S. Department of Justice Letter to Director, June 10, 1935, 1; FBI file 7-11128 serial 1726.
20. Stoll, Berry V., "Report on Jury," October 1935, 1, FBI file 7-1128 serial 2196.
21. "Stoll Case Pair Freed," *Los Angeles Times*, October 14, 1935, 1.
22. Tamm, E. A., FBI "Memorandum for The Director," October 9, 1935, 2-3; FBI file 7-1128 serial 2115.
23. Theoharis, Athan G., *The FBI: A Comprehensive Reference Guide*, (Greenwood 1998), 238.
24. Transcript of Thomas M. McDade Journal (1934-1938) 16. https://cdn.ymaws.com/socxfbi.org/resource/resmgr/Docs/MCDADEFINALTRANSCRIPT-1
25. "2 Robinsons, Cleared by Jury, Return Home," *The Courier-Journal* [Louisville, Kentucky], October 14, 1935, 2.
26. "U.S. Refuses to Ask Death for Robinsons," *The Nashville Tennessean*, October 12, 1935, 5.

27. "Robinsons to Testify in Own Defense Today," *The Courier-Journal* [Louisville, Kentucky], October 10, 1935, 2.

28. "U.S. Order Spurs Hunt for Nelson Aids Slaying," *Chicago Tribune*, December 1, 1934, 3.

29. *U. S. vs. Thomas Henry Robinson, Sr. & Mrs. Frances Robinson*, No. 18917, District Court of the United States For The Western District of Kentucky at Louisville, signed Elwood Hamilton, Judge, October 13, 1935, 1.

30. www.findagrave.com

Chapter 11 Lovebirds on the lam

1. Behrens, Jennifer L., *Beyond The Annals of Murder: The Life and Works of Thomas M. McDade*, Law Library Journal, Vol. 111:3 [2019-13], 281-306.

2. Connelley, E. J., FBI, Interview of Robinson, October 12-13, 1936, 22; FBI file 7-1128 no serial number.

3. Dewey, O. C., Letter to the Director, May 16, 1936, 1; FBI file 7-1128 no serial number.

4. Dewey, O. C., FBI Summary Report, May 20, 1936, 7-8; FBI file 7-1128 serial 2961.

5. Dewey, O. C., FBI letter to Director, May 27, 1936, 1; FBI file 7-1128 serial 3012.

6. "Forges New Link Against Dillinger," *The Times*, February 13, 1934, 25.

7. Hoover, John Edgar, Memorandum for Mr. Tamm dated May 12, 1936, 1; FBI file 7-1128 serial 2814.

8. Hunter, Stephen, "A Battle At Barrington: The Men & The Guns," *American Rifleman*, May 4, 2017, 84.

9. Keith, J. M., Federal Bureau of Investigation, Letter to the Director, November 25, 1935, 6; FBI file 7-1128 serial 2303.

10. Madala, John, L., FBI, Kansas City, Missouri, "Statement of Thomas Henry Robinson Jr.," Leavenworth, Kansas, February 23, 1937, 65-67,69-70,72-82,88; FBI file 7-1128 no serial number.

11. Nathan, H, Federal Bureau of Investigation, Memorandum for the Director, May 11, 1936, 1; FBI file 7-1128 serial 2928.

12. "One Man Successfully Evades G-Men," *Tulsa Daily World*, January 26, 1936, Section 4,11.

13. "Surrender Plan Told," *The Los Angeles Times*, May 13, 1936, 3.

14. Tamm, E.A., Federal Bureau of Investigation, Memorandum for the Director, December 2, 1935, 1; FBI file 7-1128 serial 2295.

15. "The Kidnapping of Edward George Bremer, St. Paul, Minnesota," FBI Summary Report, November 19, 1936, 59-60; FBI file 7-576 no serial number.

16. "Theater To Observe 50th John Dillinger Anniversary," *The Times Recorder* [Zanesville, Ohio] July 22, 1984, 6.

17. Transcript of Thomas M. McDade Journal (1934-1938) 38-41. https://cdn.ymaws.com/socxfbi.org/resource/resmgr/Docs/MCDADEFINALTRANSCRIPT-1

18. Wack, Larry, www.historicalgmen.squarespace.com

19. Whitley, Rhea, FBI Summary Report to Director, "Interview of Jean Breese by SA John S. Bugas," L.A. Office at New York City, June 6, 1936, 13, 15, 18, 28; FBI file 7-1128 serial 3013X.

Chapter 12 Last stop, Hellcatraz

1. "Alcatraz Horrors Doom Men, Ex-Convict Says," *The Philadelphia Enquirer*, November 29, 1937, 17.

2. "An Alcatraz Ex-Convict Talks," *The Courier-Journal* [Louisville, Kentucky], December 26, 1937, 45.

3. "Atlanta Prison Term Is Begun By Robinson, Jr." *The Washington Post*, May 13, 1936, 3.

4. Borne, Ronald F., *Troutmouth: The Two Careers of Hugh Clegg* (University Press of Mississipi 2015), 56.

5. Ferguson, Mrs. Walter, "Love, A Woman's Opinion," *The Pittsburgh Press*, August 28, 1936, 20.

6. "Fight Writ for Stoll Kidnapper," *New York Times*, October 31, 1939, 14.

7. "Kidnaper Asks Habeas Writ," *Oakland Tribune*, December 18, 1939, 11.

8. Levinson, David, *Encyclopedia of Crime and Punishment*, "Alcatraz" (Thousand Oaks: Sage Publications 2002), 8,9.

The G-men and the Heiress

9. Madala, John, L., Federal Bureau of Investigation, Kansas City, Missouri, Statement of Thomas Henry Robinson Jr, Leavenworth, Kansas, February 23, 1937, 76,99-100,102,104; FBI file 7-1128 no serial number.

10. Odier, Pierre, *The Rock, A History of Alcatraz: The Fort/The Prison* (Eagle Rock, CA: L'Image Odier Publishing, Co., 1982), 103.

11. "Robinson Begins Life Term Here," *Atlanta Georgian*, May 14, 1936, 1.

12. "Robinson Gets New Trial," *New York Times*, August 10, 1943, 1939, 21.

13. "Robinson Is In Prison, But Son Thinks He's Dead," *The Courier-Journal* [Louisville, Kentucky], May 15, 1936, 1.

14. Robinson Jr., Thomas H., Letter to Mr. Bates, Director, Bureau of Prisons, Department of Justice, Washington, DC, July 1, 1936, 1.

15. Robinson Special Progress Report, U.S. Penitentiary, Leavenworth, KS, June 12, 1936, 2.

16. Sifakis, Carl, *The Encyclopedia of American Prisons*, "Alcatraz Prison" (Thousand Oaks: Sage Publications 2003), 6-8.

17. Sullivan, Herman, F. Special Agent, Federal Bureau of Investigation Interview of Raymond Maple at San Francisco, CA, October 28, 1943, 1.

18. "Swim From Alcatraz," *The Port Arthur News*, October 5, 1974, 16.

19. "Thomas H. Robinson, Sr., Dies After Illness One week," *The Nashville Tennessean*, December 20, 1937, 1.

20. "Tom Robinson's Mother to Aid Him in Fight for his Freedom," *Nashville Banner*, September 07, 1943, 3.

21. Whitley, Rhea, FBI Summary Report to Director, Interview of Jean Breese by SA John S. Bugas, LA Office at New York City, June 6, 1936, 3,21,22; FBI file 7-1128 serial 3013X.

22. Wynn, Earl, J., Federal Bureau of Investigation Summary Report, November 28, 1943, 283; FBI file 7-1128 serial 3828.

Chapter 13 The trial: be careful what you wish for

1. "Maheu Never Met Howard Hughes face-to-face," *Honolulu Star-Bulletin*, December 13, 1970, 5.

2. "Mrs. Stoll Repeats Story of Kidnapping," *The Courier-Journal* [Louisville, Kentucky], December 02, 1943, 1.

3. "Robinson Describes Spree On Kidnap Money," *The Courier-Journal* [Louisville, Kentucky], December 8, 1943, 1.

4. "Robinson Is Pictured as Popular Squanderer," *The Courier-Journal* [Louisville, Kentucky], December 4, 1943, 4.

5. "Second Juror Becomes Ill at Stoll Case," *The Courier-Journal* [Louisville, Kentucky], December 10, 1943, 1.

6. "The Story of Charles A. Appel, Jr., Founder of the FBI Laboratory" *The Grapevine*, March 2015, 23-27.

7. *United States of America vs. Thomas H. Robinson Jr.*, District Court Western District of Kentucky at Louisville, Transcript filed February 12, 1944, 480, 483-489,491-496, 502,506-507,516,523,542, 559-560,567-568,575,578-580,583,589,592,593-594,646,658,1076,1160,1195-1196,1220-1225,1230.

8. *U.S. vs. Thomas H. Robinson Jr.*, District Court of the U.S., Western District of Kentucky at Louisville, court document dated September 30, 1943, 1.

9. Wynn, Earl J., FBI Summary Report, November 28, 1943, Pgs 1,61,102,113-114,312-313 FBI file 7-1128 serial 3828.

Chapter 14 Dead man talking

1. Connor A. H., Acting Director, U.S. Bureau of Prisons Office Memorandum to Acting Director Walter A. Hunter, Warden, United States Penitentiary at Leavenworth, July 18, 1945, 1; FBI file 7-1128 serial 3969.

2. "Court Sentences Robinson to Die," *The New York Times*, December 14, 1943, 18.

3. "Cranor Dreads Job of Executing Robinson," *The Courier-Journal* [Louisville, Kentucky], May 17, 1936, 17.

4. Gearty, Thomas J, SAC, FBI Airtel to the Director, July 11, 1956, 1; FBI file 7-1128 serial 4085.

5. "High Court Grants Test of Stoll Case," *The New York Times*, January 06, 1945, 36.

6. "Hogan Appeals Robinson Case On Legal Point," *The Courier-Journal* [Louisville, Kentucky], June 6, 1944, 1.

7. Hoover, J Edgar, Director, FBI, "Memorandum to the Attorney General," June 19, 1946, 1; FBI file 7-1128 serial 4030.

8. Hoover, J Edgar, Director, FBI, Urgent Teletype to SAC Louisville, May 25, 1955, 1; FBI file 7-1128 no serial number.

9. Hoover, J. Edgar, Director Telemeter to SAC San Francisco, October 3, 1945, 1; FBI file 7-1128 no serial number.

10. Hoover, J. Edgar, FBI Director "Memorandum to the Attorney General," June 19, 1946, 1; FBI file 7-1128 serial 4030.

11. Hoover, John Edgar, Director, Federal Bureau of Investigation, Letter to Daniel M. Lyons, Pardon Attorney, April 5, 1945, 3-4; FBI file 7-1128 serial 3970

12. "Jury Votes Death for Kidnapper Robinson," *The Courier-Journal* [Louisville, Kentucky], December 12, 1943, 16.

13. "Kidnaper Makes Final Plea To Save Life," *The Courier-Journal* [Louisville, Kentucky], December 14, 1943, 1,10.

14. "Kidnaper Robinson Goes to U. S. Prison," *The Courier-Journal* [Louisville, Kentucky], February 15, 1944, 1,4.

15. "Robinson 'Goes to Chair' Just to Try It," *The Courier-Journal* [Louisville, Kentucky], June 9, 1945, 1.

16. "Robinson 'Tried Out' Electric Chair Before Leaving," *The Messenger* [Fort Dodge, Iowa], June 9, 1945, 6.

17. "Robinson Case To Cost Public Near $30,000," *The Courier-Journal* [Louisville, Kentucky], December 17, 1943, 1,21.

18. "Robinson Has Lively Manner During Trip to Death House, *The Courier-Journal* [Louisville, Kentucky], May 31, 1945, 14.

19. "Robinson is Pictured as Popular Squanderer," *The Courier-Journal* [Louisville, Kentucky], December 4, 1943, 1.

20. Robinson Jr., Thomas H., Letter to Mr. Robert E. Hogan dated March 7, 1945, 2; FBI file 7-1128 serial 3967.

21. Robinson Jr., Thomas H., Letter to Mrs. Ernest M. Warner dated March 23, 1945, 1; FBI file 7-1128 serial 3977.

22. Robinson Jr., Thomas H., Letter to Mrs. Thomas H. Robinson Sr. dated March 15, 1945, 1; FBI file 7-1128 serial 3969.

23. Robinson Jr., Thomas H., Letter to Mrs. Thomas H. Robinson Sr. dated April 9, 1946, 1; FBI file 7-1128 no serial number.

24. Robinson Jr., Thomas H., Letter to Mrs. Thomas H. Robinson Sr., February 1945, 1; FBI file 7-1128 serial 3965.

25. Robinson Jr., Thomas H., Letter to Mrs. Thomas H. Robinson Sr., March 11, 1945, 1; no serial number.

26. Robinson Jr., Thomas H., Letter to Mrs. Thomas H. Robinson Sr., May 6, 1945, 1; FBI file 7-1128 serial 3990.

27. Robinson Jr., Thomas H., Letter to Mrs. Thomas H. Robinson Sr., May 6, 1945, 2,5; FBI file 7-1128 serial 4001.

28. Robinson Jr., Thomas H., Letter to Mrs. Thomas H. Robinson Sr., September 30, 1945, 1; FBI file 7-1128 serial 4018.

The G-men and the Heiress

29. Robinson Jr., Thomas Henry, Conduct Record, Department of Justice, Penal and Correctional Institutions, United States Penitentiary, Alcatraz, California, November 30, 1949, 1.

30. Robinson Jr., Thomas Henry, Special Progress Report, U.S. Penitentiary, Alcatraz Island, California, September 1, 1948, 1.

31. "Robinson's Death Set For March 10," *The Courier-Journal* [Louisville, Kentucky], December 14, 1943, 10.

32. "Robinson's Fate Left Up to Judge," *The Courier-Journal* [Louisville, Kentucky], December 13, 1943, 1.

33. "Robinson's Life Saved by Truman; Hearing on Sanity to Be Today," *The Courier-Journal* [Louisville, Kentucky], June 7, 1945, 8.

34. Robinson Sr., Mrs. Thomas H., Letter to Thomas H. Robinson Jr., March 6, 1945, 1; FBI file 7-1128 no serial number.

35. Rosen, Mr., FBI Memorandum to Mr. Ladd, December 4, 1952, 1-2; FBI file 7-1128 no serial number.

36. SAC Louisville, FBI Airtel to Director, No Date, 6; FBI file 7-1128 no serial number

37. "Second Juror Becomes Ill at Stoll Case, *The Courier-Journal* [Louisville, Kentucky], December 10, 1943, 1.

38. "Stoll Says He Believed Wife Had been Slain," *The Nashville Tennessean*, December 03, 1943, 1

39. "Supreme Court Dooms Stoll Kidnapper; Rules on Injuries Under Lindbergh Law," *The New York Times*, March 6, 1945, 23.

40. "Witnesses Say Robinson Lied About Dates," *The Courier-Journal* [Louisville, Kentucky], December 11, 1942, 1,9.

41. www.bop.gov/about/history/federalexecutions.jsp

Chapter 15 Robinson takes a hike & Epilogue

1. "Aged Mother Waits, Hopes," *The Nashville Tennessean*, July 24, 1962, 1,5.

2. "Alice Speed Stoll left an estate of $159 million," *The Courier-Journal* [Louisville, Kentucky], April 10, 1996, 13,15.

3. "Case Against FCI Fugitive Dropped," *Tallahassee Democrat*, August 14, 1962, 2.

4. "Case of Reluctant Parolee," *Honolulu Star-Bulletin*, August 29, 1965, 126.

5. " J.B. Speed's granddaughter leaves museum $50 million," *The Courier-Journal* [Louisville, Kentucky], April 9, 1996, 1.

6. McNeill, N. K., U. S. Bureau of Prisons Memorandum, August 30, 1962, 1-2.

7. "Nashvillian Finally Wins Parole After 34 Years, " *The Nashville Tennessean*, September 15, 1970, 9.

8. "Old Times, Ex-Con Reminisces about Life in Stir" *The Jackson Sun*, May 8, 1980, 35.

9. "Parole Progress Report," U.S. BOP, U.S. Penitentiary, Atlanta, Georgia, May 20, 1970, 1.

10. "Planes Aid Robinson Hunt," *The Nashville Tennessean*, July 24, 1962, 1,5.

11. "Robinson Caught Here," *Nashville Banner*, July 14, 1965, 1,3.

12. "Robinson Found Fit For Trial," *The Courier-Journal* [Louisville, Kentucky], October 8, 1965, 24.

13. Robinson Jr., Thomas H., Letter to Mrs. Thomas H. Robinson Sr., no date, 1; FBI file 7-1128 serial 3965.

14. Stoll, Alice Speed, Last Will and Testament, Louisville, Jefferson County, Kentucky.

15. Stoll, Berry Vincent, Last Will and Testament, Louisville, Jefferson County, Kentucky.

16. "Stoll Kidnapper Is Back in Pen," *News-Press* [Ft. Meyers, Florida] November 3, 1965, 12.

17. "Stolls in Europe, Unaware of Escape, *The Nashville Tennessean*, July 24, 1962, 5.

18. "The Kidnapers Second Choice," *The Honolulu Advertiser*, October 21, 1962, 2.

19. "Tom Robinson Sees Mother Here; Finds She's Fading," *The Nashville Tennessean*, August 29, 1962, 1,5.

Photo credits

79—National Archives, Atlanta, Georgia

81—National Archives, College Park, Maryland

80—National Archives, Atlanta, Georgia

84—National Archives, College Park, Maryland

86—Courtesy FBI

87—Courtesy of Detective Daniel E. Dewine, Springfield Police Department, Springfield, Ohio

90—National Archives College Park, Maryland

92—Archives and Rare Books Library, University of Cincinnati

95—Courtesy Thomas L. Connor

96—*The Louisville Herald-Post*

97—National Archives, College Park, Maryland

99—National Archives, College Park, Maryland

100—*The Atlanta Georgian*

104—Author's collection

107—National Archives, Atlanta, Georgia

108—Archives and Rare Books Library, University of Cincinnati

110—Archives and Rare Books Library, University of Cincinnati

113—National Archives, Atlanta, Georgia

116—Archives and Rare Books Library, University of Cincinnati

118—Author's collection

120—National Archives, Atlanta, Georgia

121—Author's collection

123—*The Pittsburgh Press*

124—Courtesy *The Investigator*

125—National Archives, College Park, Maryland

127—*Courier-Post (Delaware)*

129—Library of Congress

130—National Archives, College Park, Maryland

132—National Archives College Park, Maryland

134—Associated Press

134—Archives and Rare Books Library, University of Cincinnati

137—National Archives, San Bruno, California

141—courtesy FBI

144—National Archives, College Park, Maryland

145—National Archives, College Park, Maryland

147—Author's collection

148—National Archives Kansas City, Missouri

151—Author's collection

154—*The Nashville Tennessean*

155—National Archives San Bruno, California

157—Library of Congress

158—Associated Press

160—Author's collection

161—National Archives, Atlanta, Georgia

163—National Archives, Atlanta, Georgia

166—Courtesy FBI

168—*Louisville Courier-Journal*

170—National Archives, College Park, Maryland

173—Archives and Rare Books Library, University of Cincinnati

174—*The Louisville Herald-Post*

179—Archives and Rare Books Library, University of Cincinnati

181—Library of Congress

182—Library of Congress

185—Courtesy Kennedy Presidential Library

186—Author's collection

188—Associated Press

190—State Archives of Florida

193—National Archives, San Bruno, California

196—National Archives, College Park, Maryland

198—National Archives, Kansas City, Missouri

200—Courtesy Helen Condon Powell

203—Courtesy FBI

Photo Credits

Bibliography

Books

Alix, Ernest Kahlar. *Ransom Kidnapping in America, 1874-1974, The Creation of a Capital Crime.* (Carbondale: Southern Illinois University Press, 1978)

Becket, Henry, S. A. *The Dictionary of Espionage.* (New York: Dell Publishing Company Inc., 1986)

Bjorkman, Timothy. *Verne Sankey: America's First Public Enemy.* (Norman: University of Oklahoma Press, 2007)

Borne, Ronald, F. *Troutmouth: The Two Careers of Hugh Clegg.* (Jackson: University Press of Mississippi, 2015)

Burrough, Bryan. *Public Enemies.* (London: Penguin Books, 2004)

Clarens, Carlos. *Crime Movies, From Griffith to the Godfather and Beyond.* (New York: W. W. Norton & Company, 1980)

Cooper, Courtney Ryley. *Ten Thousand Public Enemies.* (Boston: Little, Brown & Company, 1935)

Falkner, Murry C., *The Falkners of Mississippi: A Memoir.* (Baton Rouge: Louisana State University Press, 1967)

Gerdes, Louise, I. *The 1930s.* (San Diego: Greenhaven Press Inc., 2000)

Helmer, William J. *The Complete Public Enemy Almanac.* (Frederick: Cumberland House Publishing, Inc., 2007)

Karpis, Alvin. *The Alvin Karpis Story.* (Irish Press International, 1971)

Kazanjian, Howard, and Chris Enss. *Ma Barker.* (Helena: A Twodot Book, 2017)

Levinson, David. *Encyclopedia of Crime and Punishment.* (Sage Publications, 2002)

Livesey, Robert. *On the Rock: Twenty-Five Years in Alcatraz.* (Ontario, Canada: Little Brick Schoolhouse Inc., 2008)

Odier, Pierre. *The Rock, A History of Alcatraz The Fort/The Prison.* (Eagle Rock: L'Image Odier Publishing Company, 1982)

Purvis, Alston. *The Vendetta.* (New York: Public Affairs, 2005)

Purvis, Melvin. *American Agent.* (New York: Garden City Publishing Company, Inc., 1938)

Ross, Charles Brewster. *Charlie Ross The Kidnapped Child, The Fathers' Story.* (Philadelphia: John E. Potter & Company, 1876)

Ruth, David E. *Inventing the Public Enemy, The Gangster in American Culture 1918-1934.* (Chicago: The University of Chicago Press, 1996)

Sifakis, Carl. *The Encyclopedia of American Prisons.* (Thousand Oaks: Sage Publications, 2003)

Sutton, Willie, and Edward Linn. *Where The Money Was: The Memoirs of a Bank Robber.* (New York: The Viking Press, 1976)

Theoharis, Athan, G. *The FBI: A Comprehensive Reference Guide.* (The Oryx Press, 2000)

Society of Former Special Agents of the FBI. (Nashville: Turner Publishing Company, 1998)

Weiner, Tim. *Enemies: A History Of The FBI.* (New York: Random House, 2012)

Yater, George H. *Two Hundred Years at the Falls of the Ohio: A History of Louisville and Jefferson County.* (Louisville: The Heritage Corporation, 1979)

Zierold, Norman. *Little Charley Ross, The Shocking Story of America's First Kidnapping For Ransom.* (Boston: Little, Brown and Company, 1967)

Zorn, Robert. *Cemetery John, The Undiscovered Mastermind of the Lindbergh Kidnapping* (New York: The Overlook Press, 2013)

Articles

"Absent Transvestite," *Time*, October 21, 1935, 12

"A Gift of History," *The Grapevine*, May 2014, 10

Bomar, Horace L., Jr., "The Lindbergh Law," *Law and Contemporary Problems*, 1934, 435-444, "Lindbergh Law and After," *Time*, October 29, 1934, 11

"Famous Cases of J. Edgar Hoover, Ransom Trial," *G-Men*, May 1938, 100-113

"FBI Agents Had Important Role In Solving Lindbergh Kidnaping," *The Grapevine*, November 1982, 22-23

Hunter, Stephen, "A Battle at Barrington: The Men & The Guns." *American Rifleman.* May 4, 2017, 84

Newspapers

The Arizona Republic, The New York Times, The New York Daily News, The Louisville Courier-Journal, Chicago Tribune, The Cincinnati Enquirer, Honolulu Star-Bulletin, The Honolulu Advertiser, The Indianapolis Star, The Jackson Sun, The Louisville Times, The Nashville Tennessean, The Nashville Banner, News-Press (Ft. Meyers, Florida.), *The Pittsburgh Press*

Films/Documentary

Escape From Alcatraz (1979), Don Siegel

The Real Story/Escape From Alcatraz (2008), David Hickman

Alcatraz: Beyond the Rock (2016)

Bloody Mama (1970), Roger Corman

The G-men and the Heiress

About the author

William Eric Plunkett is a former Special Agent with the FBI, having served in offices in Albany and Syracuse, New York; Cincinnati, Ohio; and Washington, D.C. During his FBI career, he was involved in joint counterintelligence operations with the Central Intelligence Agency and investigated national security (counterintelligence, terrorism, and cyber) matters. He was an original member of the Cincinnati FBI Joint Terrorism Task Force, formed after 9/11. An avid golfer he participates in various charitable law enforcement golfing events. He has articles published in multiple magazines and is the author of *The G-Man and the Diamond King* and *The G-Men and the Nurse*. *The G-Men and the Heiress* is his third book. A native of upstate New York and a graduate of the State University of New York at Oswego, he resides in one of the "Top Fun Cities" in America, Cincinnati, Ohio. His e-mail is wplunkett1958@gmail.com